Financial Risk: Theory, Evidence and Implications

Financial Risk: Theory, Evidence and Implications

Proceedings of the Eleventh Annual Economic Policy Conference of the Federal Reserve Bank of St. Louis

edited by

Courtenay C. Stone
The Federal Reserve Bank of St. Louis

Kluwer Academic Publishers
Boston Dordrecht London

Distributors for North America:
Kluwer Academic Publishers
101 Philip Drive
Assinippi Park
Norwell, Massachusetts 02061, USA

Distributors for the UK and Ireland:
Kluwer Academic Publishers
Falcon House, Queen Square
Lancaster LA1 1RN, UNITED KINGDOM

Distributors for all other countries:
Kluwer Academic Publishers Group
Distribution Centre
Post Office Box 322
3300 AH Dordrecht, THE NETHERLANDS

Library of Congress Cataloging-in-Publication Data
Economic Conference, (Federal Reserve Bank of St. Louis).
(11th: 1986: Federal Reserve Bank of Saint Louis)
Financial risk.

Bibliography: p.
1. Finance—Congresses. 2. Risk—Congresses.
I. Stone, Courtenay C. II. Title.
HG63.E36 1986 332 87-32516
ISBN-13: 978-94-010-7701-9 e-ISBN-13: 978-94-009-2665-3
DOI: 10.1007/978-94-009-2665-3

Softcover reprint of the hardcover 1st edition 1989

Typeset by Macmillan India Ltd, Bangalore 25

Contents

Contributing Authors

K. C. Chan
Department of Finance
Ohio State University
Columbus, Ohio 43210

Varadarajan V. Chari
Economist
Federal Reserve Bank of Minneapolis
Minneapolis, Minnesota 55480

George G. Kaufman
Department of Finance
Loyola University
820 N. Michigan Avenue
Chicago, Illinois 60611

Donald R. Lessard
Sloan School of Management
Massachusetts Institute of Technology
Cambridge, Massachusetts 02139

Richard A. Meese
School of Business Administration
University of California at Berkeley
Berkeley, California 94720

Richard W. Nelson
Vice President and Chief Economist
Federal Home Loan Bank
of San Francisco
P.O. Box 7948
San Francisco, California 94120

Maurice Obstfeld
Department of Economics
University of Pennsylvania
Philadelphia, Pennsylvania 19104

Charles Plosser
Department of Economics
University of Rochester
Rochester, NY 14627

Rene M. Stulz
Department of Finance
Ohio State University
Columbus, Ohio 43210

Stephen J. Turnovsky
Department of Economics
University of Washington
301 Savery Hall
Seattle, Washington 98195

Hal R. Varian
Department of Economics
University of Michigan
Ann Arbor, Michigan 48109

Thomas D. Willett
Claremont Center for Economic
Policy Studies
Claremont Colleges
Claremont, California 91711

Arnold Zellner
Graduate School of Business
University of Chicago
Chicago, Illinois 60637

Preface

The Federal Reserve Bank held its Eleventh Annual Economic Policy Conference on November 14 and 15, 1986. The topic of the conference was Financial Risk: Theory, Evidence and Implications; this volume contains the papers and discussants' comments that were presented at this conference. As the reader will note, these papers cover the broad aspects of financial risk, from some key general concepts to specific domestic and international financial risk problems. And, of equal importance, they provide some interesting insights into reasons for the continuing turmoil in domestic and international financial markets that we have witnessed in recent years.

I RISK: A GENERAL OVERVIEW

1 DIFFERENCES OF OPINION IN FINANCIAL MARKETS

Hal R. Varian

The standard models of financial markets such as the Sharpe-Lintner mean-variance model or the Rubinstein-Breeden-Litzenberger contingent consumption model both assume more-or-less homogenous probability beliefs.[1] There has been some work on extending the mean-variance model to allow for differences in beliefs across agents; see Jarrow (1980), Lintner (1969), Mayshar (1983), and Williams (1977). Differences in beliefs in contingent commodities models have received much less attention. The major references are Rubinstein (1975, 1976a), Breeden and Litzenberger (1978), Hakansson et al. (1982), and Milgrom and Stokey (1982).

Cragg and Malkiel (1982) have done some empirical work concerning the effect of the diversity of beliefs on asset prices. According to them:

This work was supported by the National Science Foundation. I thank Sudipto Bhattacharya, Fisher Black, Robert Holbrook, Jeff Mackie-Mason, Dale Morse, Paul Milgrom, Tom Russell, Duane Seppi, Sarab Seth, Joseph Swierzbinski, and Jean Tirole for helpful discussions and references.

> We found that the best single risk measure available for each company was the extent to which different forecasters were not in agreement about that company's future growth.... [These results] suggest that the variance of analysts' forecasts may represent the most effective risk proxy available. (Cragg and Malkiel, 1982, p. 4).

The strong empirical relationship between dispersion of forecasts and share performance found by Cragg and Malkiel suggests that it is appropriate to examine more deeply the theoretical relationship between dispersion of beliefs and asset prices.

One issue that must be faced at the outset is how there can be any differences of belief in equilibrium. Several authors have argued that differences in beliefs that are due solely to differences in information should tend to be eliminated in equilibrium. This literature is briefly discussed in section 1.1 and it is argued that to explain observed trading volumes, one must allow for differences in *opinions*—that is, differences in beliefs that are not shared by other agents, even when they are known to other agents. Equilibrium models that allow for both differences in opinions and differences in information are explored in sections 1.2–1.5.

Sections 1.2–1.4 study a simple mean-variance model with differential information of the sort examined by Grossman (1976, 1978). Grossman's model is generalized to allow for different prior probabilities and for two periods of trade and it is found that even when the equilibrium prices reflect all available information, the volume of trade is determined entirely by the differences of opinion. Section 1.5 examines an Arrow-Debreu contingent consumption model of the sort studied by Milgrom and Stokey (1982). A similar result emerges there: prices are determined by information, but the pattern of trade is determined by the differences in opinion.

Having established the importance of differences of opinion for trade, I then examine some of its consequences for asset market equilibrium in sections 1.6–1.10. In the context of an Arrow-Debreu equilibrium it is shown that if risk aversion does not decrease too rapidly, then assets with more dispersed opinion will have lower prices, other things being equal. If risk aversion does decrease too rapidly, then more dispersion of opinion will be associated with higher prices.[2] Under general conditions assets with more dispersion of opinion will have more equilibrium trade, other things being equal.

It is important to understand that the results in sections 1.6–1.10 involve comparisons of asset prices and trading volumes in a single Arrow-Debreu equilibrium; they are emphatically *not* comparative statics results about how an equilibrium price changes as the overall dispersion of opinion changes. Rather they are *comparative asset pricing* results that compare the prices of two different assets in the *same* equilibrium. These results are analogous to those in standard asset pricing models that compare the equilibrium relationship between the prices of assets and various characteristics of the assets such as their betas, the covariance with aggregate consumption, and so on. We have simply added a new characteristic of assets, namely, the dispersion of opinion.

Since the results describe the relationship between the *equilibrium* price and volume of trade in assets and the *equilibrium* probability beliefs about those assets, they are independent of the exact model of how equilibrium beliefs are formed. As long as one admits that probability beliefs may differ in equilibrium, the results in sections 1.6–1.10 of this chapter describe how those differences in belief will be related to asset prices, regardless of precisely *why* these beliefs differ.

1.1 No-Trade Theorems

The main results of this chapter described in sections 1.6–1.10 are independent of the exact model of why equilibrium beliefs may differ. However, it is worthwhile to investigate conditions in which equilibrium probability beliefs differ and agents actually trade on the basis of these different beliefs, since a number of authors have shown that in a speculative market composed of fully rational agents with identical priors there will be no trade in equilibrium. The basic structure of the argument has been summarized by Tirole.

> Consider a purely speculative market (i.e., a market where the aggregate monetary gain is zero and insurance plays no role). Assume that it is common knowledge that traders are risk averse, rational, have the same prior and that the market clears. Then it is also common knowledge that a trader's expected monetary gain given his information must be positive in order for him to be willing to trade. The market clearing condition then requires that no trader expect a monetary gain from his trade. (Tirole, 1982, p. 1164)

Put in more familiar terms, if one agent has information that induces him to want to trade at the current asset price, then other rational agents would be unwilling to trade with him, because they realize that he must have superior information. Papers that explore this kind of No-Trade Theorem in a variety of contexts include those by Rubinstein (1975), Bhattacharya (1976), Hakansson et al. (1982), and Milgrom and Stokey (1982).

Hence, if we to are examine models with different equilibrium beliefs and nonzero trading volume, we must consider models that lack one of the necessary hypotheses for the No-Trade Theorems described above. Tirole (1982, p. 1167) describes the possibilities: (1) there may be some risk loving or irrational traders; (2) insurance and diversification considerations may play a significant role; or (3) agents may have different prior beliefs.

The first option is compelling on grounds of casual empiricism: clearly *some* participants in speculative markets behave in apparently irrational ways. Black (1986) explores some of the implications of this observation. It has sometimes been argued that introducing a "fringe" of irrational traders into traditional models will not significantly alter the analysis of these models, since the irrational traders will only introduce a nonsystematic "error term" on top of the traditional results. However, if the rational traders know that irrational traders are present in a market they would rationally attempt to exploit them. *The introduction of irrational traders will, in general, alter the behavior of the rational players and thereby change the nature of the equilibrium.* The problem with pursuing this approach lies in deciding what kinds of irrational behavior are plausible. Some interesting leads are being examined in this area, but, as yet, little progress has been made.

The second way to get around the No-Trade Theorems is the route that most of the literature in finance has taken. All trade in speculative markets is taken to be due to differences in endowments and risk aversion, and observed portfolio holidings are taken to be the outcome of pure "hedging" rather than "speculation" per se.

However, attributing all trade to hedging seems implausible empirically and does not really get around the No-Trade Theorems. Suppose that agents do have different risk aversion and different endowments, so that there is some gain from trade on these characteristics. After a single round of trading based on hedging and insurance considerations, there is no further reason to trade when new information arrives for exactly the same reasons described by Tirole: in a market of rational individuals there would be no one to trade with. Trading on the arrival of new information can arise only if agents *interpret* the information differently, that is, if the information affects their posterior beliefs differently. This point will be explored in greater detail below.

This leaves us with the third option: different prior beliefs. This is the motive force for trade that we will explore in this chapter. If differences in prior beliefs can generate trade, then these differences in belief cannot be due to *information* as such, but rather can only be pure differences in *opinion.* Let us consider the difference between information and opinion more closely.

The distinction between what counts as differences in information and differences of opinion must lie in the eyes of the beholder. According to Bayesian decision theory, a rational agent will combine his prior probability beliefs and his likelihood function via Bayes' law to determine his posterior probability beliefs. If I convey a probability belief to another agent and he updates his posterior just as though this probability belief were objective evidence, then he has interpreted my probability beliefs as information: he has accepted my beliefs as being *credible.* If he does not update his posterior at all, then he has interpreted my beliefs as opinion, or as being *noncredible.* The extent that one agent's beliefs are capable of influencing another agent's beliefs determines to what extent one agent conveys information or opinion to the others. We will refer to an agent's belief about what fraction of other agents' beliefs are opinion and what fraction is information as the first agent's beliefs about the *credibility* of the other agents' views.

One hardly needs to consider speculative markets to encounter this distinction. In any kind of human communication it is necessary for one party to determine how credible the other's "information" is. When is someone really conveying information and when is he just conveying his opinion? How much weight should be attached to another individual's pronouncements?

The same sort of question arises in financial markets. If a firm introduces a new product that I find attractive, but the stock market value of the firm falls, what am I to conclude? How much of the price fall is due to superior information of others, and how much is due to differences in opinion? What credibility should we attach to market price movements? As we will see below, the nature of the market equilibrium will depend crucially on the degree of credibility that agents attach to the "information" conveyed by the market price.

Allowing for differences of opinion in this sense can be viewed as allowing for a certain kind of irrational agents. If each agent truly believed that all other agents were rational, doesn't that mean that each agent would accept the other agents' beliefs as being due solely to different information? If I "weight" another agents' beliefs differently than hard evidence, doesn't this mean that I view the other agent as having some degree of irrational behavior? Harsanyi (1983), for example, has argued that under certain conditions fully rational agents must have the same prior beliefs. According to this view, having different priors—differences of opinion—is tantamount to irrationality in some cases. However, Harsanyi's discussion certainly allows that there also exist cases where rational people can agree to disagree at least with respect to prior probability beliefs.[3]

I prefer to remain agnostic on this issue. It seems to me that agents do have different beliefs in practice, and that they do have different degrees of credibility. This is enough to generate equilibrium trade, and nothing in particular hinges on whether we want to call this "rational" or "irrational," at least for the purpose of this chapter.

1.2 A Mean-Variance Model

We first consider a simplified version of a model of the sort studied by Grossman (1976, 1978). There are two assets, one with an unknown payoff and one with a certain payoff. We let v denote the unknown value of the risky asset next period. For simplicity we assume that the certain asset has a zero rate of return.

Each investor i has a subjective prior distribution for the value of the risky asset which we take to be Normally distributed with mean v_i and precision α.[4]

We assume that investor i has a constant absolute risk-tolerance utility function with coefficient of risk tolerance τ.[5] For simplicity we assume for now that all agents have the same risk tolerance; this assumption will be relaxed in section 1.3. It can be shown that the demand function for the risky asset for each agent will have the linear form

$$D_i = \frac{\tau[E_i(v) - P]}{\text{var}_i(v)}, \tag{1.1}$$

where $E_i(v)$ is the expected value of v in the opinion of agent i, $\text{var}_i(v) = 1/\alpha$ is the variance v of the opinion of agent i, and P is the market price. Thus, the demand function for agent i is

$$D_i = \tau\alpha(v_i - P). \tag{1.2}$$

Each agent has a supply S_i of the risky asset, and we suppose that the price P adjusts so as to equate aggregate demand and supply, which yields an equilibrium price of

$$P^* = \bar{v} - \bar{S}/\tau\alpha, \tag{1.3}$$

where bars over a variable denote the arithmetic mean of that variable across the agents.

Inserting this into the demand function of agent i we find the equilibrium demand for the risky asset to be

$$D_i^* = \tau\alpha(v_i - \bar{v}) + \bar{S}. \tag{1.4}$$

Note that each agent's equilibrium demand depends on the deviation of his opinion from the average opinion.

Up until now, the trade has been due entirely to differences in opinion. Now suppose that some information arrives that allows each agent to improve his estimate of the value of the asset. In particular, we suppose that each agent i observes a signal V_i where

$$V_i = v + \varepsilon_i \tag{1.5}$$

and ε_i is IID Normal with mean zero and precision ω. Each agent will have a different piece of information about the value of the asset, but all agents will have information of the same precision. Of course, the information set of agent i is not limited to just this piece of information; he will also use the market price in forming a final estimate of the value of the asset.

Given the n observations (V_i), an omniscient observer could calculate the sample mean

$$\bar{V} = \sum_{i=1}^{n} \frac{V_i}{n}, \tag{1.6}$$

which will have a Normal distribution with mean v and precision $\beta = n\omega$. In this model the equilibrium price turns out to be fully revealing, so that each agent will be able to calculate $\bar{V}$ in equilibrium.

Being good Bayesians, each investor will then form a posterior distribution for the value of the risky asset by combining his prior and his sample information in accord with Bayes' law. Given the distributional assumptions we have made, the posterior distribution of investor i will be Normal with precision of $\gamma = \alpha + \beta$ and mean of

$$\frac{\alpha}{\gamma} v_i + \frac{\beta}{\gamma} \bar{V}. \tag{1.7}$$

Using the assumption of constant absolute risk tolerance, the demand for the risky asset will have the linear form

$$D_i = \frac{\tau[E(v \mid I_i) - P]}{\operatorname{var}(v \mid I_i)}, \tag{1.8}$$

where $E(v \mid I_i)$ is the expected value of the asset conditional on the information set of agent i, $\operatorname{var}(v \mid I_i)$ is the variance of the asset conditional on i's information, and P is the market price.

Inserting the expressions for the expected value and the variance given in equation 1.7 into equation 1.8, the demand of agent i reduces to

$$D_i = \tau(\alpha v_i + \beta \bar{V} - \gamma P). \tag{1.9}$$

We suppose that the market price P adjusts so as to equate aggregate demand and supply which gives us a postinformation equilibrium price of

$$\hat{P} = \frac{\alpha \bar{v} + \beta \bar{V} - \bar{S}/\tau}{\gamma}, \tag{1.10}$$

where, as before, bars over a variable denote the mean across the population.

Let us consider the information structure in this market more closely. Suppose that all agents agree on the value of the *information* (V_i) observed by the other agents but disagree about the value of the other agents' opinions (v_i). Then knowing the average prior mean $\bar{v}$ would not lead any agent to revise his own posterior mean, but knowing the average *information* $\bar{V}$ would induce an agent to change his posterior mean. That is, each agent would agree that $\bar{V}$ would be a superior estimate of the true value of the asset compared to any agent's individual information V_i. The distinction being drawn here is the distinction between the other agent's *opinions*—which do not change a given agent's beliefs—and other agents' pieces of *information*—which do change a given agent's beliefs.

But, if each consumer knows the value of the coefficients in the aggregate demand function, he or she can estimate $\bar{V}$ from the observed equilibrium price and the formula:

$$\bar{V} = \frac{\bar{S}/\tau + \gamma\hat{P} - \alpha\bar{v}}{\beta}. \tag{1.11}$$

As in the original Grossman (1976) model, the equilibrium price aggregates all of the information in the economy and thus provides a superior estimate of the "true" expected value of the asset.

In Grossman's original paper all agents had the same prior beliefs but different tastes. In that paper he argues for the rational expectations equilibrium by appealing to a long-run equilibrium where agents can tabulate the empirical distribution of the $\hat{P}$, $\bar{V}$) pairs and thus infer $\bar{V}$ from observations of $\hat{P}$. The agents do not have to know the structure of the model, only the reduced form relationship between $\hat{P}$ and $\bar{V}$.

This sort of argument does not work here, for if the events were repeated a large number of times, the different prior beliefs would tend to converge to identical posterior beliefs. Instead it appears that we must assume that agents have some understanding of the structure of the model and are able to disentangle the information contained in the market price directly rather than to simply use a reduced form model. It appears that a model with different prior opinions demands even more "rational expectations" than does Grossman's model.

Luckily this is not the case, for we have an extra feature not present in the original Grossman model. We have assumed that the agents can observe an equilibrium price prior to the arrival of the information. And certainly the *change* in the equilibrium price when new information arrives should reveal more about the new information than simply the *level* of the equilibrium price. In particular, if we rearrange expressions (1.3) and (1.10), which characterize the preinformation and postinformation equilibrium prices, we have

$$\alpha P^* = \alpha\bar{v} - \bar{S}/\tau \tag{1.12}$$

$$\gamma\hat{P} = \alpha\bar{v} + \beta\bar{V} - \bar{S}/\tau. \tag{1.13}$$

These equations can be solved for $\bar{V}$ to yield

$$\bar{V} = \frac{\gamma\hat{P} - \alpha P^*}{\beta}. \tag{1.14}$$

Using the definitions of the precisions, $\beta = n\omega$ and $\gamma = \alpha + n\omega$, this expression can be rewritten as

$$\bar{V} = \hat{P} + \frac{\alpha}{n\omega}(\hat{P} - P^*). \tag{1.15}$$

Thus, if the agents are able to observe the *change* in the equilibrium prices when information arrives, they need to know only the precisions α and ω to estimate the aggregate information. The number ω/α is the ratio of the precision of the likelihood to the precision of the prior opinion, and can be thought of as a measure of credibility. A credible agent gives a larger weight to the evidence than to his opinions; therefore, the ratio ω/α should be large. If all agents believe that all agents are very credible—or that there is a very large number of not-so-credible agents—then the market price will essentially be equal to $\bar{V}$, the average information in the population.

If agents perceive the other agents' beliefs as not being particularly credible in the sense that ω/α is small, then they will attempt to use the change in the equilibrium price, appropriately weighted, to try to sort out the "information" from the "opinion."[6]

Inserting the "rational expectations" estimate of $\bar{V}$ into the demand function for agent i and simplifying we have the equilibrium demand of agent i:

$$D_i = \tau\alpha(v_i - \bar{v}) + \bar{S}. \tag{1.16}$$

Note the interesting feature of this expression: all of the information variables have dropped out—an agent's trade in equilibrium is determined solely by the deviation of his or her opinion from the average opinion.

The size of agent i's position in the risky asset depends positively on his risk tolerance τ and his *prior* precision α. This latter point is somewhat surprising. The sample precision of $\beta = n\omega$ may be much larger than the prior precision α, and one might have thought that for large n it would swamp the prior precision. Nevertheless, the equilibrium demand for the risky asset is exactly the same as if the agent had no sample information at all! An agent's posterior *beliefs* may be dominated by the sample information but his *trades* will depend only on the prior information. The explanation of this seeming paradox is that the market price adjusts to reveal all information in the economy and thus eliminates the value of the sample information to any one agent. Trade can occur only when people are different, and in this model the only difference that people have are in their prior opinions.

Note that the equilibrium demand for each agent in the postinformation equilibrium is exactly the same as in the preinformation equilibrium. The arrival of the information will have zero impact on the volume of trade. This is because each agent is able to extract the same information from the market price. The only differences among the agents are the differences in their prior opinions, and trade on the differences in opinions has already taken place. Thus, there is nothing left to trade on when the information arrives.

Of course, the equilibrium *price* will respond to arrival of information; if $\bar{V}$ is large in some particular realization, then the market price will be large. Indeed, the price responds in such a way as to perfectly offset the desire to trade. But it has to be that way in a fully revealing equilibrium—if the price reveals all information, there is nothing left to be revealed by the volume of trade. Thus, the volume of trade cannot depend in any independent way on the information signals received by the agents.[7]

These observations become even more striking if we consider what happens as the information becomes more and more precise, relative to the prior. According to equation 1.10 as n goes to infinity, for example, the precision of the information goes to infinity, and the equilibrium postinformation price becomes $\bar{V}$. Thus, as the sample information becomes more and more informative, the price of the asset approaches its average perceived value: the postinformation equilibrium price reflects all available information. Nevertheless, the equilibrium trade of each agent, as given in equation 1.16, is entirely determined by the initial dispersion of opinion and remains unaffected by a change in the accuracy of the information. When information is very informative the equilibrium price is determined almost entirely by the information, while the equilibrium trade is determined entirely by the differences in opinion.

What are the implications of opinion differences for the volume of trade? Agent i's net trade in the risky asset is

$$T_i = \tau\alpha(v_i - \bar{v}) - (S_i - \bar{S}) \tag{1.17}$$

so that the equilibrium volume depends on both the differences in opinions and the differences in endowments. Suppose for simplicity that each agent has an identical endowment $\bar{S}$ of the risky asset. Then the net trade of agent i is simply $T_i = \tau\alpha(v_i - \bar{v})$ and the overall volume of trade is given by

$$\sum_{i=1}^{n} \tau\alpha|v_i - \bar{v}|/2, \tag{1.18}$$

which clearly depends only on the dispersion of opinion. An increase in the dispersion of opinion, as measured by the sum of the absolute deviations of the priors, will necessarily increase the volume of trade, regardless of the private information received by the market participants.

1.3 Different Tastes

In Grossman's original model of all agents had identical priors but different risk tolerances; the equilibrium volume was therefore due solely to the differences in tastes. In the model above the agents all have the same tastes, but different prior opinions, and the equilibrium volume depends only on the differences of opinion. What if agents have different tastes and different opinions?

Letting τ_i denote the risk tolerance of agent i, the preinformation price is determined by solving

$$\sum_{i=1}^{n} \tau_i \alpha(v_i - P) = \sum_{i=1}^{n} S_i \tag{1.19}$$

and the postequilibrium price is determined by solving

$$\sum_{i=1}^{n} \tau_i(\alpha v_i + \beta \bar{V} - \gamma P) = \sum_{i=1}^{n} S_i. \tag{1.20}$$

Subtracting equation 1.19 from 1.20 and solving for $\bar{V}$, we find that the rational expectations estimate of $\bar{V}$ is exactly the same that given in equation 1.15:

$$\bar{V} = \frac{\gamma \hat{P} - \alpha P^*}{\beta} = \hat{P} + \frac{\alpha}{n\omega}(\hat{P} - P^*). \tag{1.21}$$

The agents do not need to know anything about the taste differences in the population to estimate $\bar{V}$, as long as they can observe the preinformation and postinformation prices. Everything hinges on the magnitude of "credibility" of the market price, as determined by α relative to $n\omega$.

Using this estimate of $\bar{V}$ it can be shown that the equilibrium demand of agent i is

$$D_i = \tau_i \alpha \left(v_i - \sum_{j=1}^{n} \theta_j v_j \right) + \omega_i \sum_{j=1}^{n} S_j, \tag{1.22}$$

where

$$\theta_i = \frac{\tau_i}{\sum_{j=1}^{n} \tau_j}.$$

The volume of trade still depends on the deviation of agents opinion from the average opinion, but now it is weighted average rather than the simple average we had before.

1.4 Differences in Interpretation

The no-trade result may appear to fly in the face of common sense; certainly the arrival of new information in real markets may contribute to volume. It seems that this view is held by those who have examined the empirical determinants of the volume of trade. For example:

> One reason to suggest a relationship between changes in price and transactions volume is that both are related to the type and flow of information in the market. New information can simultaneously spur trading and lead to new equilibrium prices. (Karpoff, 1985)

Casual empiricism (i.e., the nightly news) suggests that volume does react to new information. Empirical work by Epps and Epps (1976), Tauchen and Pitts (1983), Harris (1983), and others suggests that volume is highly correlated with the absolute value of the price change for daily stock returns. How can we reconcile this observation with the model described above?

One assumption of the above model was that agents interpreted the information in the same way. That is, all agents agree that the observation of V_i contributed to their posterior estimate of v in the same way. For some kinds of information this may be plausible, but for other types it may be quite implausible. If OPEC were to break up tomorrow would everyone agree on the impact of this event on all asset prices? When Apple introduces a new computer line does everyone agree on the impact of this product on the market value of Apple stock?

We might model this by distinguishing between the *arrival* of the information and the *interpretation* of the information. Let Y_i be a random variable denoting the "magnitude" of a piece of information, and let $V_i = \delta_i Y_i$ be agent i's estimate of the impact of this information on the mean value of the risky asset. That is, agent i views $\delta_i Y_i$ as a signal about the value of the risky asset in the sense that he believes the model

$$V_i = \delta_i Y_i = v + \varepsilon_i. \tag{1.23}$$

All agents agree on the magnitude of the information Y_i but the "interpretation" of the information δ_i differs from agent to agent. That is, each agent i has a potentially different belief δ_i about how the information Y_i will affect the equilibrium value of the asset.

Let us assume that the interpretations (δ_i) and the observations (Y_i) are distributed independently across the set of agents so that $\bar{V} = \bar{\delta}\bar{Y}$. Substituting this into equation 1.15 and solving for $\bar{Y}$ yields

$$\bar{Y} = \frac{\hat{P}}{\bar{\delta}} + \frac{\alpha}{n\omega}\frac{(\hat{P} - P^*)}{\bar{\delta}}. \tag{1.24}$$

Thus, as long as the average value of δ is common knowledge, each agent will be able to estimate $\bar{Y}$ from the observed change in equilibrium price. After observing the equilibrium price of the asset, agent i should then revise his own estimate of the expected value of the risky asset to be $\delta_i \bar{Y}$. This leads to an equilibrium demand of the form

$$D_i = \tau(\alpha v_i + \beta\delta_i \bar{Y} - \gamma P). \tag{1.25}$$

Solving for the postinformation equilibrium price we have

$$\hat{P} = \frac{\alpha\bar{v} + \beta\overline{\delta Y} - \bar{S}/\tau}{\gamma}. \tag{1.26}$$

Substituting this back into the demand function of agent i and subtracting his endowment to get his equilibrium net trade T_i we have

$$T_i = \tau[\alpha(v_i - \bar{v}) + \beta(\delta_i - \bar{\delta})\bar{Y}] + (S_i - \bar{S}). \tag{1.27}$$

The interpretation of this equation is rather nice. The equilibrium net trade of an agent depends on the difference in his opinion, his interpretation, and his endowment from the averages of these variables. In this model, the agents can use the market price to estimate whether or not the events have occurred, but then put their own interpretation on the events themselves. In equilibrium the arrival of the information affects the volume of trade, but only through the differences of opinion about how the information should be interpreted, not through the difference in information itself.

1.5 An Arrow-Debreu Model

The model described in the first part of this chapter is a mean-variance model. However, the ideas described there are robust; we will demonstrate that by considering the same issues in the context of a contingent-consumption model, which is a simplification of the model described in Milgrom and Stokey (1982). Let $s = 1, \ldots, S$ index states of nature and $i = 1, \ldots n$ index the economic agents. Use $\pi_i(s)$ to denote agent i's prior probability belief about the occurrence of state s, and c_{is} to denote agent i's contingent consumption in state s. Finally, let $u_i(c)$ be agent i's von Neumann-Morgenstern utility function and p_s the Arrow-Debreu price for consumption in state s.

We suppose that all agents trade to an equilibrium which will be characterized by the first-order conditions for utility maximization:

$$\pi_i(s)u_i'(c_{is}) = \lambda_i p_s, \tag{1.28}$$

where λ_i is agent i's marginal utility of wealth.

Now suppose that each agent observes a private signal y_i that is a realization of a random variable that affects the probability of occurrence of state s. We suppose that if agent i could observe the signals of all the agents, $y = (y_1, \ldots, y_n)$, he would calculate the probability of occurrence of state s via Bayes' law, and that all agents agree on the form of the likelihood function, which we denote by $\pi(y|s)$.

After each agent observes his private signal, markets are reopened and all agents can revise their contingent consumption plans. Given the new information, we would expect that prices of the various states would change. As in the model presented above, the agents can take these price changes into account and use them to infer something about what signals the other agents observed. What will the new postinformation equilibrium look like?

Given this framework, Milgrom and Stokey establish a remarkable result: there will always be a postinformation equilibrium that reveals all the information observed by all the agents and, furthermore, the new equilibrium involves no trade by any agent.[8]

The proof is simply to consider what happens if the price of state s consumption changes to $\hat{p}_s = \pi(y|s)p_s$. In this case, each agent can extract the likelihood function $\pi(y|s)$ by dividing the postinformation price by the preinformation price and use this likelihood to revise his prior probability via Bayes' law. The resulting equilibrium is characterized by the first-order conditions

$$\pi_i(s|y)u_i'(c_{is}) = \frac{\pi(y|s)\pi_i(s)}{\pi_i(y)}u_i'(c_{is}) = \frac{\lambda_i}{\pi_i(y)}\pi(y|s)p_s = \hat{\lambda}_i\hat{p}_s, \qquad (1.29)$$

where $\hat{\lambda}_i = \lambda_i/\pi_i(y)$. Since the new prices $(\hat{p}_s)$ the new beliefs $(\pi_i(s|y))$, and the original consumption levels (c_{is}) satisfy the appropriate first-order conditions, we do indeed have an equilibrium in the postinformation market that involves no trade due to the arrival of the information.

As before, one could question the assumption of a common likelihood function. If agents have different opinions about the effect of a given piece of information on the probability of occurrence of a state of nature, the Milgrom-Stokey result need no longer hold. Arrival of new information will in general cause agents to trade in this case, but only because agents *interpret* the information differently, not because it is different information.

This observation can be sharpened; Milgrom and Stokey show that if everyone has the same likelihood function there will always exist an equilibrium that is fully revealing and that involves no trade. But there is a partial converse: if there is no trade after information is revealed, then all agents must have essentially the same likelihood function and equilibrium will be fully revealing. So the relationship between differences of opinions and the volume of trade is an if-and-only-if relationship—common opinions about how information affects state probabilities mean zero volume, and zero volume means essentially common opinions.

This proposition is a small extension of arguments given by Rubinstein (1975, Nonspeculation Condition), Milgrom and Stokey (1982, Theorem 3), and Hakansson et al. (1982, Lemma 2). However, it seems worthwhile to give a brief exposition of the result.

Following Hakansson et al. (1982), we will say that likelihood functions are *essentially homogenous* if

$$\pi_i(y_i, \hat{p}|s) = k_i(y_i, \hat{p})\pi_1(y_i, \hat{p}|s)$$

for all $i = 1, \ldots, n$. If two likelihood functions are essentially homogenous, then Bayes' law implies that they will generate the same posterior probabilities, since the $k_i(y_i, \hat{p})$ terms will cancel out from the numerator and the denominator. Thus, agents that have essentially homogenous likelihood functions will make the same inferences from the information they observe.

Theorem 1: Let (c_{is}, p_s) be an equilibrium before the information y is revealed and let $(c_{is}, \hat{p}_s)$ be a no-trade equilibrium after y_i is revealed to each agent. Then the value of each agent's likelihood function is given by

$$\pi_i(y_i, \hat{p}|s) = k_i(y_i, \hat{p})\frac{\hat{p}_s}{p_s}$$

so that agents' likelihood functions must be essentially homogenous.

Proof: Choose two states, s and t. Since the economy is in equilibrium before and after the information is revealed, we must have

$$\frac{\pi_i(s)u_i'(c_{is})}{\pi_i(t)u_i'(c_{it})} = \frac{p_s}{p_t}$$

and

$$\frac{\pi_i(s|y_i, \hat{p})u_i'(c_{is})}{\pi_i(t|y_i, \hat{p})u_i'(c_{it})} = \frac{\hat{p}_s}{\hat{p}_t}.$$

By Bayes' law we can write the latter expression as

$$\frac{\pi_i(y_i, \hat{p}|s)\pi_i(s)u_i'(c_{is})}{\pi_i(y_i, \hat{p}|t)\pi_i(t)u_i'(c_{it})} = \frac{\hat{p}_s}{\hat{p}_t}.$$

Dividing by the first equation gives

$$\frac{\pi_i(y_i, \hat{p}|s)}{\pi_i(y_i, \hat{p}|t)} = \frac{\hat{p}_s/p_s}{\hat{p}_t/p_t}.$$

This implies that

$$\pi_i(y_i, \hat{p}|s) = k_i(y_i, \hat{p})\frac{\hat{p}_s}{p_s}$$

for all s as required. ▌

As indicated above, this result is essentially a corollary to theorem 3 in Milgrom and Stokey (1982). However, the focus is different; Milgrom and

Stokey show that if all agents have the same likelihood function, then in a postinformation, no-trade equilibrium, each agent's posterior probability must depend only on the postinformation prices and be independent of his private signal. We show something a bit different: *if* there is no trade in a postinformation equilibrium, then all agents must have essentially the same likelihood value, and the equilibrium price change must reveal this common likelihood value. Hakansson et al. (1982) have essentially the same result in a somewhat different setting, whereas Bhattacharya (1976) has shown that this result is closely related to Rubinstein's (1975) Nonspeculation Condition.

1.6 The Effect of Differences of Opinion on Asset Prices

The results of the last section suggest that the volume of trade in an Arrow-Debreu model is due primarily to the differences of opinion. In a one-period model, these can be differences of opinion about the prior probabilities; in a two-period model, trade requires differences of opinion about likelihood functions—that is, the interpretation of information.

How far can this insight be pushed? If two assets are otherwise identical but one has "more diverse" beliefs, which asset will have the larger volume of trade? Which asset will have the higher price? It is important to note that these questions can be addressed independently of the particular model of information transfer, for the questions are phrased in terms of *equilibrium* differences in beliefs. They are questions about comparative asset pricing, not about comparative statics.

Varian (1985a) has described some results concerning relative pricing in this framework. Here we review these results and consider the implications for the volume of trade. In this section we will consider only the case of identical utility functions; the case of different utility functions is considered in sections 9 and 10.

Letting $f(\cdot)$ be the inverse of $u'(\cdot)$, we can write the Arrow-Debreu first-order conditions in equation 1.28 as

$$c_{is} = f[\lambda_i p_s / \pi_i(s)],$$

where $\pi_i(s)$ is now interpreted as either a prior or a posterior probability. Let us define $q_{is} = \pi_i(s)/\lambda_i$ to be a "weighted" probability for agent *i*. In general, we would expect wealthier agents to have lower marginal utilities of wealth in equilibrium so that their beliefs will get a higher weight in the q_{is} expression. (It is easy to show that if two agents have the same probability beliefs and the same utility function, the wealthier one will have a lower marginal utility of wealth.)

Then we can sum the first-order conditions across the agents to derive an expression for aggregate consumption in state s:

$$C_s = \sum_{i=1}^{n} c_{is} = \sum_{i=1}^{n} f(p_s/q_{is}).$$

Theorem 2: The function $f(p_s/q_{is})$ is always an increasing function of q_{is}. It will be a concave (convex) function of q_{is} as the derivative of risk tolerance is less (greater) than 1.

Proof: The first part of the theorem is proved in Varian (1985a). The same paper shows that $f(p_s/q_{is})$ will be concave in q_{is} iff $r'(c) > -r(c)^2$ where $r(c) = -u''(c)/u'(c)$ is the Arrow-Pratt measure of absolute risk aversion. This condition can be rearranged to give

$$-\frac{r'(c)}{r(c)^2} = \frac{d}{dc}\frac{1}{r(c)} < 1,$$

which establishes the second statement. ▮

It is easy to check that the derivative of risk tolerance for a logarithmic utility is precisely one, so we can conclude that $f(p_s/q_{is})$ will be a concave function of q_{is} when risk tolerance increases less rapidly than it does in the case of logarithmic utility. This seems like a very natural assumption.

Following Varian (1985a) we now consider two different states, s and t, such that $C_s = C_t$, but the probability beliefs for state t are a mean-preserving spread of the probability beliefs for state s in the sense of Rothschild and Stiglitz (1970). It follows from the strict concavity of $f(\cdot)$ that

$$\sum_{i=1}^{n} f(p_s/q_{it}) < \sum_{i=1}^{n} f(p_s/q_{is}) = C_s = C_t = \sum_{i=1}^{n} f(p_t/q_{it})$$

and, therefore, $p_t < p_s$.

This argument proves:

Theorem 3: Consider two Arrow-Debreu assets that pay off in states with the same level of aggregate consumption. Then if all agents have identical tastes and risk tolerance does not increase too rapidly, the asset with the more dispersion of weighted probability beliefs will have the lower equilibrium price.

Thus, increased dispersion of beliefs should be associated with lower prices in equilibrium. It is important to understand that this is *not* a comparative statics statement; we are not examining two different equilibria. Rather we are examining two different assets in a *given* equilibrium. Theorem 3 followed solely from the first-order conditions and the assumption about risk tolerance; it is therefore compatible with any model of how equilibrium beliefs are formed. Equilibrium beliefs could be due to differences in likelihoods, nonrational behavior, or whatever, as long as the first-order conditions for an Arrow-Debreu equilibrium hold.

1.7 The Effect of Differences of Opinion on Volume

To get a result concerning the relative volume of trade in different assets we must refine the meaning of "other things being equal" and use a more restrictive notion of "increased dispersion of opinion." Since the final volume of trade depends on the pattern of initial endowments across the agents, we will further assume that assets s and t have the same pattern of initial endowments: $\bar{c}_{is} = \bar{c}_{it}$ for all $i = 1, \ldots, n$.

In a given equilibrium and state s, let D_s be the set of net demanders—those agents for whom $f(p_s/q_{is}) > \bar{c}_{is}$—and let S_s be the set of net suppliers, defined in a similar manner. Since the amount bought equals the amount sold in equilibrium, we can express the volume of trade in state s by

$$V_s = \sum_{i \in D_s} [f(p_s/q_{is}) - \bar{c}_{is}] = \sum_{i \in S_s} [\bar{c}_{is} - f(p_s/q_{is})].$$

Now consider two states, s and t, and suppose that all of the agents who purchase asset s feel that state t is at least as likely as state s, and that all agents who sell asset s feel that t is less likely that s. That is

$$q_{it} \geq q_{is} \qquad \text{for all } i \in D_s$$

$$q_{it} \leq q_{is} \qquad \text{for all } i \in S_s.$$

Informally, we are assuming that all of the net demanders for state s securities are even more optimistic about state t occurring than they are about state s occurring, and all of the net suppliers of state s securities are even more pessimistic about state t occurring that they are about state s occurring. Thus, there is certainly more dispersion of equilibrium beliefs about state t than about state s.

Theorem 4: If all of the net demanders in state s are more optimistic about state t occurring than state s occurring and all of the net suppliers in state s are more pessimistic about state t occurring than state s occurring, then the volume of trade in state t must be higher than the volume of trade in state s.

Proof: Suppose first that $p_t > p_s$, and let agent i be a net supplier of asset s in equilibrium. By the hypothesis of the theorem, $q_{it} < q_{is}$. The function $f(p_s/q_{is})$ is increasing in q_{is} and decreasing in p_s by Theorem 2, so we have

$$f(p_s/q_{is}) > f(p_t/q_{it}).$$

Since $\bar{c}_{is} = \bar{c}_{it}$, by assumption we have

$$\bar{c}_{is} - f(p_s/q_{is}) < \bar{c}_{it} - f(p_t/q_{it}).$$

Summing over the net suppliers shows that $V_s < V_t$.

Now suppose that $p_t < p_s$. Then let agent i be a net *demander* of asset s in equilibrium. By exactly the same argument, we have

$$f(p_s/q_{is}) - \bar{c}_{is} > f(p_t/q_{it}) - \bar{c}_{it}.$$

Summing shows that $V_t > V_s$, as required. ∎

It is worth observing that this argument does not depend on agents having identical tastes or on the earlier assumption about risk tolerance; it is true in complete generality. Furthermore, the argument holds for the unweighted beliefs $\pi_i(s)$ as well as the weighted beliefs q_{is}. In fact, the argument has a very simple graphical proof, which is depicted in figure 1–1A. The assumption that all net demanders become more optimistic implies that the aggregate demand curve shifts to the right, and the assumption that all net suppliers become more pessimistic implies that the aggregate net supply curves shifts to the right. Hence the volume of trade must increase, as shown in figure 1–1A.[9]

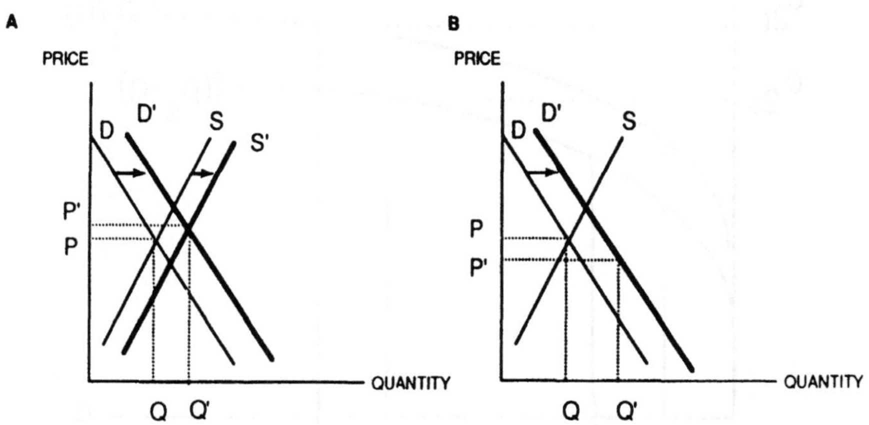

Figure 1–1. (A) An increase in the dispersion of beliefs of both demanders and suppliers must increase volume. (B) If the buyers become more optimistic and the equilibrium price decreases, then the volume must increase, regardless of what happens to the beliefs of suppliers.

However, this particular kind of increase in the dispersion of opinion is rather special. We can get a different result using a weaker definition of an increase in the dispersion of belief. In particular, let us consider a mean-preserving spread that does not decrease q_{is} for any agent who is a net purchaser of the asset. That is, we assume that the mean-preserving spread in beliefs is such that

$$q_{it} \geq q_{is} \qquad \text{for all } i \text{ such that } c_{is} > \bar{c}_{is}.$$

Let us also assume that the derivative of risk tolerance is less than 1, so that $f(p_s/q_{is})$ is concave. Then we have the situation illustrated in figure 1–2. Here we have plotted the weighted probabilities q_{is} on the horizontal axis, and $c_{is} = f(p_s/q_{is})$ on the vertical axis. When we consider the movement from q_{is} to q_{it} we see that

$$f(p_s/q_{is}) \leq f(p_s/q_{it}) < f(p_t/q_{it})$$

for all net purchasers of the asset where the first inequality follows from the monotonicity of $f(\cdot)$ and the second from the fact that $p_t < p_s$, which we established in theorem 3. Since all of the net purchasers of the asset are now buying more, the net sellers of the asset must be selling more, and the volume of the trade is therefore larger. The volume of trade has increased for two

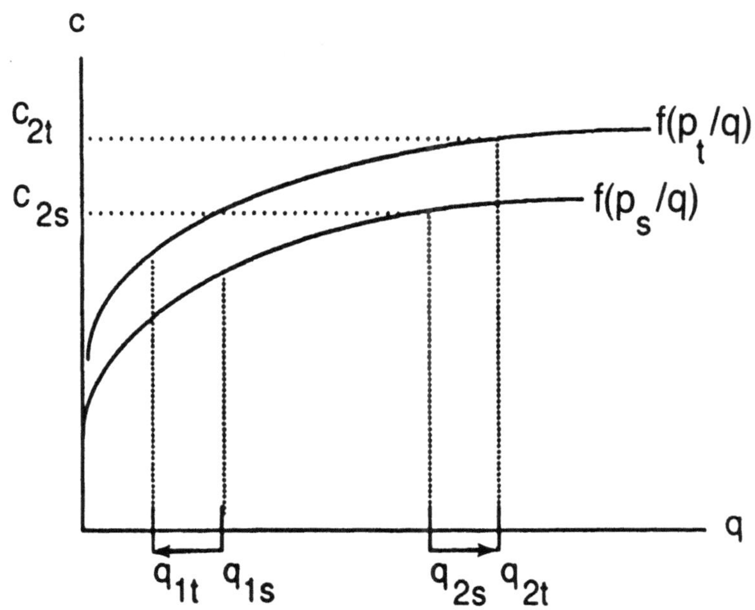

Figure 1–2. A mean-preserving spread in weighted beliefs increases volume.

reasons: each net purchaser wants to buy more at the same price, and the price decrease makes him want to buy even more again.

This can also be demonstrated using the supply and demand graph in figure 1–1. If the demand increases and the equilibrium price decreases, then it follows that the equilibrium volume must be larger, as shown in figure 1–1B. This result holds regardless of the change in the beliefs of the sellers of the asset, although it must be the case that on the average their beliefs have become more pessimistic.

If it appears obvious that making buyers more optimistic will increase the volume of trade, it might be worth considering the case where $f(\cdot)$ is a *convex* function of q_{is}. For example, take constant relative risk averse utility functions with $\rho < 1$. Then increasing the dispersion of opinion will *increase* asset prices, so the two effects described above work in opposite directions and the volume of trade can go either way. We give an algebraic example of this below.

An example can also be constructed using the supply and demand framework in figure 1–1. Simply imagine the case where the demand curve shifts to the right as illustrated in figure 1–1B, but the supply curve shifts far enough to the left so that the equilibrium price rises and the equilibrium transactions decrease.

1.8 Constant Relative Risk Aversion

The case of constant relative risk averse utility functions, $u(c_{is}) = c_{is}^{1-\rho}/(1-\rho)$, serves as a convenient example of the above discussion. The first-order conditions take the form

$$c_{is}^{\rho} = \frac{\lambda_i p_s}{\pi_{is}}.$$

Straightforward but tedious calculations show that the equilibrium value of λ_i is given by

$$\lambda_i = \left(\frac{\sum_{s=1}^{S} p_s^{(\rho-1)/\rho} \pi_{is}^{1/\rho}}{m_i} \right)^{-\rho},$$

where m_i is agent i's equilibrium wealth. As indicated earlier, λ_i is a decreasing function of equilibrium wealth. If $\rho = 1$, λ_i is simply $1/m_i$.

Letting $q_i = \pi_{is}/\lambda_i$ the first-order conditions may be rewritten as

$$c_{is}^{-\rho} = \frac{p_s}{q_{is}}$$

so that

$$c_{is} = \left(\frac{q_{is}}{p_s}\right)^{1/\rho}$$

This in turn implies

$$C_s = \sum_{j=1}^{n} \left(\frac{q_{js}}{p_s}\right)^{1/\rho}$$

and

$$p_s = C_s^{-\rho}\left(\sum_{j=1}^{n} q_{js}^{1/\rho}\right)^{\rho}.$$

This function gives us the explicit equilibrium relationship between aggregate consumption, probability beliefs, and equilibrium prices. Inserting this into the first equation, we see that the equilibrium demand of agent i takes the form

$$c_{is} = w_{is} C_s,$$

where

$$w_{is} = \frac{q_{is}^{1/\rho}}{\sum_{j=1}^{n} q_{js}^{1/\rho}}.$$

Thus the equilibrium demand of agent i is completely determined by his weighted probability, relative to the weighted probabilities of the other agents.

We can use this expression to present the example promised above. Suppose that $\rho = 0.5$, $C_s = C_t = 1$, and q_{is} and q_{it} are as given in table 1–1. Note that in state s all agents have the same value of q_{is} so that any mean-preserving change in the equilibrium beliefs about state s will be a mean-preserving spread. In the case illustrated in the table, both of the net demanders have the same probability beliefs about state t as state s while one of the net suppliers is more optimistic and one is more pessimistic about state s as compared to state t.

Using the formula given above it is straightforward to calculate the net trades x_{is} and x_{it}. We find that state s has a volume of 0.200 and state t has a volume of 0.190. Even though the dispersion of opinion has increased, and no

Table 1–1. Example of Decreased Volume of Trade

	q_{is}	q_{it}	$\bar{c}_{is}$	x_{is}	x_{it}
1	0.250	0.200	0.300	−0.050	−0.143
2	0.250	0.300	0.400	−0.150	−0.047
3	0.250	0.250	0.100	0.150	0.145
4	0.250	0.250	0.200	0.050	0.045

net purchaser has become more pessimistic, the volume of trade has decreased. This is not, of course, a violation of theorem 4, since one of the net demanders of the Arrow-Debreu security is more optimistic about state t than about state s. Nevertheless, the example is somewhat surprising since it shows that without the curvature assumption on demands somewhat perverse results can arise.

1.9 Different Tastes and Different Opinions

Here we discuss the general case where tastes differ across the agents. Letting $f_i(\cdot)$ be the inverse of agent i's marginal utility function, and following the derivation in section 6 we have

$$C_s = \sum_{i=1}^{n} f_i(p_s/q_{is}).$$

For fixed values of $(q_{1s}, \ldots, q_{ns})$, $f_i(\cdot)$ is a decreasing function of p_s. Thus we can invert it to get $p_s = F(C_s, q_s)$ where $q_s = (q_{1s}, \ldots, q_{ns})$. It is easy to show, following Varian (1985a), that $F(C_s, q_s)$ is a decreasing function of C_s and an increasing function of q_{is} in a given Arrow-Debreu equilibrium. What about the curvature of $F(C_s, q_s)$? The results of Varian (1985b) show that increasing risk tolerance (i.e., decreasing absolute risk aversion) implies that $F(C_s, q_s)$ is a convex function of C_s. With some more effort we can show:

Theorem 5: If risk tolerance increases less rapidly than in the case of logarithmic utility, $F(C_s, q_s)$ will be a quasiconcave function of q_s.

Proof: Fix C at $\bar{C}$, say, and consider three different sets of prices and weighted probabilities such that

$$\sum_{i=1}^{n} f_i(p''/q_i'') = \sum_{i=1}^{n} f_i(p'/q_i') = \sum_{i=1}^{n} f_i(p/q_i) = \bar{C},$$

where $q_i'' = tq_i + (1-t)q_i'$.

To establish quasiconcavity, we need to show that

$$F(C, q'') \geq \min\{F(C, q), F(C, q')\}$$

or, equivalently, that

$$p'' \geq \min\{p, p'\}.$$

Without loss of generality let $p = \min\{p, p'\}$.

The assumption that risk tolerance does not increase too rapidly implies that $f_i(p/q)$ is concave in q. This implies that

$$f_i(p/q_i'') \geq tf_i(p/q_i) + (1-t)f_i(p/q_i').$$

By the negative monotonicity of $f_i(p/q_i)$ in p and the assumption that $p' \geq p$ we have

$$tf_i(p/q_i) + (1-t)f_i(p/q_i') \geq tf_i(p/q_i) + (1-t)f_i(p'/q_i').$$

Putting these two inequalities together and summing we have

$$\begin{aligned}\sum_{i=1}^{n} f_i(p/q_i'') &\geq t\sum_{i=1}^{n} f_i(p/q_i) + (1-t)\sum_{i=1}^{n} f_i(p'/q_i') \\ &= t\bar{C} + (1-t)\bar{C} = \bar{C} \\ &= \sum_{i=1}^{n} f_i(p''/q_i'').\end{aligned}$$

It follows that $p \leq p''$. ▮

This result suggests that even if preferences are different, there is a tendency for divergence of opinion to lead to lower asset prices. Consider figure 1–3 where we have illustrated a level set of $F(C, q_1, q_2)$. In this example we have two states of nature with the same value of aggregate consumption and state prices but different weighted subjective probabilities, (q_1, q_2) and (q_1', q_2'). As established above, the upper contour set is convex and monotonic. Therefore, if we take a weighted average of (q_1, q_2) and (q_1', q_2') to get (q_1'', q_2''), the equilibrium value of p'' must increase. In this sense, taking an average of "extreme" distributions of beliefs will tend to increase state prices.

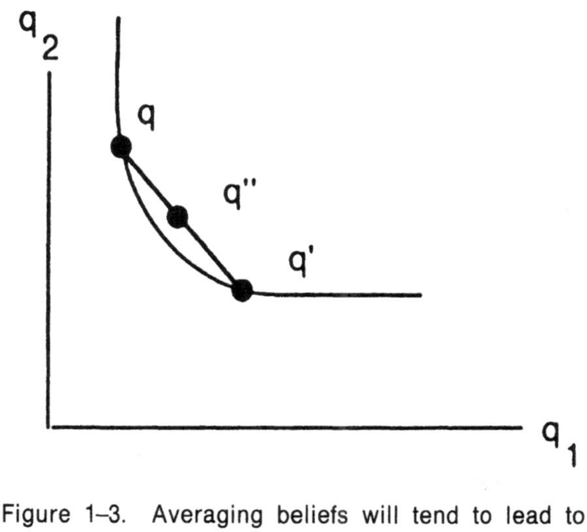

Figure 1–3. Averaging beliefs will tend to lead to lower asset prices.

It is instructive to consider this geometry when the tastes are identical. In figure 1–4A we have illustrated a typical level set of $F(C, q_1, q_2)$. We can also describe this level set implicitly as the set of all (q_1, q_2) such that

$$C = f(p/q_1) + f(p/q_2),$$

where p and C are fixed.

Consider the slope of this level set along the diagonal, where $q_1 = q_2$. Since $f(p/q_i)$ is independent of i along the diagonal, the slope of the level set must be -1. Thus, if we take a "spread" in (q_1, q_2) away from the diagonal that preserves the mean of (q_1, q_2) we are moving along a 45° line and must therefore move to a lower level set. At any other point on the curve a mean-preserving spread will necessarily move us to a lower level set, as illustrated.

Now consider the general case with different utilities as depicted in figure 1–4B. Here the level curve does not necessarily have slope of -1 at the diagonal so that a spread in beliefs may easily move us to a higher level set.

1.10 Moving from Homogenous to Diverse Beliefs

The geometric analysis of the last section can be used to describe another sense in which increases in the dispersion of opinion will tend to lower asset prices. Consider figure 1–4 once again. It is true that the level curve may not have a slope of -1 at the diagonal, but we can compute its slope easily enough. The level curve is defined by the identity

$$f_1(p/q_1) + f_2(p/q_2) = C.$$

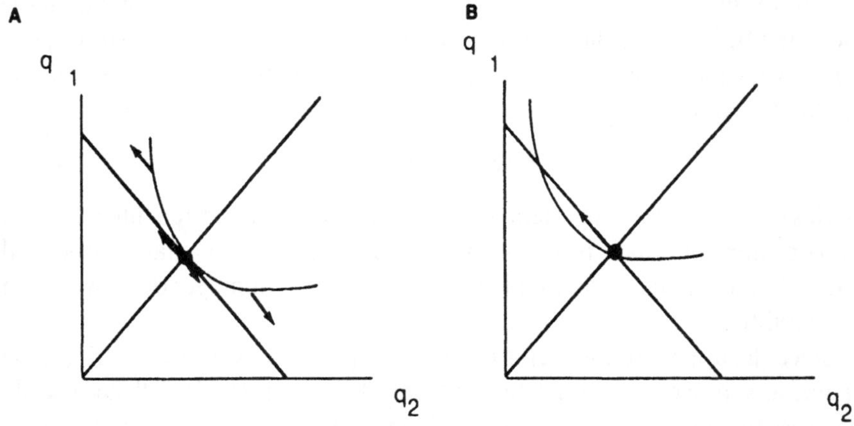

Figure 1–4. A mean-preserving spread with (A) identical tastes and (B) different tastes.

Totally differentiating this expression gives us

$$-f'_1(p/q_1)\frac{p}{q_1^2}dq_1 - f'_2(p/q_2)\frac{p}{q_2^2}dq_2 = 0.$$

Now use the facts that $f'_i = 1/u''_i$ and $u'_i = p/q_i$ to write

$$-\frac{u'_1(c_1)}{u''_1(c_1)}\frac{dq_1}{q_1} + \left(-\frac{u'_2(c_2)}{u''_2(c_2)}\right)\frac{dq_2}{q_2} = 0. \tag{1.30}$$

Using τ_i to represent individual i's risk tolerance, and evaluating this expression where $q_1 = q_2$ we have

$$\tau_1 dq_1 + \tau_2 dq_2 = 0 \tag{1.31}$$

or

$$\frac{dq_2}{dq_1} = -\frac{\tau_1}{\tau_2}. \tag{1.32}$$

This gives us the slope of the level set when the weighted beliefs are the same. A change in (q_1, q_2) that keeps the *weighted* sum in equation 1.31 constant represents an increase in the dispersion of beliefs which preserves the *weighted* mean. By the convexity of the level set, any such change must reduce the state price, starting from equal weighted beliefs.

In this expression an agent's beliefs are weighted by both his marginal utility of wealth and his risk tolerance. Generally speaking, the beliefs of wealthy and risk tolerant agents will have a larger weight in the above expression. Thus, an increase in the dispersion of those agents' beliefs will have a larger impact than an increase of the dispersion of beliefs of poorer and more risk averse agents, as one might expect.

This result can also be stated in terms of the absolute beliefs rather than the weighted beliefs. By definition of q_i, we have that $dq_i/q_i = d\pi_i/\pi_i$ since the λ_i terms will cancel from the numerator and denominator. Thus, if we evaluate (1.30) at a state where $\pi_1 = \pi_2$, we have

$$\tau_1 d\pi_1 + \tau_2 d\pi_2 = 0. \tag{1.33}$$

In this expression the risk tolerances τ_1 and τ_2 are evaluated at a different level of consumption than before—the consumption in the state associated with homogenous probabilities rather than homogenous weighted probabilities.

Since the upper contour set is convex in (π_1, π_2) space as well as in (q_1, q_2) space, any movement along tangent line defined in (1.33) will necessarily decrease the state price. Thus, moving from a state with homogenous beliefs to a state with heterogenous beliefs but the same level of aggregate consumption will necessarily lower the state price, as long as the *weighted* average of probability beliefs remains constant—where the weights are given by the risk tolerances.

Summarizing the above discussion we have:

Theorem 6: Assume that risk tolerance decreases less rapidly than in the case of logarithmic utility. Suppose the agents have homogenous beliefs about the probability of occurrence of state s. Then, if state t has identical aggregate consumption, and identical "weighted mean opinion," $\bar{\pi}$, but more dispersed probability beliefs, it must have a lower state price.

1.11 Other Equilibrium Models

The basic analytic tool used in the last few sections is the relationship between a mean-preserving spread in opinions and the concavity of the "demand functions." This observation can be applied to a variety of other equilibrium models.

The simplest case is that of a single risky asset. Let v_i be agent i's estimate of the expected value of this asset, and let p be the market price. Suppose that all agents have identical demand functions $D(p, v_i)$ and that the equilibrium price is determined by demand and supply:

$$\sum_{i=1}^{n} D(p, v_i) = S.$$

Suppose that the demand function is a concave function of v_i. Then a mean-preserving spread in v_i will decrease the sum of the demands. To restore equilibrium, the price must rise. The reverse result holds if the demand function is convex in v_i. These statements, unlike those of the last few sections, *are* comparative statics results since they refer to how the equilibrium values change when opinions become more dispersed, rather than how different asset values compare in a given equilibrium.

So the problem of how an increase in the dispersion of some variable affects equilibrium prices can be reduced to the question of whether demand functions are concave or convex in that variable. How can that be determined? The answer comes from examining the structure of the maximization model that lies behind the demands.

The standard comparative static technique to determine the slope of a demand function with respect to some parameter is to differentiate the first-order conditions. To determine the *curvature* of a demand function, it is necessary to take the *second derivative* of the first-order conditions, which will typically involve the third derivatives of the utility function. In the case investigated in this chapter we were able to give a simple interpretation of the conditions for concavity of the demand function in terms of how risk tolerance changes as wealth changes. In general, these third-order terms are rather messy, but it seems that there is hope of interpreting them in special cases.

Of course, in some models one can derive explicit forms for demand functions. For example, a constant relative risk aversion model with a single, Normally distributed asset gives rise to a demand function of the form

$$D_i = \frac{\tau_i(v_i - P)}{\sigma_i^2},$$

where τ_i is agent i's risk tolerance, v_i is his expected value, and σ_i^2 is his variance. In this case, demand is linear in the "weighted beliefs" $\tau_i v_i/\sigma_i^2$, so that a mean-preserving spread in these weighted beliefs will leave asset prices unchanged. However, demand is a *convex* function of the variances (σ_i^2), so a mean-preserving spread in the agents' beliefs about the variance of the risky asset will tend to *increase* the equilibrium price.[10]

Similar conclusions emerge in a CAPM or continuous-time model.[11] Since asset demand functions are linear functions of expected values for each agent, the equilibrium prices of assets will simply depend on the average expected values; assets with different degrees of dispersions of opinion will have the same equilibrium prices, other things being equal.

1.12 Summary

The first part of this chapter examined the distinction between information and opinions and showed that in equilibrium the pattern and volume of trade would be determined by differences of opinion, not differences in information.

The second part of the chapter, examined a model with pure opinion differences and derived the implications for comparative asset pricing. Maintaining the assumption that risk tolerance decreases, but not too rapidly, it was shown that if tastes are identical, asset prices would be decreasing functions of the dispersion of opinion. If tastes are different, asset prices will be quasiconcave functions of the vector of weighted probability beliefs, so that averaging beliefs will tend to increase asset prices. The curvature of the demand function is the crucial feature in determining how asset prices relate to different degrees of dispersion of beliefs.

Appendix: A Continuous-Time Model

This appendix examines a continuous-time model in which there are heterogenous beliefs about asset returns. Models of this sort have been extensively investigated by Williams (1977) and Grossman and Shiller (1982), with a somewhat different emphasis. By combining the insights of these authors we can adapt their results to the problem at hand.

Let r_s be the (instantaneous) random return on security s, and let r_0 be the (instantaneous), risk-free rate. Suppose that all asset returns and the optimal consumption of each agent follow an Ito process. Then in our notation Grossman and Shiller's equation 1.11a takes the form

$$r_{is} = r_0 + A_i \mathrm{cov}_i(r_s, dc_i/c_i),$$

where r_{is} is agent i's expected return on security s, $\mathrm{cov}_i(r_s, dc_i/c_i)$ is agent i's belief about the covariance of the rate of growth of his consumption and the rate of return on security s, and

$$A_i = -\frac{u_i''(c_i)}{u_i'(c_i)} c_i$$

is agent i's coefficient of *relative* risk aversion. This is simply the first-order condition for optimal choice in a continuous-time model, combined with Ito's lemma. Using the linearity of the covariance operator and that fact that c_i is nonstochastic at the time the optimal choice is made we have

$$r_{is} = r_0 + \frac{1}{\tau_i} \mathrm{cov}_i(r_s, dc_i), \tag{1.34}$$

where $\tau_i = -u'(c_i)/u_i''(c_i)$ is agent i's absolute risk tolerance.

Williams (1977) and Merton (1980) have argued that if security returns follow an Ito process, it is possible to estimate the covariance matrix of security returns arbitrarily accurately in an arbitrarily short time interval. The expected returns of the assets, on the other hand, will always be estimated imprecisely. Thus, following the argument of Williams (1977), we will assume that agents agree about the covariance matrix of the returns, and disagree only in their beliefs about the expected returns. This allows us to drop the subscript i on the covariance term in (1.34) and write it simply as $\mathrm{cov}(r_s, dc_i)$.

Cross multiply (1.34), sum over the agents $i = 1, \ldots, n$, and use the linearity of the covariance operator to get

$$\sum_{i=1}^{n} \tau_i r_{is} = r_0 \sum_{i=1}^{n} \tau_i + \mathrm{cov}(r_s, dC), \tag{1.35}$$

where $dC = \Sigma_{i=1}^{n} dc_i$ is the change in aggregate consumption.

Now define

$$\gamma_i = \frac{\tau_i}{\sum_{j=1}^{n} \tau_j}$$

and

$$\kappa = \frac{C}{\sum_{j=1}^{n} \tau_j}$$

and rewrite this expression as

$$\sum_{i=1}^{n} \gamma_i r_{is} = r_0 + \kappa \operatorname{cov}(r_s, dC/C). \tag{1.36}$$

To interpret this equation, we note that the left side is the weighted average of expected returns, where the weight given to agent i's beliefs is proportional to his risk tolerance. The right side of the equation is the risk-free return plus a constant depending on the average risk tolerance in the economy times the covariance of the asset return with the rate of growth of aggregate consumption.

This calculation is similar to the derivation of Grossman and Shiller (1982) but with a different interpretation. They take expectations with respect to the set of common information available to the agents at the time their consumption decisions are made. The left side of equation 1.36 in their framework is the expected return on security s based on the publicly available information at a given time. In our framework, the left side of (1.36) is a weighted average of subjective beliefs about the expected returns.

Following Williams (1977) we have assumed that agents have homogenous beliefs about the covariance structure of the asset returns, but differ in their expected values for asset returns. The expectations in equation 1.36 are the actual expectations of the agents, based on their own private information and beliefs, not the expectations based on some common information as in Grossman and Shiller.

Equation 1.36 is the analog of Williams (1977) continuous-time CAPM with heterogenous beliefs, but because we use the covariance with consumption rather than the covariance with respect to wealth, the "hedging portfolios" in his equation are not needed here. (See Breeden (1979) for further discussion of why "hedging portfolios" are not needed in general in consumption-based pricing models in continuous time.)

For our purposes, the interesting thing about equation 1.36 is what it says about comparative asset pricing. If two securities have the same "consumption beta" then they have to have the same "average expected return." This in turn implies that the pricing of securities is independent of the dispersion of opinion about their expected values. To see this, let v_s be the market value of security s at a specific time and let dv_s be the random change in its value in the next instant. Then, since the instantaneous return is given by $r_{is} = dv_{is}/v_s$, we can solve (1.36) to get

$$v_s = \frac{\sum_{i=1}^{n} \gamma_i dv_{is} - \kappa \operatorname{cov}(dC/C, dv_s)}{r_0}.$$

Here dv_{is} is agent i's belief about the expected change in value of asset s. Thus, two securities that have the same "consumption beta" and the same *average* expected return must have the same price.

It is interesting to compare this result with equation 1.33. In that equation π_1 and π_2 are the expected returns on the Arrow–Debreu asset under consideration, since it pays zero in all states but one. Theorem 6 established that an increase in dispersion of opinion that keeps the weighted average of opinions constant will decrease the state price. In the continuous-time framework examined above, such an increase in dispersion of opinion will leave the state price unchanged.

The insensitivity of asset prices to differences of opinion arise in this framework because of the linearity of the asset demand functions in the expected returns. Since only the first two derivatives of utility enter into the portfolio choice problem, the higher order curvature properties of utility considered earlier will not affect asset price in equilibrium.

A similar result occurs in a discrete-time model, if we are willing to postulate that individuals believe that their optimal consumption in future periods and asset returns will be Normally distributed. Since the algebra is almost the same as that given above, we will sketch only the details.

The first-order conditions for utility maximization by individual i will take the form

$$E_i u_i'(c_i)(r_s - r_0),$$

where E_i stands for expectation with respect to agent i's subjective beliefs about the asset returns. (The expectations are at time 0 for some given time in the future, but we omit the time subscript so as not to clutter the notation.)

Using the standard covariance identity, and rearranging, we can write this as

$$r_{is} = r_0 - \frac{\operatorname{cov}_i(u_i'(c_i), r_s)}{E_i u'(c_i)},$$

where $r_{is} = E_i r_s$, as before. Assume now that c_i and r_s are perceived as bivariate Normal by investor i. Applying a theorem from Rubinstein (1976b) we have

$$r_{is} = r_0 + \left(- \frac{E_i u_i''(c_i)}{E_i u_i'(c_i)} \right) \operatorname{cov}_i(c_i, r_s).$$

Letting $\tau_i = -E_i u_i'(c_i)/E_i u''(c_i)$, we can write this as

$$r_{is} = r_0 + \frac{1}{\tau_i} \operatorname{cov}_i(c_i, r_s). \tag{1.37}$$

This equation is virtually the same as (1.34). If we assume that agents have the same beliefs about the covariance structure of the asset returns, then the same algebraic manipulations as before gives us

$$\sum_{i=1}^{n} \gamma_i r_{is} = r_0 + \kappa \operatorname{cov}(C, r_s). \tag{1.38}$$

The only difference between (1.36) and (1.38) is that γ_i and κ have slightly different interpretations in the two equations, and that (1.38) is expressed in levels rather than instantaneous rates of change.

Equations 1.36 and 1.38 are on the verge of being estimable, at least given survey data on expectations and the time-series estimates of the covariance between asset returns and aggregate consumption that are beginning to appear. Perhaps the addition of heterogenous beliefs about assets returns will improve the performance of the empirical estimates of consumption-based asset pricing models.

Finally, we consider the volume of trade in this kind of model. If we increase dispersion of opinion in the way described earlier—where the net demanders become more optimistic and the endowments of the two assets across the consumers are the same—and we keep the weighted sum of expected returns constant, then it is easy to see that the volume of trade must increase, for an increase in the expected return on an asset must increase net demand for it by an individual, and we have established above that the asset price remains unchanged. Thus, the transactions volume in the asset with the more dispersed beliefs must unambiguously be larger.

Notes

1. More precisely, the mean-variance model requires that agents agree on the mean returns and covariance matrix of the assets; the contingent consumption model requires that agents agree on the probability of occurrence of different levels of aggregate consumptions.
2. The precise meaning of "too rapidly" is given below.
3. Aumann's (1976) famous paper on this topic establishes only that rational individuals with *identical* priors and likelihoods who communicate their posteriors cannot disagree.
4. The precision of a random variable is the reciprocal of the variance.
5. Risk tolerance is given by $-u'(c)/u''(c)$; it is the reciprocal of the Arrow-Pratt measure of absolute risk aversion. For a discussion of the Arrow-Pratt measure see Varian (1984).

6. Milgrom and Stokey (1982) also make use of the change in equilibrium prices to convey information. We will examine their model shortly. I thank Sarab Seth for suggesting that a similar approach would be useful in the mean-variance context considered here.

7. Of course, this model leads directly to the Grossman paradox as well: if the market price reveals all information, why does anyone bother to acquire information? Various resolutions of this paradox can be found in Grossman and Stiglitz (1980), Hellwig (1980), and Diamond and Verrecchia (1981).

8. Related insights can be found in Marshall (1974), Rubinstein (1975), Bhattacharya (1976), Hakansson, et al. (1982), and Verrecchia (1981).

9. The fact that theorem 4 has an elementary graphical argument was pointed out to me by Duanne Seppi.

10. For an interesting analysis of an equilibrium in a futures market in which traders have different variances, see Stein (1986).

11. See the appendix for a discussion of dispersion of beliefs in a continuous-time framework.

References

Aumann, R. (1976), "Agreeing to Disagree," *Annals of Statistics*, **4**, 1236–1239.

Bhattacharya, S. (1976), "Information Efficiency and Inter-temporal Rates of Return," Sloan School mimeo.

Black, F. (1986), "Noise," *Journal of Finance*, **41**, 529–543.

Breeden, D. (1979), "An Intertemporal Asset Pricing Model with Stochastic Consumption and Investment Opportunities," *Journal of Financial Economics*, **7**, 265–296.

Breeden, D. and M. Litzenberger (1978), "Prices of State-Contingent Claims Implicit in Option Prices," *Journal of Business*, **51**, 621–651.

Cragg, J. and B. Malkiel (1982), *Expectations and the Structure of Share Prices*, University of Chicago Press, Chicago.

Diamond, D. and R. Verrecchia (1981), "Informational Aggregation in a Noisy Rational Expectations Economy," *Journal of Financial Economics*, **9**, 221–235.

Epps, T. and M. Epps (1976), "The Stochastic Dependence of Security Price Changes and Transaction Volumes: Implications for the Mixture-of-Distribution Hypothesis," *Econometrica*, **44**, 305–321.

Grossman, S. (1976), "On the Efficiency of Competitive Stock Markets Where Traders Have Diverse Information," *The Journal of Finance*, **31**, 573–585.

——— (1977), "The Existence of Futures Markets, Noisy Rational Expectations, and Informational Externalities," *Review of Economic Studies*, **44**, 431–449.

——— (1978), "Further Results on the Informational Efficiency of Competitive Stock Markets," *Journal of Economic Theory*, **18**, 81–101.

Grossman, S. and R. Shiller (1982), "Consumption Correlatedness and Risk Measurement in Economies with Non-Traded Assets and Heterogeneous Information," *Journal of Financial Economics*, **10**, 195–210.

Grossman, S. and J. Stiglitz (1980), "On the Impossibility of Informationally Efficient Markets," *American Economic Review*, **70**, 393–408.

Hakansson, N., J. Kunkel, and J. Ohlson (1982), "Sufficient and Necessary Conditions for Information to have Social Value in Pure Exchange," *Journal of Finance*, **37**, 1169–1181.

Harris, L. (1983), "The Joint Distribution of Speculative Prices and of Daily Trading Volume," University of Southern California Working Paper.

Harsanyi, J. (1983), "Bayesian Decision Theory, Subjective and Objective Probabilities, and Acceptance of Empirical Hypotheses," *Synthese*, **57**, 341–365.

Hellwig, M. (1980), "On the Aggregation of Information in Competitive Markets," *Journal of Economic Theory*, **22**, 477–498.

Jarrow, R. (1980), "Heterogeneous Expectations, Restrictions on Short Sales, and Equilibrium Asset Prices," *Journal of Finance*, **35**, 1105–1113.

Karpoff, J. (1985), "The Relationship between Stock Prices and Volume," *Center for the Study of Banking and Financial Markets Digest*, University of Washington, Seattle.

Lintner, J. (1969), "The Aggregation of Investors' Diverse Judgements and Preferences in Purely Competitive Markets," *Journal of Financial and Quantitative Analysis*, **4**, 347–400.

Marshall, J. (1974), "Private Incentives and Public Information," *American Economic Review*, **64**, 373–390.

Mayshar, J. (1983), "On Divergence of Opinion and Imperfections in Capital Markets," *American Economic Review*, **73**, 114–128.

Merton, R. (1980), "On Estimating the Expected Return on the Market," *Journal of Financial Economics*, **8**, 323–361.

Milgrom, P. and N. Stokey (1982), "Information, Trade and Common Knowledge," *Journal of Economic Theory*, **26**, 17–27.

Rothschild, M. and J. Stiglitz (1970), "Increasing Risk I: A Definition," *Journal of Economic Theory*, **2**, 225–243.

Rubinstein, M. (1975), "Security Market Efficiency in an Arrow-Debreu Economy," *American Economic Review*, **65**, 812–824.

——— (1976a), "The Strong Case for the Generalized Logarithmic Utility Model as the Premier Model of Financial Markets," *Journal of Finance*, **31**, 551–571.

——— (1976b), "The Valuation of Uncertain Income Streams and the Pricing of Options," *Bell Journal of Economics*, **7**, 407–425.

Stein, J. (1986), "Real Effects of Futures Speculation: Asymptotically Rational Expectations," *Economica*, **53**, 159–180.

Tauchen, G. and M. Pitts (1983), "The Price Variability–Volume Relationship on Speculative Markets," *Econometrica*, **51**, 485–506.

Tirole, J. (1982), "On the Possibility of Speculation Under Rational Expectations," *Econometrica*, **50**, 1163–1182.

Varian, H. (1984), *Microeconomic Analysis*, Norton, New York.

——— (1985a), "Divergence of Opinion in Complete Markets," *Journal of Finance*, **40**(1), 309–317.

——— (1985b), "Observable Implications of Changes in Risk Aversion," University of Michigan Working Paper. To appear in *Econometrica*.

Verrecchia, R. (1981), "On the Relationship between Volume Reaction and the Consensus of Investors: Implications for Interpreting Tests of Information Content," *Journal of Accounting Research*, **19**, 271–283.

Williams, J. (1977), "Capital Asset Prices with Heterogeneous Beliefs," *Journal of Financial Economics*, **5**, 219–239.

Commentary by V. V. Chari

All of economics concerns itself with prices and quantities. Why should asset markets be any different? The need for satisfactory models of volume and price changes in asset markets is self-evident. Let me start by taking a vastly oversimplified view of this issue. If I ask a layman why anybody might sell shares in a firm, I think the obvious answers are (1) the individual needs the money to buy something else, be it a house or a six-pack of beer, and (2) the individual thinks the price of the stock will fall. Conversely, a buyer either (1) has received income that he desires to invest, or (2) thinks the stock will go up.

Trade due to differences in endowments or desired consumption is the cornerstone of economics. Presumably we understand the forces here reasonably well. Varian, in this chapter, has attempted to begin developing models of speculative behavior. There are three main messages in this chapter.

1. Trade can occur due to difference of opinion, which can formally be understood as differences in prior beliefs.
2. Trade can occur due to difference in how information is interpreted.
3. The volume of trade and the determination of prices are extraordinarily

complicated functions of preferences, endowments, and prior beliefs but under a limited set of conditions, theory imposes restrictions on the qualitative properties of trade and prices as functions of prior beliefs.

Varian also has a great deal to say about the so-called No-Trade Theorems, about which I will say a little.

Let me take these one at a time.

1. Clearly trade can be due to differences in prior beliefs. We know from the original work of Arrow and Debreu, however, that there is little or no content in their models to suggest a distinction between preferences and prior beliefs. Unless one can come up with an operational measurement of prior beliefs, this distribution is wholly without content. And what is this operational measure? Is it going out and asking people what their prior beliefs are? Well, if we could do that why don't we ask them what their preferences are, to boot? In which case we can dispense with prior beliefs anyway. There is a more serious objection to using this approach to understand prices and volume, in my view. A fundamental theorem of Bayesian statistics is that no matter what your prior beliefs are, after enough observations posterior probability assessments will converge. Combine that with the theorems from the rational expectations literature on the information revealed by market prices themselves and it is difficult to think of a sensible theory with vastly different beliefs that are sustained over any period of time. So it is difficult to know how seriously we, as theorists, should take differences in prior beliefs as useful in explaining trade in asset markets.

2. Let me turn now to differences in interpretation of information. I found this short section very difficult to understand and let me explain why. It will help to examine equation 1.23. Let me ignore $\delta_i Y_i$ temporarily. If the agent's estimate about the impact of information on the risky asset is normally distributed with mean v and precision ω as the equation seems to say, then the analysis of section 1.3 goes through unchanged. Just above equation 1.24 Varian seems to say that the sample mean of the estimates v_i equals the product of the sample mean of δ_i and Y_i. This is true only if the number of agents is infinite, in which case equation 1.24 makes no sense. Setting that aside, Varian claims just above equation 1.25 that agent i's estimate of the risky asset postinformation should be $\delta_i \bar{Y}$. But this is entirely inconsistent with Bayesian decision making, which is an absolutely crucial assumption behind section 1.3 and is used in equation 1.24. All told, I think there is a role for differences in interpretation, but this section does not make the case as far as I can tell.

3. Let me now discuss the No-Trade Theorems. First, let me point out that differences in prior beliefs do not get around the No-Trade Theorems. Exactly like differences in preferences and endowments after an initial round of trading, new information will not cause agents to trade. The No-Trade Theorems do not rest on the assumption that prior beliefs are identical at all.

Let me conclude by suggesting that the obvious ways around the No-Trade Theorems are suggested by the assumptions of the theorems themselves. Throw out complete contingent markets or competitive behavior and agents will trade even if it is common knowledge that other traders have superior information. Work on micro models of asset markets, including market makers by Glosten and Milgrom and by Kyle, has taken exactly this promising route. Why should we descend into a morass of non-Bayesian decision-making agents or throw out rationality when the implications of this rich and promising branch of the literature have not even been scratched?

2 RISK, EXCHANGE MARKET INTERVENTION, AND PRIVATE SPECULATIVE BEHAVIOR IN A SMALL OPEN ECONOMY

Stephen J. Turnovsky

2.1 Introduction

The increased fluctuations in exchange markets during the past decade or so have stimulated interest in exchange rate management and exchange market intervention; see, for example, Boyer (1978), Roper and Turnovsky (1980), Aizenman and Frenkel (1982), and papers in Bhandari (1985). By far, most of the analyses have considered official intervention in the spot market and have derived optimal intervention rules under a variety of assumptions regarding such things as (1) the types of disturbances and (2) the information sets available to the agents in the economy.[1]

But from time to time, economists have advocated that intervention in the forward exchange market may serve as an important instrument of monetary policy. This view was put forward by Keynes (1930) and later by Spraos (1959) who argued that "the forward rate should not only be supported, as a defense against speculative attack, but should be actually pegged." One of the advantages of forward market intervention is that it does not entail any tightening of domestic credit conditions and may therefore eliminate certain sources of fluctuations that may be generated by a contractionary monetary policy. More recently, Niehans (1984) has expressed a more skeptical view of forward market intervention as an instrument of stabilization policy.

In contrast to the extensive literature on spot market intervention, little work has been devoted to studying the merits of forward market intervention. One recent study of this issue is by Eaton and Turnovsky (1984), but their analysis abstracts from one important aspect.[2] Specifically, they assume that the coefficient of speculation, which determines the demand for forward exchange, is a given parameter. However, as several authors have shown, when one derives this demand from the underlying optimization of risk-averse agents in the economy, this coefficient is not fixed. Rather, under reasonable conditions it varies inversely with the one-period variance of the spot exchange rate and thereby becomes endogenously determined, along with this variance. Moreover, since the spot exchange rate is a function of government intervention policy, this coefficient becomes dependent upon the policy regime. But the Eaton-Turnovsky analysis ignores this channel, whereby government policy impacts on private behavior.

In effect, what is at issue here is the Lucas critique. As a result of Lucas' important insights, it has become accepted that reduced form parameters are not invariant with respect to government policy, so that a correct assessment of the effects of government policy needs to take account of these induced changes. In the present context, we have a somewhat stronger version of this proposition, namely that certain *structural parameters*, which in this case describe some aspect of private behavior, are also not invariant with respect to government policy.

This structural aspect of the Lucas critique, while receiving much less attention, particularly in the policy-related literature, has not gone unnoticed. It was first incorporated into a model of the foreign exchange market, based on mean-variance utility maximization by Driskill and McCafferty (1980). More recently, Kawai (1984) has used a similar framework to develop a model of spot and formal exchange rate determination, although his treatment of intervention is very brief. Some discussion of spot market intervention in this type of model is given by Black (1985), but he does not address issues pertaining to intervention in the forward exchange market.

This chapter analyzes the effects of both spot and forward market intervention, taking account of the endogeneity of private speculation and how it is influenced by government policy. The model we employ is a slightly simplified version of the Eaton-Turnovsky model. This model has the advantage of expositional simplicity, which enables most of the analysis to be conducted graphically. By dispensing with a lot of the formal analytics, we are able to see more clearly the issues that are involved.

As many authors have noted, once one endogenizes the degree of private speculation, the rational expectations equilibrium becomes nonlinear. This immediately raises questions of (1) existence and (2) nonuniqueness of equilibrium.[3] These are not simply esoteric issues, but are of relevance for policy. For example, is it the case that government intervention will succeed in helping resolve these problems? Or may what may seems to be a perfectly reasonable form of intervention generate structural imbalances in the market and thereby preclude the existence of an equilibrium? Our analysis highlights the way in which government policy exercises an influence through its impact on the behavior of private speculators. We show how in some cases this channel may dominate any direct effects, so that neglecting it can be seriously misleading.

The chapter is structured as follows. Section 2.2 outlines the model, then the equilibrium under perfectly flexible exchange rates is discussed in section 2.3. Section 2.4 analyzes the effects of increased risk. Spot market and forward market intervention rules are discussed in sections 2.5 and 2.6. Section 2.7 briefly compares the perfectly flexible rate, with not only the fixed spot rate, but a fixed forward rate as well. The main conclusions are reviewed in the final section.

2.2 The Analytical Framework

We shall consider a slightly simplified version of the Eaton-Turnovsky (1984) model by taking output to be fixed at its full employment level. Specifically, we assume there is a single traded commodity, the price of which in terms of foreign currency is given, set at unity, say. Also, we assume that the domestic bond is a perfect substitute for a traded world bond, when fully covered against exchange risk. Thus, purchasing power parity (PPP) and covered interest parity (CIP) are assumed to hold.

The model is summarized by the following equation

$$m_t - e_t = -\alpha r_t + u_t \qquad \alpha > 0 \tag{2.1a}$$

$$r_t = \omega_t + f_t - e_t \tag{2.1b}$$

$$h_t = \beta r_t + v_{1t} \qquad \beta > 0 \tag{2.1c}$$

$$s_t = \gamma(e^*_{t+1,t} - f_t) + v_{2t} \qquad \gamma > 0 \tag{2.1d}$$

$$h_t = (1-\mu)(b_t + g_t - p_t) + \mu s_t \qquad 0 \le \mu \le 1 \tag{2.1e}$$

where

e_t = current spot exchange rate (measured in terms of units of domestic currency per unit of foreign currency),

$e^*_{t+1,t}$ = expectation of the spot exchange rate at time $t+1$, conditional on information at time t,
f_t = forward exchange rate (measured in terms of units of domestic currency per unit of foreign currency),
m_t = domestic nominal money supply,
b_t = domestic nominal supply of bonds,
h_t = domestic demand for real bonds,
s_t = speculative demand for forward exchange,
g_t = nominal value in domestic currency units of official purchases of forward exchange, expressed as a share of outstanding bonds,
r_t = domestic nominal interest rate,
ω_t = world nominal interest rate,
u_t = stochastic disturbance in demand for money,
v_{1t} = stochastic disturbance in demand for bonds,
v_{2t} = stochastic disturbance in speculators' demand for forward exchange.

All variables, except r_t, ω_t, and g_t are expressed as logarithmic deviations from steady-state levels; r_t and ω_t are deviations in natural units and g_t is defined below. Given PPP and the normalization of the foreign price level, the domestic price level is simply e_t.

Equation 2.1a describes domestic money market equilibrium, in which, with output fixed, the demand for money depends only upon the domestic interest rate. All domestic money is held by domestic residents, who in turn hold no foreign money. Equation 2.1b specifies covered interest parity and embodies the assumption that domestic bonds and foreign bonds are perfect substitutes on a covered basis.

Equation 2.1c specifies the domestic demand for bonds. Because the bond market interacts in a crucial way with the forward exchange market, we depart from the standard practice of specifying a commodity market equilibrium or a savings or absorption equation, and suppressing the bond market equilibrium condition. Instead, we explicitly include the bond market and leave savings to be defined residually from conditions for money market and bond market equilibrium. This specification is also the most convenient in a log-linear framework and is frequently invoked in such models; see, for example, Lucas (1975). We postulate a simple demand for bonds function, which depends positively upon the domestic interest rate.

The specification of the forward market is given in equations 2.1d and 2.1e and can be derived from intertemporal portfolio maximization; see, for example, Solnik (1973), Kouri (1976), Fama and Farber (1979), and Eaton and Turnovsky (1981). In our model, this market has two functions. First, it provides holders of foreign bonds with a means of eliminating exchange risk by selling the foreign currency proceeds of their bonds forward. Such sales constitute *arbitrage* activity on this market. Second, the forward market provides a means of *speculating* on exchange rate movements.[4] A first-order approximation to the rate of return on the forward purchase of a unit of foreign currency is $(e_{t+1} - f_t)$. In (2.1d) we postulate that the demand of foreign exchange for speculation s_t is an increasing function of the expected difference $(e^*_{t+1,1} - f_t)$.

Equilibrium in the forward exchange market is described by (2.1e). This equation asserts that the demand for forward exchange consisting of (1) demand for speculation and (2) demand by intervention authorities for stabilization purposes equals the supply for arbitrage. This equation is perhaps the least familiar aspect of the model and requires further explanation. Because of the assumption that domestic and foreign bonds are perfect substitutes, there is in fact only a single demand function for total bonds h_t; the demand for foreign bonds is simply the difference between the aggregate national demand and the supply from domestic sources; that is [5]

$$H_t - B_t/P_t = H^f_t,$$

where

H = the total real bond demand,
B = the domestic nominal bond supply,
P = the domestic price level,
H^f = the real demand for foreign bonds,

all these quantities being expressed in levels.

Since foreign bonds are covered, forward market equilibrium requires that

$$H_t - B_t/P_t = S_t + E_t G_t/P_t,$$

where G_t denotes government purchases of forward exchange and E_t is the level of the current spot exchange rate. The net private supply of forward exchange to cover foreign bonds equals the net private speculative demand plus net government purchases of forward exchange. Defining the quantity g_t to be the nominal value in domestic current units of these government purchases, expressed as a share of outstanding bonds,

$$g_t = \frac{E_t G_t}{B_t},$$

we obtain

$$H_t - (1 + g_t)\frac{B_t}{P_t} = S_t.$$

Equation 2.1e is obtained as a log-linear approximation to this relationship, where the parameter $\mu \equiv \bar{H}^f/\bar{H}$ is the average holdings of foreign bonds, as a share of total bond demand, and arbitrary constants are deleted.[6]

An important consequence of (2.1e) is that variations in the stock of domestic government bonds and in the government's forward market position are not linearly independent. Forward market intervention is equivalent to sterilized intervention in the spot market.

Finally, the stochastic disturbances u_t, v_{1t}, v_{2t} are assumed to have zero means, finite second moments, and to be identically and independently distributed over time. The foreign interest rate ω_t is also assumed to be stochastic and to have these same properties.

The key parameter in the model is γ, which describes the elasticity of speculation. Eaton and Turnovsky (1984) take this to be a given constant. However, when the basic model (2.1a)–(2.1e) is derived from underlying optimization of the private agents, γ becomes an endogenously determined parameter. Specifically, Eaton and Turnovsky (1981) and others have shown that optimizing a mean-variance utility function over two periods leads to a speculative demand for forward exchange in which

$$\gamma \simeq \frac{1}{R\sigma_e^2(1)}, \tag{2.2}$$

where $\sigma_e^2(1)$ is the one-period variance of the spot exchange rate and R is the coefficient of absolute risk aversion.[7]

It is clear from equation 2.2 that γ is jointly determined with the one-period variance of the spot rate, and is therefore endogenous. It is this nonlinearity between these variables that is the source of the possible nonexistence and nonuniqueness problems mentioned earlier. In the limiting case when investors are risk neutral ($R \to 0$), $\gamma \to \infty$. Speculation is infinitely elastic, and the forward market equilibrium condition reduces to $f_t = e^*_{t+1,t}$, so that uncovered interest parity prevails. This is the assumption made in much of the intervention literature, when infinitely elastic speculation renders the forward market redundant.

2.3 Equilibrium under Flexible Exchange Rates

We begin by solving the model outlined in section 2.2 under perfectly flexible exchange rates, when there is no government intervention in either the spot or forward exchange market. We therefore set $m_t = b_t = g_t = 0$ for all t, so that domestic nominal money, bonds, and forward market positions remain fixed at their constant steady-state levels. Taking conditional expectations of the system (2.1) at time t for time $t+i$, we can show that expectations of future spot rates satisfy a difference equation of the form

$$e^*_{t+i,t} = \phi e^*_{t+i-1,t} \qquad i = 1, 2, \ldots, \tag{2.3}$$

where $\phi > 1$ is a function of the underlying parameters. Thus, if exchange rate expectations are to remain bounded as $i \to \infty$, we require

$$e^*_{t+i,t} = 0 \qquad i = 1, 2, \ldots. \tag{2.4}$$

Otherwise, expectations become unbounded and this in turn implies that the asymptotic variances of the spot and forward exchange rates will become infinite. To rule this out, we therefore focus on the bounded solution given by (2.4).[8] Setting expectations to zero in (2.1), we can reduce the system to the following three relationships:

Money Market $\qquad -e_t + \alpha r_t = u_t \qquad$ (2.5a)

Covered Interest Parity $\qquad r_t - f_t + e_t = \omega_t \qquad$ (2.5b)

Forward Market $\qquad \beta r_t + (1-\mu)e_t + \gamma\mu f_t = v_t \quad v_t \equiv v_{1t} + v_{2t}. \qquad$ (2.5c)

Writing the relationships in this way highlights how the three disturbances impact on the domestic economy. The domestic monetary shock is introduced via the money market; the foreign interest rate shock occurs through the covered interest parity relationship. The disturbance v_t is a composite one and can reflect a stochastic shift either in the demand for bonds or in speculation. It can also be interpreted as reflecting a stochastic disturbance in the supply of bonds and to this extent can be identified as being a domestic fiscal disturbance. The three relationships (2.5a)–(2.5c) determine simultaneously the equilibrium levels of the spot rate e_t, the forward rate f_t, and the domestic interest rate r_t.

The solutions to these equations are given by the expressions

$$e_t = \frac{1}{D}[-(\beta + \mu\gamma)u_t + \alpha v_t + \alpha\mu\gamma\omega_t] \tag{2.6a}$$

$$f_t = \frac{1}{D}\{(1 - \mu - \beta)u_t + (1 + \alpha)v_t - [\alpha(1 - \mu) + \beta]\omega_t\} \tag{2.6b}$$

$$r_t = \frac{1}{D}[(1 - \mu + \mu\gamma)u_t + v_t + \mu\gamma\omega_t], \tag{2.6c}$$

where

$$D \equiv \beta + \mu\gamma + \alpha(\mu\gamma + 1 - \mu) > 0.$$

These solutions are expressed in terms of γ, the elasticity of speculation, which we have argued depends upon the one-period variance of the spot rate. Since with white noise disturbances and future expectations therefore all zero, the model is in fact static; the one period variance of the spot rate (and also the asymptotic variance) is simply given by the variance of (2.6a). Assuming, for simplicity, that u_t, v_t, ω_t are uncorrelated, this is given by

$$\sigma_e^2 = \frac{1}{D^2}[(\beta + \mu\gamma)^2\sigma_u^2 + \alpha^2\sigma_v^2 + \alpha^2\mu^2\gamma^2\sigma_\omega^2]. \tag{2.7a}$$

The solutions for σ_e^2, σ_f^2, and σ_r^2, are therefore (2.7a), together with

$$\sigma_f^2 = \frac{1}{D^2}\{(1 - \mu - \beta)^2\sigma_u^2 + (1 + \alpha)^2\sigma_v^2 + [\alpha(1 - \mu) + \beta]^2\sigma_\omega^2\} \tag{2.7b}$$

$$\sigma_r^2 = \frac{1}{D^2}[(1 - \mu + \mu\gamma)^2\sigma_u^2 + \sigma_v^2 + \mu^2\gamma^2\sigma_\omega^2], \tag{2.7c}$$

where

$$\gamma = \frac{1}{R\sigma_e^2}. \tag{2.7d}$$

In particular, equations 2.7a and 2.7d highlight the joint determination of the variance of the spot rate and the elasticity of speculation. The nonlinearity of the relationship raises the question of (1) the existence, and (2) the possible multiplicity of equilibria. This issue can be studied by substituting (2.7d) into (2.7a), to yield the following cubic equation in the variance σ_e^2:

$$\begin{aligned}&[\beta + \alpha(1 - \mu)]^2R^2(\sigma_e^2)^3 + \{2\omega(1 + \alpha)[\beta + \alpha(1 - \mu)]R - \beta^2R^2\sigma_u^2\\&\quad - \alpha^2R^2\sigma_v^2\}(\sigma_e^2)^2\\&\quad + [\mu^2(1 + \alpha)^2 - 2\beta R\mu\sigma_u^2]\sigma_e^2 - \mu^2(\sigma_u^2 + \alpha^2\sigma_\omega^2] = 0.\end{aligned} \tag{2.8}$$

The existence question revolves around whether or not there is a solution to (2.8) with $\sigma_e^2 > 0$, so that the variance of the spot rate is indeed positive.

The answer to this question depends upon the sources of shocks. If either $\sigma_u^2 > 0$ or $\sigma_\omega^2 > 0$, the constant term in this cubic equation is strictly postive, implying that the product of the three roots is positive. This means that there are either one or three positive solutions to σ_e^2. At least one equilibrium therefore exists. The conditions for a unique equilibrium are complicated and not very illuminating. The characterization of the equilibria, however, does simplify when one focuses on one disturbance at a time.

1. If the only disturbance is in the domestic monetary sector ($\sigma_u^2 > 0$, $\sigma_v^2 = \sigma_\omega^2 = 0$), then one can show that there may be either one or three equilibrium solutions. For plausible parameter values it seems likely that a

unique solution will prevail. For example, a sufficient, but not necessary, condition for a unique solution is

$$\beta < 1 - \mu. \tag{2.9}$$

Inequality 2.9 is the condition for a positive disturbance in the demand for money to impact positively on the forward exchange rate; see (2.6b). On the one hand, a postive shock in u_t tends to raise the interest rate, while simultaneously leading to an appreciation of the domestic currency. The net effect on the forward rate f_t depends upon which of these two effects is dominant.

2. If the only disturbance is in the foreign interest rate ($\sigma_\omega^2 > 0$, $\sigma_u^2 = \sigma_v^2 = 0$), then one can show that equation 2.8 has a unique solution for $\sigma_e^2 > 0$.

3. If the only disturbance is in the bond market ($\sigma_v^2 > 0$, $\sigma_u^2 = \sigma_\omega^2 = 0$), then (2.8) reduces to

$$\sigma_e^2 [\![[\beta + \alpha(1-\mu)]^2 R^2 (\sigma_e^2)^2 + \{2\mu(1+\alpha)[\beta + \alpha(1-\mu)]R - \alpha^2 R^2 \sigma_v^2\} \sigma_e^2 + \mu^2 (1+\alpha)^2]\!] = 0. \tag{2.8$'$}$$

Ruling out $\sigma_e^2 = 0$, leaves a quadratic equation in σ_e^2, the product of the roots of which is positive. The condition for (2.8′) to have real roots is

$$\alpha^2 R \sigma_v^2 > 4\mu(1+\alpha)[\beta + \alpha(1-\mu)]. \tag{2.10}$$

Hence, with the only disturbances occurring in the bond market, the solution will have either *two* equilibria or *no* equilibrium according to whether (2.10) is or is not met. In particular, it is of interest, and rather counterintuitive, to observe that a larger variance in bond disturbances is more conductive to the existence of an equilibrium.

The reason for this can be seen by substituting from (2.5a) and (2.5b) into the forward market equilibrium condition (2.5c):

$$\left[\frac{1}{\alpha}(\beta + \mu\gamma) + \mu\gamma + 1 - \mu\right] e_t = -\frac{1}{\alpha}(\beta + \mu\gamma)u_t + v_t + \mu\gamma\omega_t. \tag{2.11}$$

The left side reflects the endogenous variation in the excess demand for forward exchange due to fluctuations in the exchange rate; the right side represents the fluctuations due to the exogenous random disturbances.

Suppose that the exogenous fluctuations in the bond market v_t are small, so that σ_v^2 is small. These small fluctuations in v_t will, for a given degree of speculation γ and other parameters, lead to small fluctuations in the spot exchange rate; that is, σ_e^2 will be small. But this will encourage private speculation, thereby increasing γ. This in turn will exacerbate the endogenous fluctuations in the demand for forward exchange. But the variations due to the exogenous fluctuations on the right side of (2.11) remain fixed. Indeed, if σ_v^2 is sufficiently small so that γ is large, it is possible for the induced fluctuations in excess demand to exceed the exogenous fluctuations given by the right side, so that no equilibrium exists. By contrast, for fluctuations in either u_t or ω_t, as γ increases, the exogenous fluctuations on the right side and endogenous fluctuations on the left side both increase together, and the problem of imbalance and disequilibrium does not arise.

Equations 2.7a–2.7d determine simultaneously the solutions for σ_e^2, σ_f^2, σ_r^2, and γ. The possible nonuniqueness of equilibrium was discussed originally by McCafferty and Driskill (1980). This condition raises the question of how to choose among the various equilibria. One possibility is to choose the one having the minimum (or smaller) variance. However, as McCafferty and Driskill note, this may or may not yield the maximum (or higher) level of utility. A more appropriate criterion is to select the equilibrium having the highest expected welfare.

In the present context, the only function derived from explicit welfare considerations is the speculation function (2.1d). The profits of speculators are given by the expression

$$\pi_t = (e_{t+1} - f_t)s_t. \tag{2.12}$$

Suppose that speculators wish to maximize the one-period mean variance objective function

$$W_{t,t-1} = \pi^*_{t,t-1} - \tfrac{1}{2}RE_{t,t-1}(p_t - p^*_{t,t-1})^2, \tag{2.13}$$

where E_{t-1} denotes expectations, conditional on information at time $t-1$. Calculating the expected value and one-period variance of (2.12) yields

$$\pi^*_{t,t-1} = (e^*_{t,t-1} - f_t)s_t$$

$$E_{t-1}(\pi_t - \pi^*_{t,t-1})^2 = \sigma_e^2 s_t^2, \tag{2.14}$$

and optimizing (2.13) subject to (2.14) with respect to s_t leads to (2.1d) of the model, with γ defined by (2.7d).

Now, substituting for s_t into $W_{t,t-1}$, we find that with $e^*_{t+1,t} = 0$ the optimized value of $W_{t,t-1}$, denoted by $\hat{}$, is[9]

$$\hat{W}_{t,t-1} = \frac{f_t^2}{2R\sigma_e^2}$$

so that

$$E(W) = \frac{\sigma_f^2}{2R\sigma_e^2}$$

and substituting for σ_e^2, σ_f^2, from (2.7a) and (2.7b), leads to

$$E(\hat{W}) = \frac{(1-\mu-\beta)^2\sigma_u^2 + (1+\alpha)^2\sigma_v^2 + [\alpha(1-\mu)+\beta]^2\sigma_\omega^2}{(\beta+\mu\gamma)^2\sigma_u^2 + \alpha^2\sigma_v^2 + \alpha^2\mu^2\gamma^2\sigma_\omega^2}.$$

This is a decreasing function of γ. Faced between the choice of (1) a high-variance σ_e^2–low-speculative elasticity γ, and (2) a low-variance σ_e^2–high-speculative elasticity γ equilibrium, speculators will prefer the former. They will choose a point such as A, rather than A'' in figure 2–1B. Accordingly, this is the equilibrium point on which we will focus. While our welfare justification is obviously seriously incomplete, as will become evident below, the comparative statics around A as equilibrium are much more plausible than those around A''.

2.4 Increased Risk

In this section we consider the effects of increased risk, as measured by increases in the exogenous variances σ_u^2, σ_v^2, σ_ω^2 on the variances σ_e^2, σ_f^2, σ_r^2. We maintain our assumption of a perfectly flexible exchange rate, with no intervention. We consider one disturbance at a time, thereby enabling us to conduct our analysis graphically. The qualitative results are summarized in table 2–1A.

2.4.1 Domestic Monetary Shocks

Figure 2–1 illustrates the equilibrium for the case of monetary shocks ($\sigma_u^2 > 0$, with $\sigma_v^2 = \sigma_\omega^2 = 0$). This and all subsequent figures are constructed in the following manner. On the right side of the first panel we have drawn two graphs in $\gamma - \sigma_e^2$ space. The first of these, illustrated by the locus WW, is (2.7d), which is a rectangular hyperbola. The second, described by XX, is the solution for σ_e^2 given in (2.7a), setting $\sigma_v^2 = \sigma_\omega^2 = 0$. For given σ_u^2 and other parameters, this also defines a relationship between γ and σ_e^2. It can be easily verified that the slope of XX is positive or negative, depending upon whether $\beta < 1 - \mu$ or $\beta > 1 - \mu$. Accordingly, these two cases are illustrated separately in parts A and B of the figure. The lines can also be shown to have the curvature indicated.

In the case where $\beta < 1 - \mu$ (figure 2–1A), XX is upward sloping so that it intersects WW at a unique point A, which defines the equilibrium solutions for the variance of the spot rate, σ_e^2 and the implied elasticity of speculation γ. When $\beta > 1 - \mu$ (figure 2–1B), XX is downward sloping and may intersect

Table 2–1. Summary of Qualitative Effects

	Source		
Effect on	σ_u^2	σ_v^2	σ_ω^2
	A. Increased Risk		
σ_e^2	+	+	+
σ_f^2	+	+	+
σ_r^2	+ if $\beta < 1-\mu$? if $\beta > 1-\mu$	+	+
	B. Spot Market Intervention		
σ_e^2	−	−	−
σ_f^2	−	? if $\beta < 1-\mu$ − if $\beta > 1-\mu$	− if $\beta < 1-\mu$? if $\beta > 1-\mu$
σ_r^2	− if $\beta < 1-\mu$? if $\beta > 1-\mu$	?	+
	C. Forward Market Intervention		
σ_e^2	+ if $\beta < 1-\mu$ − if $\beta > 1-\mu$	−	+
σ_f^2	−	−	−
σ_r^2	− if $\beta < 1-\mu$ + if $\beta > 1-\mu$	−	+

WW in either one or three points. Only the case of a unique equilibrium is illustrated.

The line *YY* on the left side of the first panel graphs the relationship between σ_f^2 and γ implied by (2.7b). Since an increase in γ raises *D*, it lowers σ_f^2 and the locus is therefore a negatively sloped one. Also, the curvature is as indicated. Corresponding to the equilibrium value of γ obtained from the point of intersection *A* of the *WW* and *XX* loci is point *C* on the *YY* locus, which in turn yields the equilibrium value for the variance of the forward rate σ_f^2.

Similarly, the locus *ZZ* in the second panel defines the relationship between γ and σ_r^2 implied by (2.7c). Like *YY*, its slope depends upon $\beta - (1-\mu)$. In (A) it is downward sloping, in (B) it is upward sloping, having the

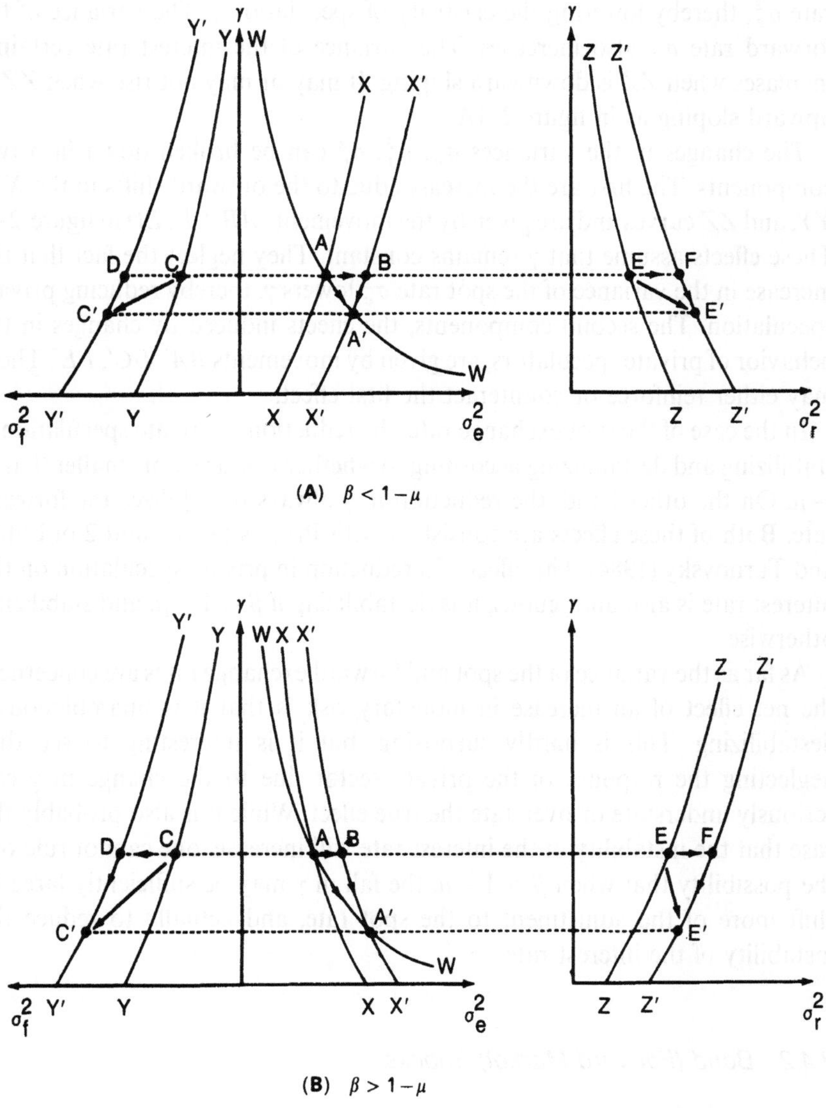

Figure 2–1. Increased risk due to domestic monetary disturbances.

indicated curvature. The equilibrium variance of the interest rate σ_r^2 is at the point *E*, which corresponds to the solution for γ, on the *ZZ* curve.

Consider now an increase in monetary risk σ_u^2. What this does is to shift the *XX*, *YY*, and *ZZ* curves out; the *WW* curve remains unchanged, because the position of this curve is independent of σ_u^2. The upshot of these shifts is that the equilibria move from points *A*, *C*, and *E* to *A′*, *C′*, and *E′*, respectively. In particular, the increase in monetary risk σ_u^2 increases the variance of the spot rate σ_e^2, thereby lowering the elasticity of speculation γ. The variance of the forward rate σ_f^2 also increases. The variance of the interest rate certainly increases when ZZ is downward sloping. It may or may not rise when ZZ is upward sloping as in figure 2–1A.

The changes in the variances σ_e^2, σ_f^2, σ_r^2 can be broken down into two components. The first are the increases due to the outward shifts in the XX, YY, and ZZ curves and are given by the movements AB, CD, ED in figure 2–1. These effects assume that γ remains constant. They neglect the fact that the increase in the variance of the spot rate σ_e^2 lowers γ, thereby reducing private speculation. The second components, the effects induced by changes in the behavior of private speculators, are given by movements BA', DC', FE'. These may either reinforce or counteract the first effect.

In the case of the spot exchange rate, the reduction in private speculation is stabilizing and destabilizing according to whether β is larger or smaller than $1 - \mu$. On the other hand, the reduction in γ always destabilizes the forward rate. Both of these effects are consistent with Propositions 1 and 2 of Eaton and Turnovsky (1984). The effect of a reduction in private speculation on the interest rate is also ambiguous; it is destabilizing if $\beta < 1 - \mu$, and stabilizing otherwise.

As far as the variance of the spot and forward exchange rates are concerned, the net effect of an increase in monetary risk is that it is unambiguously destabilizing. This is hardly surprising, but it is interesting to see that neglecting the response of the private sector due to the change in γ can seriously understate or overstate the true effect. While it is also probably the case that the instability of the interest rate will increase, one cannot rule out the possibility that when $\beta > 1 - \mu$, the fall in γ may be sufficiently large to shift more of the adjustment to the spot rate, and actually to reduce the instability of the interest rate.

2.4.2 Bond (Forward Market) Shocks

As indicated, v_t may reflect shocks in either the bond market or the forward market. The interesting feature about this disturbance is that the XX locus is downward sloping and intersects the WW locus either in zero points, when there is no equilibrium, or in two points, when multiple equilibria exist. The latter case is illustrated in figure 2–2. On the basis of the welfare analysis given in section 2.3, we assume that the equilibrium is initially at point A on the right side of the first panel, rather than at A''. The YY and ZZ curves are basically the same as before, except now they correspond to given values of σ_v^2, rather than σ_u^2.

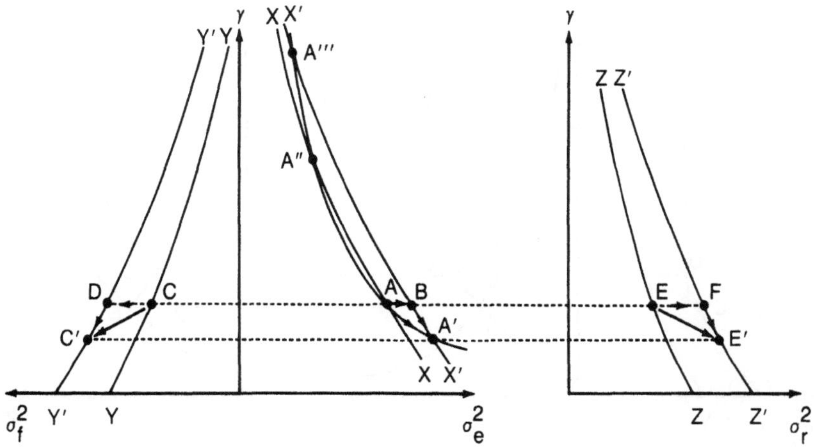

Figure 2–2. Increased risk due to domestic bond disturbances.

An increase in the variance of bond shocks shifts the XX, YY, ZZ curves outward as indicated. The equilibrium variance of the spot rate σ_e^2 and the speculative coefficient γ moves from A to A'; σ_e^2 increases and γ falls. This seems perfectly reasonable. By contrast, at intersection point A'', the increase in σ_u^2 causes a shift to point A''', with a reduction in σ_e^2. This is a less plausible response and supports our choice of the low-γ–high-σ_e^2 equilibrium as being the appropriate one.

The increase in the variance of bond shocks increases the three variances $\sigma_e^2, \sigma_f^2, \sigma_r^2$. In all cases, the reduction in private speculation, resulting from the higher variability in the spot rate, reinforces the destabilizing effects of the shift, which is again consistent with Propositions 1 and 2 of Eaton and Turnovsky.

2.4.3 Foreign Interest Rate Shocks

Foreign interest rate shocks are illustrated in figure 2–3. In this case, the XX and ZZ curves are upward sloping and pass through the origin. The increase in the foreign interest rate therefore generates rotations in these curves through the origin. Again, an increase in the variance of the foreign interest rate leads to higher variances in σ_e^2, σ_f^2, and σ_r^2. The increases in the variances of the spot and forward rates is apparent from the figure. The increase in σ_r^2 is not obvious, but follows from (2.7a) and (2.7c), which in the presence of only interest rate shocks yields

$$\frac{\sigma_r^2}{\sigma_e^2} = \alpha^2.$$

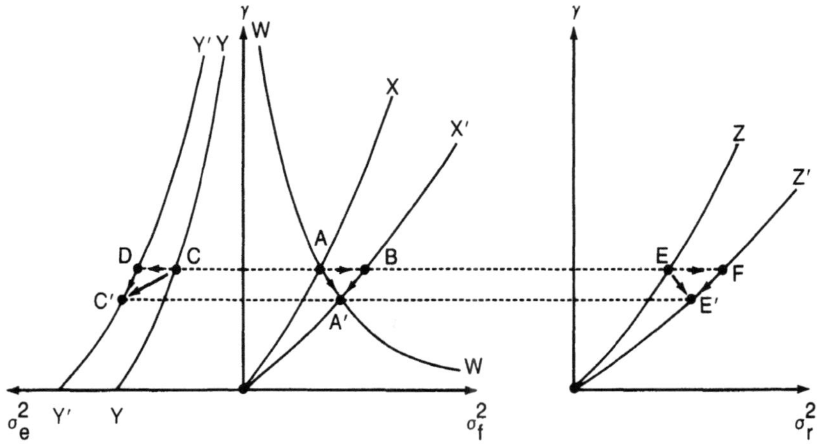

Figure 2–3. Increased risk due to foreign interest rate disturbances.

Since this ratio is independent of γ, we see that the increase in the variance of the spot rate leads to a proportional increase in the variance of the interest rate as well. As in previous cases, the shift in equilibria from A, C, and E, to A', C', and E', respectively, can be broken down into a direct shift and the induced response through γ. In particular, the reduction in private speculation has stabilizing effects on the spot rate and the interest rate, but a destabilizing effect on the forward rate.

2.5 Spot Market Intervention

We now consider the effects of official intervention in exchange markets. This section deals with intervention in the spot market; forward market intervention is discussed in section 2.6.[10]

The intervention is hypothesized to take the form

$$m_t = -ae_t \qquad a > 0. \tag{2.15}$$

This describes a policy of "leaning against the wind" and has been widely discussed in the exchange rate management literature.[11] Equation 2.15 specifies that the monetary authority expands or contracts the money supply by an amount that is proportional to the extent to which the exchange rate has appreciated or depreciated. The limiting cases of perfectly flexible and perfectly fixed spot exchange rate are parameterized by setting $a = 0$ and letting $a \to \infty$, respectively.

Continuing to set $b_t = g_t = 0$ and substituting the rule (2.15) into the basic system (2.1a)–(2.1e), one can derive a difference equation in exchange rate expectations of the form

$$e^*_{t+i+1,t} = \phi' e^*_{t+i,t}, \tag{2.16}$$

where ϕ' depends upon the intervention parameter a, as well as the other parameters of the system. It can be shown that for $a > 0$, $\phi' > 1$ and the only stable solution is $e^*_{t+i,t} = 0$.

The solution for e_t, f_t, and r_t, with intervention become

$$e_t = \frac{1}{D_a}[-(\beta + \mu\gamma)u_t + \alpha v_t + \alpha\mu\gamma\omega_t] \tag{2.17a}$$

$$f_t = \frac{1}{D_a}\{(1 - \mu - \beta)u_t + (1 + \alpha + a)v_t - [\alpha(1 - \mu) + \beta(1 + a)]\omega_t\} \tag{2.17b}$$

$$r_t = \frac{1}{D_a}[(1 - \mu + \mu\gamma)u_t + (1 + a)v_t + (1 + a)\mu\gamma\omega_t], \tag{2.17c}$$

where

$$D_a \equiv (1 + a)(\beta + \mu\gamma) + \alpha(\mu\gamma + 1 - \mu),$$

the variances of which are

$$\sigma_e^2 = \frac{1}{D_a^2}[(\beta + \mu\gamma)^2\sigma_u^2 + \alpha^2\sigma_v^2 + \alpha^2\mu^2\gamma^2\sigma_\omega^2] \tag{2.18a}$$

$$\sigma_f^2 = \frac{1}{D_a^2}\{(1 - \mu - \beta)^2\sigma_u^2 + (1 + \alpha + a)^2\sigma_v^2 + [\alpha(1 - \mu) + \beta(1 + a)]^2\sigma_\omega^2\} \tag{2.18b}$$

$$\sigma_r^2 = \frac{1}{D_a^2}[(1 - \mu + \mu\gamma)^2\sigma_u^2 + \sigma_v^2 + (1 + a)^2\mu^2\gamma^2\sigma_\omega^2], \tag{2.18c}$$

where

$$\gamma = \frac{1}{R\sigma_e^2}. \tag{2.18d}$$

Questions of existence and uniqueness of equilibrium again arise. In fact, the same general characterization exists as before. Namely, with monetary shocks there may be either one or three equilibria, with bond shocks zero or two equilibria, and with foreign interest rate shocks a unique equilibrium exists. Furthermore, it is possible for spot market intervention to actually exacerbate problems with respect to the existence of equilibrium. For example, in the case of bond shocks, $\sigma_v^2 > 0$, it was seen that existence problems arise if σ_v^2 is "too small." Since intervention taking the form of leaning against the wind typically leads to smaller variances, it will tend to increase private speculation γ, thereby increasing endogenous fluctuations in the demand for foreign exchange and affecting unfavorably the possible imbalance in equation 2.11, which was shown to be the cause of potential nonexistence of equilibrium. In other words, it is possible for the equilibrium to exist under perfectly flexible rates, but to cease to exist when the monetary authority attempts to stabilize the spot exchange rate in accordance with a rule such as (2.15).[12]

We consider the qualitative effects of an increase in intervention. This can be viewed as being either a move from a perfectly flexible regime to a managed float, or alternatively as an increase in the degree of intervention a The qualitative effects are summarized in table 2–1B and are illustrated in figures 2–4, 2–5, and 2–6. Again each disturbance is considered sequentially.

2.5.1 Domestic Monetary Shocks

Figure 2–4 illustrates the effects of an increase in spot market intervention in the face of monetary shocks ($\sigma_u^2 > 0$, $\sigma_v^2 = \sigma_\omega^2 = 0$). As before, WW is the rectangular hyperbola defined by (2.18d). The XX, YY, and ZZ curves define the solutions for σ_e^2, σ_f^2, and σ_r^2, respectively, given by (2.18a)–(2.18c), in terms of γ, for $\sigma_u^2 > 0$, with $\sigma_v^2 = \sigma_\omega^2 = 0$. These curves have the same properties as before. In particular, if $\beta < 1 - \mu$, XX is upward sloping, giving rise to a unique intersection point with WW. Otherwise, although figure 2–4B considers only a unique equilibrium, the possible of multiple equilibria exist in that case as well.

As the curves are drawn, the initial equilibria are at points A, C, and E, as before. We consider now an increase in the degree of intervention a. This leaves the WW curve unchanged. By increasing the quantity D_a, it lowers σ_e^2, σ_f^2, for any given value of γ, thereby leading to inward shifts in the XX, YY, and ZZ curves to $X'X'$, $Y'Y'$, and $Z'Z'$, respectively.

The new equilibria are at points A', C', and E'. The spot and forward rates are stabilized unambiguously, while the domestic interest rate is stabilized if $\beta < 1 - \mu$ and the ZZ curve is negatively sloping. The effects on the interest rate are less clear-cut when ZZ is positively sloped.

The effects of intervention can be decomposed into two components. The first, measured by the movements AB, CD, and EF, is due to the direct shifts in the curves. The second, measured by the movements BA', DC', and FE',

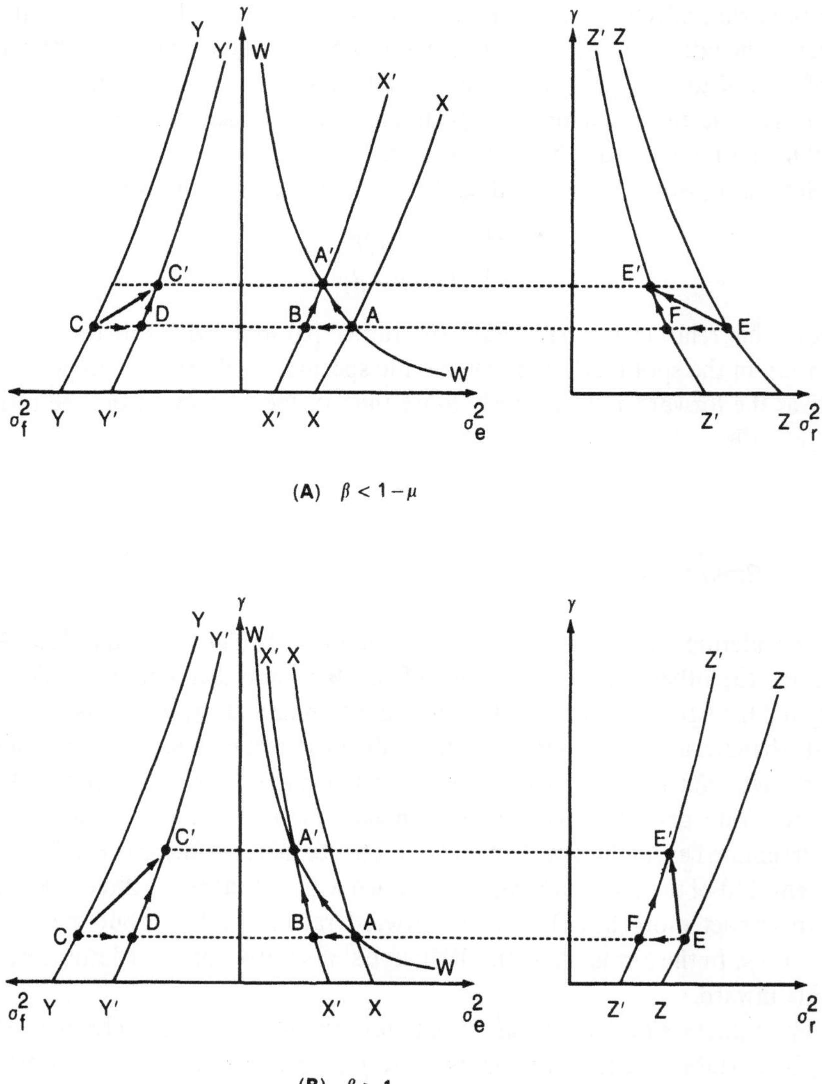

Figure 2–4. Spot market intervention: Domestic monetary disturbances.

represents the effects of increased private speculation resulting from the lower variance in the spot rate. In the case where $\beta < 1-\mu$, this latter effect tends to destabilize the spot rate while stabilizing the interest rate; when $\beta > 1-\mu$, these two responses are reversed. While spot market intervention will always lead to a lower variance of the spot rate, it is possible when $\beta > 1-\mu$ for the destabilizing effects of increased speculative activity to dominate, so that overall the interest rate is actually destabilized. This occurs when the leftward shift in ZZ to $Z'Z'$ in figure 2–4B is small and E' lies to the right of E. By contrast, the increased private speculation always provides an additional stabilizing influence on the forward rate.

Setting $\sigma_v^2 = \sigma_\omega^2 = 0$ and dividing (2.7a) by (2.7b), one can also show

$$\frac{\sigma_e^2}{\sigma_f^2} = \frac{(\beta + \mu\gamma)^2}{(1 - \mu - \beta)^2}.$$

From this relationship we obtain the rather paradoxical result that intervention in the spot market, by raising the speculative elasticity γ, in fact stabilizes the forward rate relatively more than it does the spot rate; the ratio σ_f^2/σ_e^2 falls.

2.5.2 Bond Shocks

In considering this case we focus on only one of the two possible equilibria. As drawn, the other intersection point of the WW and XX curves would be beyond the figure. Leaning against the wind stabilizes the spot rate against all disturbances, including in this case bond disturbances v_t. The XX curve shifts to the left. But in so doing, more of the adjustments to v_t are shifted to the interest rate and the forward rate. In fact, an increase in the degree of intervention causes the direct impact of v_t on r_t to increase, thereby resulting in a right shift of the ZZ curve. An increase in a will also cause the direct effect of v_t to impact more heavily on the forward rate if $\beta < 1 - \mu$, but less so if $\beta > 1 - \mu$. In the former case, the YY curve shifts outward; in the latter case it shifts inward.

The reduction in the spot rate stimulates private speculation. This increase in γ has a stabilizing effect on the spot rate, measured by BA', which reinforces the direct stabilizing shift AB. The increase in γ also has a stabilizing influence on the forward rate, which is therefore definitely stabilized by the intervention rule (2.15) as long as YY is shifted inward, as it is in figure 2–5B. However, if, as in figure 2–5A, the YY curve is shifted out, it is quite likely that the destabilizing outward shift CD dominates the stabilizing effects of increased private speculation DC', so that, on balance, the variance of the forward rate σ_f^2 is increased. Finally, the net effects on the interest rate are unclear. On the one hand, the outward shift in ZZ is destabilizing. On the other hand, increased private speculation is stabilizing. Either effect may dominate, and spot market intervention may either increase or decrease the variance σ_r^2.

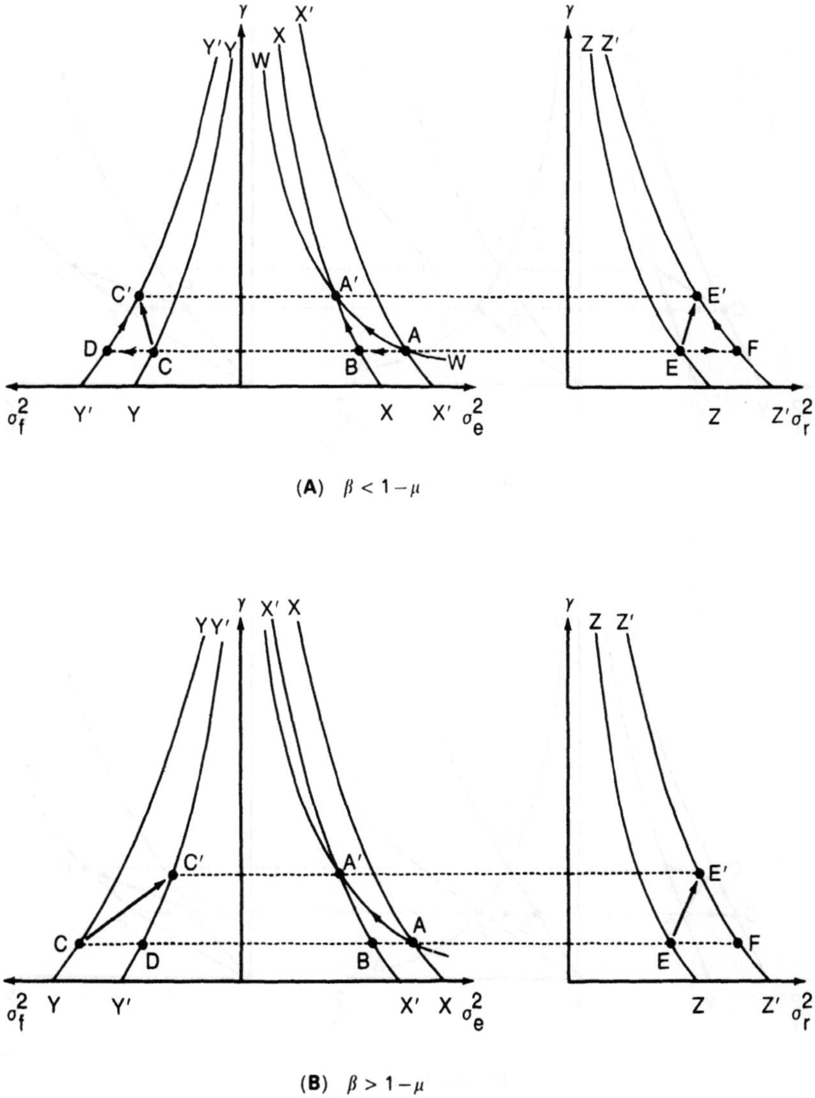

Figure 2–5. Spot market intervention: Bond disturbances.

2.5.3 Foreign Interest Rate Shocks

The effects of spot market intervention in the face of foreign interest rate disturbances are illustrated in figure 2–6. An increase in a causes the XX curve to rotate inward and the ZZ curve to rotate outward. The YY curve shifts inward if $\beta < 1 - \mu$ and outward otherwise. By now the reasons for these shifts

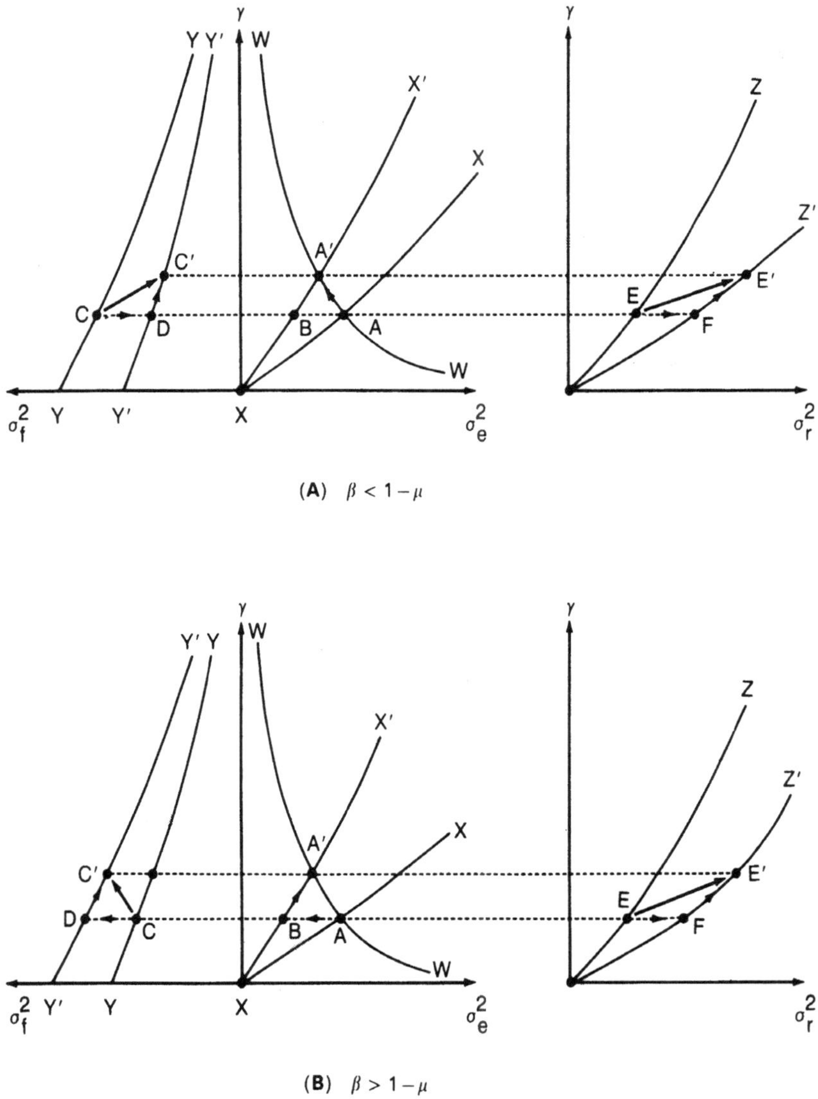

Figure 2–6. Foreign interest rate disturbances.

are clear. The direct effects of the increased intervention are given by *AB*, *CD*, and *EF*, respectively, which measure the shifts in the *XX*, *YY*, and *ZZ* curves. For given γ, it is seen that more intensive speculation stabilizes the spot rate, while destabilizing the interest rate. The forward rate is stabilized as long as $\beta < 1-\mu$, and is destabilized otherwise. But the reduction in σ_e^2 raises γ, thereby increasing private speculation. This has a destabilizing effect on the spot rate, which, however, is stabilized overall. This is evident from the move

A to A' along the WW curve. The increased private speculation has a stabilizing effect on the forward rate, which in case (A) when the YY is shifted in, leads to an unambiguous reduction in the variance σ_f^2. However, in case (B) when the YY curve shifts out, σ_f^2 may either rise or fall, depending upon which effect dominates. Finally, the increase in private speculation tends to destabilize the domestic interest rate, thereby exacerbating the destabilizing effects of the outward rotation in the ZZ curve.

2.6 Forward Market Intervention

We now turn to forward market intervention. We begin by introducing the following two rules:

$$g_t = -bf_t \tag{2.19a}$$

$$g_t = b(e^*_{t+1,t} - f_t) \qquad b > 0. \tag{2.19b}$$

The first of these is a leaning against the wind rule in the forward market. The government buys forward exchange when the forward rate is low and sells when it is high. The second rule specifies that the government intervenes as if it were a private speculator. The government buys forward exchange when the spot price is expected to exceed the current forward rate and sells otherwise.

In our present model, these two modes of intervention are equivalent. To show this, we substitute (2.19a) or (2.19b) into the basic model. This leads to a difference equation of the usual form

$$e^*_{t+i+1,t} = \phi'' e^*_{t+i,t}.$$

In either case $\phi'' > 1$, so that the only stable solution is $e^*_{t+i,t} = 0$, in which case the two rules (2.19a) and (2.19b) coincide. But for other models these rules will be quite distinct.

Hence the stable solutions under forward market intervention are

$$e_t = \frac{1}{D_b}\{-[\beta + \mu\gamma + (1-\mu)b]u_t + \alpha v_t + \alpha[\mu\gamma + (1-\mu)b]\omega_t\} \tag{2.20a}$$

$$f_t = \frac{1}{D_b}\{(1-\mu-\beta)u_t + (1+\alpha)v_t - [\alpha(1-\mu) + \beta]\omega_t\} \tag{2.20b}$$

$$r_t = \frac{1}{D_b}\{[(1-\mu+\mu\gamma) + (1-\mu)b]u_t + v_t + [\mu\gamma + (1-\mu)b]\omega_t\}, \tag{2.20c}$$

where

$$D_b \equiv (\beta + \mu\gamma) + \alpha(\mu\gamma + 1 - \mu) + (1-\mu)(1+\alpha)b,$$

the variances of which are

$$\sigma_e^2 = \frac{1}{D_b^2}\{[\beta + \mu\gamma + (1-\mu)b]^2\sigma_u^2 + \alpha^2\sigma_v^2 + \alpha^2[\mu\gamma + (1-\mu)b]^2\sigma_\omega^2\} \quad (2.21a)$$

$$\sigma_f^2 = \frac{1}{D_b^2}\{(1-\mu-\beta)^2\sigma_u^2 + (1+\alpha)^2\sigma_v^2 + [\alpha(1-\mu)+\beta]^2\sigma_\omega^2\} \quad (2.21b)$$

$$\sigma_f^2 = \frac{1}{D_b^2}\{[1-\mu+\mu\gamma+(1-\mu)b]^2\sigma_u^2 + \sigma_v^2 + [\mu\gamma+(1-\mu)b]^2\sigma_\omega^2\}, \quad (2.21c)$$

with

$$\gamma = \frac{1}{R\sigma_e^2}. \quad (2.21d)$$

The same characteristics of existence and possible multiplicity of equilibria apply as before. Intervention in the forward market is shown to stabilize the spot rate against domestic bond disturbances and this can exacerbate existence problems, as it did before.

We now discuss the effects of an increase in forward market intervention. The qualitative effects are summarized in table 2–1C and are illustrated in figures 2–7, 2–8, and 2–9. Since the reasons are analogous to those given previously, our discussion can be brief.

2.6.1 Domestic Monetary Shocks

In figure 2–7 the *WW*, *XX*, *YY*, and *ZZ* curves are defined as before with the initial equilibria being at points *A*, *C*, and *E*. Consider now an increase in forward market intervention. This leaves the *WW* curve affected. If $\beta < 1-\mu$, an increase in intervention shifts the *XX* curve to the right and the *ZZ* curve to the left; if $\beta > 1-\mu$, these shifts are reversed. In all cases, the *YY* curve shifts inward.[13]

An increase in forward market intervention in accordance with (2.19) shifts the equilibria to A', C', and E'. The forward rate is always stabilized. In the case that $\beta < 1-\mu$, such a rule destabilizes the spot rate, although the interest rate is probably, but not necessarily, stabilized. By contrast, if $\beta > 1-\mu$, then intervention stabilizes the spot rate, but destabilizes the interest rate.

The reasons for these effects can be seen by considering the two components of the shifts. In the first case, when forward market intervention destabilizes the spot price, the decrease in the elasticity of speculation γ is stabilizing. This is represented by the movement BA', which partially, but not totally, offsets the destabilization resulting from the outward shift in the *XX* curve. In the

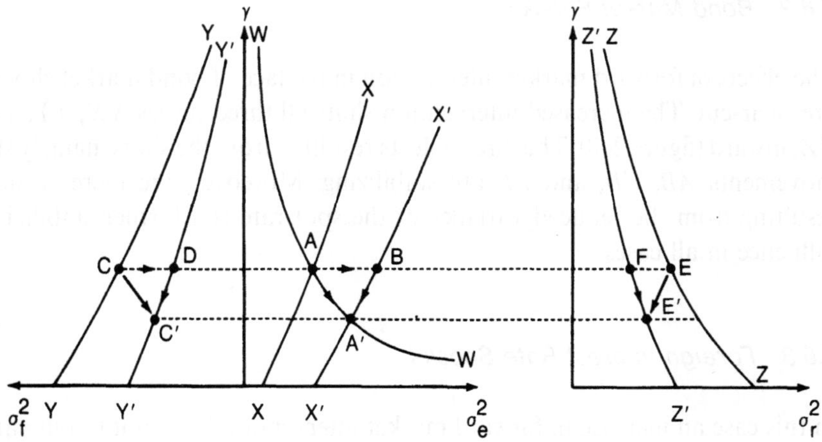

(A) $\beta < 1-\mu$

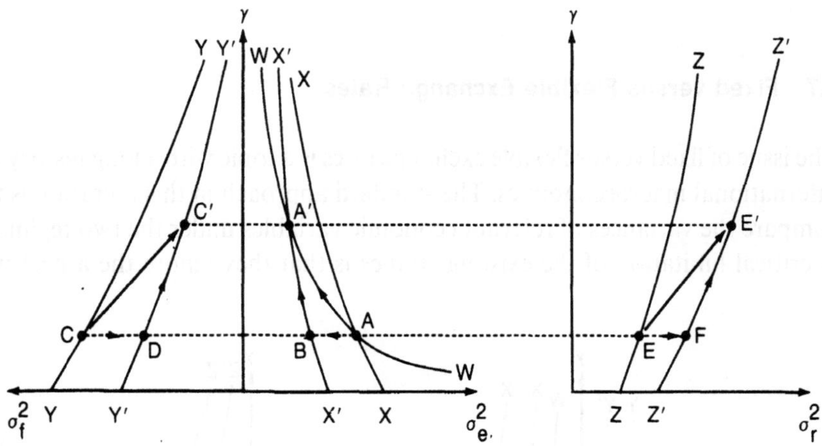

(B) $\beta > 1-\mu$

Figure 2–7. Forward market intervention: Domestic monetary disturbances.

case of the forward rate and the domestic interest rate, the decrease in γ is destabilizing. With respect to the former, it only partially offsets the stabilizing inward shift of the YY curve. In the case of the latter, it may dominate the inward movement of the ZZ curve and lead to a larger variance σ_r^2. On the other hand, when $\beta > 1 - \mu$, the increase in γ tends to stabilize σ_e^2, σ_f^2, but to destabilize σ_r^2, in both cases accentuating the direct effects stemming from the shifts in the respective curves.

2.6.2 *Bond Market Shocks*

The effects of forward market intervention in the face of bond market shocks are clear-cut. The increased intervention shifts all three curves XX, YY, and ZZ, inward (figure 2–8). The direct effects resulting from the shifts, namely the movements AB, CD, and EF are stabilizing. Moreover, the increase in γ resulting from the reduced variance of the spot rate is a further stabilizing influence in all cases.

2.6.3 *Foreign Interest Rate Shocks*

In this case an increase in forward market intervention leads not to outward shifts in the XX and ZZ curves, but to an inward shift in the YY curve (figure 2–9). The spot exchange rate and the interest rate are destabilized, while the forward rate is stabilized. In all cases, the reduction in γ partially, but not totally, offsets the direct effects resulting from the shifts in the curves.

2.7 Fixed versus Flexible Exchange Rates

The issue of fixed versus flexible exchange rates is a topic with a long history in international macroeconomics. The standard approach in this literature is to compare the variances of relevant economic variables under the two regimes. A critical limitation of the existing studies is that they ignore the aspect we

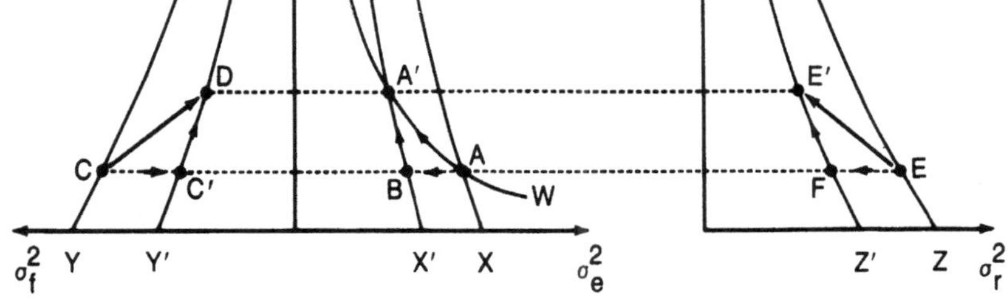

Figure 2–8. Forward market intervention: Bond disturbances.

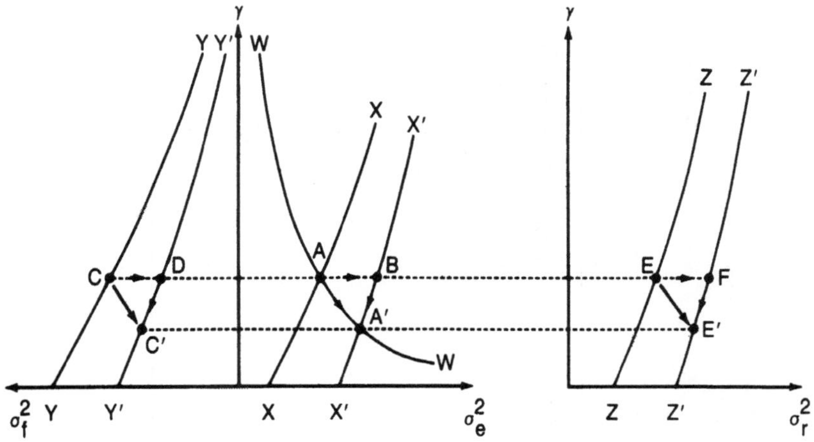

Figure 2–9. Forward market intervention: Foreign market rate disturbances.

have been emphasizing, that certain key parameters, in our case the behavior of private speculators, will change with the regime.[14] The effects of this induced change in behavior needs to be taken into account in the overall evaluation of the two regimes. Moreover, as we noted in the introduction, Spraos (1959) has argued that fixing the forward rate should also be a policy decision.

Table 2–2 compares the variances σ_e^2, σ_f^2, σ_r^2, under three regimes:

1. A perfectly flexible exchange rate
2. A fixed spot exchange rate
3. A fixed forward exchange rate.

In considering the fixed spot rate, we report two subcases. The first ignores the change in γ induced by the regime, assuming it to remain the same as under a flexible rate. In the second, the change in γ as we move to a fixed rate is taken into account. Specifically, we see from (2.7d) that as $\sigma_e^2 \to 0$, $\gamma \to \infty$. The following observations can be made from table 2–2.

Any comparison between fixed and flexible rates that ignores the adjustment in γ is misleading. For example, if γ is assumed to remain fixed at its flexible rate level, it would appear that there will be fluctuations in the forward rate in response to the stochastic disturbances v_t, ω_t. But when the fact that fixing the spot rate makes $\gamma \to \infty$ is taken into account, we find that infinitely elastic speculation stabilizes the forward rate. In other words, fixing the spot rate fixes the forward rate as well.

Table 2–2. Fixed vs. Flexible Exchange Rates

Rate	σ_e^2	σ_f^2	σ_r^2
A. Flexible Rates	$\frac{(\beta+\mu\gamma)^2\sigma_u^2+\alpha^2\sigma_v^2+\alpha^2\mu^2\gamma^2\sigma_\omega^2}{[\beta+\mu\gamma+\alpha(\mu\gamma+1-\mu)]^2}$	$\frac{(1-\mu-\beta)^2\sigma_u^2+(1+\alpha)^2\sigma_v^2+[\alpha(1-\mu)+\beta]^2\sigma_\omega^2}{[\beta+\mu\gamma+\alpha(\mu\gamma+1-\mu)]^2}$	$\frac{(1-\mu+\mu\gamma)^2\sigma_u^2+\sigma_v^2+\mu^2\gamma^2\sigma_\omega^2}{[\beta+\mu\gamma+\alpha(\mu\gamma+1-\mu)]^2}$
B. Fixed Spot Rate γ constant	0	$\frac{\sigma_v^2+\beta^2\sigma_\omega^2}{(\beta+\mu\gamma)^2}$	$\frac{\sigma_v^2+\mu^2\gamma^2\sigma_\omega^2}{(\beta+\mu\gamma)^2}$
C. Fixed Spot Rate $\gamma\to\infty$	0	0	σ_w^2
D. Fixed Forward Rate	$\frac{\sigma_u^2+\alpha^2\sigma_\omega^2}{(1+\alpha)^2}$	0	$\frac{\sigma_u^2+\sigma_\omega^2}{(1+\alpha)^2}$

Also, if one compares σ_r^2 between rows A and B of table 2–2, it would appear that fixing the spot rate destabilizes the domestic interest rate in the face of σ_v^2, and σ_ω^2. But again, taking account of the induced behavior of speculators, we find in row C that it actually stabilizes the domestic interest rate against σ_v^2. On the other hand, it destabilizes the domestic interest rate in the face of foreign interest rate shocks by an even greater amount.

Finally, we may address Spraos' suggestion for pegging the forward rate. Whereas fixing the spot rate will also peg the forward rate, the reverse is not true. Pegging the forward rate completely stabilizes the spot rate for σ_v^2 and partially stabilizes it for σ_ω^2, but it may actually destabilize the spot rate against σ_v^2. Also, fixing the forward rate may be better or worse than fixing the spot rate from the viewpoint of interest rate stability, depending upon the sources of the disturbances. Thus, the desirability of the Spraos suggestion of fixing the forward rate would appear to be questionable.

2.8 Conclusions

This chapter has emphasized the fact that private speculative behavior is endogenous. The consequences of this for the effects of (1) increased risk and (2) exchange market intervention policies have been analyzed at some length using a simple model. Space limitations preclude any detailed review of specific results. The main general conclusion is that any structural change to the economy, whether exogenous or due to a changing policy regime, has two effects: (1) the direct effects of the change itself; (2) effects induced through changes in private speculative behavior. In some cases these two partial effects may reinforce one another; in other cases they are offsetting. But both need to be taken into account, and any analysis that ignores the latter effect may be seriously misleading. Indeed, the analysis suggests the possibility that the private effects can quite plausibly be sufficiently strong to dominate and reverse the direct effects.

The policy rules we have analyzed are of the "leaning against the wind" type. The effects of such rules are not always clear-cut and depend upon the source of the disturbances impinging on the economy. For example, stabilizing the spot rate may destabilize the forward rate, and vice versa. In fact, it is even possible under cetain circumstances for leaning against the wind in the spot market to generate such an increase in private speculative behavior that the spot rate itself is destabilized rather than stabilized.

By introducing risk-averse speculators, the model introduces a second instrument of exchange rate management, namely forward market intervention. In fact, in the latter part of the chapter we have used the model to address the desirability of actually fixing the forward rate, as has been suggested in the past. Our results suggest that the desirability of such a policy is very much open to question.

Of course, we should not lose sight of the fact that the specific results pertain to a special model. We have chosen a specification that is purely static and disturbances that are purely random, so that exchange rate expectations play no role. This choice has been made intentionally because it enables much of the analysis to proceed graphically and exposes the issues that are involved. But, the principles, if not the specific details, will apply to more general models.

Notes

1. Most of the existing studies deal with white noise disturbances arising from different sources of domestic and foreign origin. More recent work has investigated the dichotomy between transitory and permanent shocks, and unanticipated and anticipated disturbances, as well as information differentials between public and private agents; see for example, Aizenman and Frenkel (1985) and Turnovsky (1987).

2. Reference should be made to two earlier papers by Tsiang (1959) and Day (1976, 1977). Both authors discuss intervention in the partial equilibrium context of the foreign exchange market. They do not discuss intervention as a more general instrument of macroeconomic stabilization policy.

3. These issues were first identified and discussed by McCafferty and Driskill (1980) in the context of speculation in commodities markets; see also Kawai (1983) and Turnovsky (1983). They were also analyzed at about the same time in the context of foreign exchange markets by Driskill and McCafferty (1980), who encountered the problem of nonuniqueness but not nonexistence of equilibrium. These issues were also noted by Kawai (1984) as well as Black (1985), although in his model neither problem arises.

4. We find it analytically convenient to separate forward market participation into pure speculation and pure arbitrage. We implicitly treat the acquisition of an amount x of uncovered bonds as combining a covered investment of x in foreign bonds and a speculative purchase of foreign currency forward in amount x. In a portfolio model of foreign investment, we identify a third motive for participating in the forward market as hedging against domestic inflation. Foward positions for hedging purposes depend upon the relative variability of the domestic and foreign price levels and do not respond to the variables we are concerned with here. We may thus treat the forward position due to hedging as a constant absorbed in s_t; see Eaton and Turnovsky (1981).

5. The domestic bond market equilibrium condition is based on the assumption that foreigners hold zero stocks of domestic bonds. In Eaton and Turnovsky (1981), we show that this is more likely to arise when the domestic price level is more sensitive to the exchange rate than is the foreign price level.

6. The approximation is obtained as follows:

$$\frac{H_t-\bar{H}}{\bar{H}}=\left(\frac{(1+g_t)\dfrac{B_t}{P_t}-\dfrac{\bar{B}}{\bar{P}}}{\bar{B}/\bar{P}}\right)\frac{\bar{B}/\bar{P}}{\bar{H}}+\left(\frac{S_t-\bar{S}}{\bar{S}}\right)\frac{\bar{S}}{\bar{H}}.$$

Assuming that g_t is small

$$(1+g_t)\frac{B_t}{P_t} \simeq \frac{\bar{B}}{\bar{P}} + \frac{\bar{B}}{\bar{P}}\left(g_t + \left(\frac{B_t - \bar{B}}{\bar{B}}\right) - \left(\frac{P_t - \bar{P}}{P}\right)\right).$$

Now, for any variable X,

$$\frac{X_t - \bar{X}}{\bar{X}} \simeq \ln\left(1 + \frac{X_t - \bar{X}}{\bar{X}}\right) = \ln\frac{X_t}{\bar{X}} = x_t - \bar{x},$$

where $x = \ln X$. Assuming that in equilibrium $\bar{S} \simeq \bar{H}^f$, we may write

$$h_t = (1-\mu)(b_t + g_t - p_t) + \mu s_t.$$

7. The microeconomics underlying our model is contained in Eaton and Turnovsky (1981). In that model, the speculative coefficient γ is the only one to be endogenized in this way. See also Black (1985).

8. This requirement that the asymptotic variance be finite may be justified by appealing to some appropriate transversality condition for a corresponding model derived from optimizing behavior. Under appropriate conditions this requirement also imposes boundedness on price expectations.

9. This analysis is ignoring v_{2t}, so that v_t must be attributed totally to fluctuations in the bond market v_{1t}.

10. The consequences of forward market intervention for the consolidated balance sheet of the fiscal authority and central bank are discussed in the appendix to Eaton and Turnovsky (1984).

11. See, for example, the papers in Bhandari (1985).

12. As discussed below, leaning against the wind in the spot market moves the XX curve to the left. In the case of bond shocks, it is possible for this curve to move sufficiently far to the left that there is no intersection point such as A' with the WW curve.

13. Alternatively, if one interprets our specification of intervention as being equivalent to increased private speculation, it can be represented graphically as an outward shift in the WW curve, with all other curves remaining fixed. This representation yields precisely the same qualitative implications to those presented.

14. To the extent that this literature assumes uncovered interest parity ($\gamma \to \infty$), it is, of course, immune to this criticism.

References

Aizenman, J. and J. A. Frenkel (1985), "Optimal Wage Indexation, Foreign Exchange Market Intervention, and Monetary Policy," *American Economic Review*, **75**, 402–423.

Bhandari, J. S. (Ed.) (1985), *Exchange Rate Management under Uncertainty*, MIT Press, Cambridge, MA.

Black, S. W. (1985), "The Effect of Alternative Policies on the Variability of Exchange Rates: The Harrod Effect," in J. S. Bhandari (Ed.), *Exchange Rate Management under Uncertainty*, MIT Press, Cambridge, MA.

Boyer, R. (1978), "Optimal Foreign Exchange Market Intervention," *Journal of Political Economy*, **86**, 1045–1056.

Day, W. H. L. (1976), "The Advantages of Exclusive Forward Exchange Rate Support," *IMF Staff Papers*, **23**, 137–163.

——— (1977), "Flexible Exchange Rates: A Case for Official Intervention," *IMF Staff Papers*, **24**, 330–343.

Driskill, R. and S. McCafferty (1980), "Speculation, Rational Expectations, and Stability of the Foreign Exchange Market," *Journal of International Economy*, **10**, 91–102.

Eaton, J. and S. J. Turnovsky (1981), "Exchange Risk, Political Risk and Macroeconomic Equilibrium," Discussion Paper No. 388, Economic Growth Center, Yale University, New Haven, CT.

——— (1984), "The Forward Exchange Market, Speculation, and Exchange Market Intervention," *Quarterly Journal of Economics*, **99**, 45–69.

Fama, E. and A. Farber (1979), "Money, Bonds, and Foreign Exchange," *American Economic Review*, **69**, 639–649.

Frenkel, J. A. and J. Aizenman (1982), "Aspects of the Optimal Management of Exchange Rates," *Journal of International Economics*, **13**, 231–256.

Kawai, M. (1983), "Price Volatility of Storable Commodities under Rational Expectations in Spot and Futures Market," *International Economic Review*, **24**, 435–459.

——— (1984), "The Effect of Forward Exchange on Spot-Rate Volatility under Risk and Rational Expectations," *Journal of International Economics*, **19**, 155–172.

Keynes, J. M. (1930), *A Treatise on Money*, Vol. 2, MacMillan, London.

Kouri, P. J. K. (1976), "The Determinants of the Forward Premium," Institute for International Economic Studies, Paper No. 62

Lucas, R. E., Jr. (1975), "An Equilibrium Model of the Business Cycle," *Journal of Political Economy*, **83**, 1113–1144.

McCafferty, S. and R. Driskill (1980), "Problems of Existence and Uniqueness in Nonlinear Rational Expectations Models," *Econometrica*, **48**, 1313–1317.

Nichans, J. (1984), *International Monetary Economics*, Johns Hopkins Press, Baltimore.

Roper, D. E. and S. J. Turnovsky (1980), "Optimal Exchange Market Intervention in a Simple Stochastic Macro Model," *Canadian Journal of Economics*, **13**, 296–309

Solnik, B. (1973), *European Capital Markets*, Heath, Lexington, MA.

Spraos, J. (1959), "Speculation, Arbitrage, and Sterling," *Economic Journal*, **69**, 1–21.

Tsiang, S. C. (1959), "The Theory of Forward Exchange and the Effects of Government Intervention on the Forward Exchange Market," *IMF Staff Papers*, **6**, 75–106.

Turnovsky, S. J. (1983), "The Determination of Spot and Futures Prices with Storable Commodities," *Econometrica*, **51**, 1363–1387.

——— (1987), "Optimal Monetary Policy and Wage Indexation under Alternative Disturbances and Information Structures," *Journal of Money, Credit, and Banking*, **19**, 157–180.

Commentary by Charles I. Plosser

Turnovsky's chapter illustrates in a simple model the consequences of various intervention policies in the spot and forward exchange rate markets. A key element of the model is that risk aversion on the part of agents leads to a nonzero premium in the forward market. Since these premia are endogenous, they may be influenced by the intervention policies of the central bank. It is difficult to argue with the spirit of the analysis in the chapter. Economists have recognized since Lucas' insightful work, if not before, that the behavior of private agents frequently depends on a number of factors including the relevant policy regime. My comments are primarily directed toward the model used and whether it provides a framework for a substantive analysis of the questions raised, or is simply an illustrative exercise with limited applicability for policy. Unfortunately, I'm inclined toward the latter view.

The chapter focuses on the international features of the model and policies associated with exchange market intervention. To illustrate the sort of difficulties I have with the model, it is useful to take the model out of its international context. It turns out that this is quite easy to do. In fact, the chapter is only indirectly related to exchange rates. To see this recall that (1) foreign prices are fixed, so there is no foreign inflation; (2) foreign bonds are always "covered", which means they are domestic bonds; and (3) real outputs are fixed. These assumptions mean that the exchange rate in Turnovsky's model is equivalent to the domestic price level. Consequently, with no terms of trade shocks, the only disturbances that can be considered are exogenous shocks to the demand for bonds, money, or the world interest rate. Increases in variance in the exogenous disturbances in the model have effects on the variance of the price level, either in the spot market and/or the forward market. The difference in the two markets arises from the endogeneity of the forward premium. Intervention involves the central bank attempting to target the current consumer price index (CPI) or, alternatively, targeting the CPI forward price. The results can be restated in terms of the implications for the domestic price level rather than the exchange rate. For example, spot market control does not eliminate variance in the forward market unless all agents are risk neutral. Controlling the forward rate leaves the spot rate free to fluctuate.

Looking at the model in this light raises two issues that are not clearly handled in the chapter. First, why do agents in this economy care about variance in the price level? And second, which is related to the first, what motivates intervention in these markets in this model? I am uncertain as to the answer to these questions in the context of the model presented, but I suspect that part of it arises from the fact that in the model there is no opportunity to hedge or diversify price level risk perfectly. In reality, however, we see numerous instruments created in financial markets to help agents cope with volatility which indicate that intervention may not be the most productive way to think about these issues. Unless restricted in some way, markets and, in particular, financial markets are very adept at adapting to risk through price changes and the creation of new instruments that enable agents to diversify the risk. Thus, from the standpoint of the issues of interest at this conference, it is crucial to make explicit the nature of these risks and the market structures that make the risks important.

In attempting to put the model back into some international perspective, the observation that the model is about the domestic price level also says that there are no real exchange rate fluctuations in the model. Yet, most of the empirical work on exchange rates with which I am familiar strongly suggests that fluctuating real exchange rates are the predominant source of variation, at least since 1972, in nominal exchange rates movements. So the model really does not address the largest part of exchange rate movements. Is this important? The answer is maybe. If, as in the monetary models of Lucas, Stockman, or Stultz, portfolio decisions depend on both the real and monetary equilibrium, then by incorporating movements in the terms of trade, many of the results in this chapter may be altered through the adjustment of individual portfolios. If the decisions are separable, then this model just does not have much to say about the effects of intervention on observed exchange rates.

There is an alternative strategy. For example, one could set up, what is by now a standard equilibrium model of the sort used by Lucas. One could retain the key features emphasized by Turnovsky, such as risk-averse agents, and thus premia in the forward markets, but the advantage would be an integration of the real and monetary aspects of the model explicitly describing how individual portfolio decisions influence the outcomes. At that point one may feel more comfortable with the robustness of the results.

In summary, I want to reiterate that I am very sympathetic to the spirit of the analysis in Turnovsky's chapter. My fundamental concern rests with the narrowness of the specific model employed and, therefore, whether the results will carry over to richer environments.

II RISK: A DOMESTIC OVERVIEW

3 RISK AND THE ECONOMY: A FINANCE PERSPECTIVE

K. C. Chan and Rene M. Stulz

3.1 Introduction

In their introduction to a recent conference volume, Brunner and Meltzer identify "the integration of risk and uncertainty, a standard feature of research in finance, into the type of general equilibrium models used by macroeconomists" as one of the "major areas of interest to macroeconomists in the years ahead."[1] Macroeconomists are concerned with the economy as a whole and changes in risk and uncertainty affect the economy as a whole. While macroeconomists were always aware of this simple truth, they are now more likely to act on it and to take it into account explicitly in their models. The Lucas critique has convinced many of them of the necessity of building their models on the actions of optimizing households. Unless households are risk-neutral, changes in risk affect their consumption and investment plans, and hence have macroeconomic implications.

We are grateful to Wayne Ferson, Ken Singleton, and Arnold Zellner for useful comments.

In this chapter we provide an analysis of those changes in risk that affect the expected returns of risky assets. These are the changes that financial economists have focused on. From a macroeconomic perspective, these changes in risk are of crucial importance because they have direct, pervasive effects throughout the economy even in simple optimizing general equilibrium models. This point is made in section 3.2 where we construct an optimizing growth model in which an increase in risk brings about a fall in consumption, investment, and output as households reallocate their invested wealth across risky technologies.

Changes in risk that affect expected returns are not the only changes in risk that have effects on the economy as a whole. To see this, consider a change in the variance of an individual asset. Such a change may have no effect or only a negligible effect on the asset's expected return. However, if the asset is the common stock of a bank, an increase in the variance of its return signifies that bankruptcy has become more likely for that bank. Such an event can have implications for the economy as a whole. To take another example, an increase in the variance of some asset can increase the bid–ask spread for that asset and hence increase the transaction costs of trading that asset. Higher transaction costs on asset markets can have economy-wide effects, because they make financial markets less efficient. In this chapter, we do not focus on such effects of changes in risk, as they are more of a microeconomic nature.

Measures of risk are used by macroeconomists both in theoretical and in empirical work. In sections 3.3–3.5 we discuss the theoretical motivation for three different measures of risk and review the empirical evidence on the ability of these measures of risk to explain asset returns. We show that measures of risk that are widely used in finance may not be useful to macroeconomists because they are generally concerned about the effects on risk of policy changes that have no role in models used by financial economists. We argue that the lesson from the empirical evidence most relevant for macroeconomists is that the most popular approach, the mean-variance approach, fails to adequately explain differences in expected returns among risky assets. Since most of the empirical evidence in the finance literature focuses on the stock market, we provide in section 3.6 an empirical analysis of the risk measures by applying them to an issue of great interest among macroeconomists. We show how the risk of government bonds changed following the change in the operating procedures of the Fed in 1979. This empirical section allows us to document how much risk measures differ when applied to assets whose risk has not been extensively studied in the finance literature. Section 3.7 provides concluding comments.

3.2 Risk and Economic Activity

In this section, we use a simple optimizing growth model to emphasize the relation between risk and economic activity. The model is related to those used in the "real business cycle" literature.[2] In that literature, households have perfect information and choose how to invest among various technologies. The model used here is more primitive than most of those used in the real business cycle literature, since there is only one commodity produced with only one input, the commodity itself. Contrary to most of the real business cycle literature, we use a continuous-time model. The use of continuous-time techniques, which are popular in finance, makes it easier to derive the comparative statics of a change in risk as we need to focus only on the first two moments of the joint distribution of asset returns if asset prices follow jointly a diffusion process.[3]

3.2.1 The Model

We consider an economy in which all markets are perfect: that is, there are no taxes, no transaction costs, no restrictions to short sales, and all households have the same information and are price takers. In this economy, there is only one costlessly storable commodity. The per capita stock of the commodity at time t. $K(t)$, can be invested in n different constant stochastic returns to scale production processes. $K_i(t)$, $i = 1, \ldots, n$, is the per capita investment in the ith production process. The instantaneous output of the investment in the ith production process is

$$dK_i(t) = \mu_{K_i} K_i(t)dt + \sigma_{K_i} K_i(t)dz_{K_i}, \tag{3.1}$$

where μ_{K_i} and σ_{K_i} are assumed to be constant for all i's and dz_{K_i} is the increment of a standard Brownian notion. In this economy, each household can invest in n production processes and a bond that pays $r(t)$ per unit of time. One can think of households investing in risky assets that are claims to the output of firms or of households producing the commodity directly. For the sake of continuity, we assume that households invest in risky assets sold by firms. These risky assets are claims to the output of production processes. With the assumption of constant returns to scale, a claim worth one unit of commodity in a firm that uses the ith production process has the same payoff as an investment of one unit of commodity in the ith production process. Bonds are in zero net supply. Each household has wealth $W(t)$ and maximizes the same expected utility function of lifetime consumption. We assume that households have a time-additive utility function with constant relative risk aversion and that they are infinitely lived. More precisely, we assume that each household maximizes

$$E_t \int_t^{\infty} e^{-\rho\tau} \frac{1}{\gamma} C(\tau)^{\gamma} \, d\tau, \tag{3.2}$$

where E_t is the expectation conditional on the information set of households at date t.

The wealth of each household must evolve according to a flow budget constraint. Let $n_i(t)$ be the fraction of a household's wealth invested in the ith asset, $i = 1, \ldots, n$. With this notation, the wealth of the household must evolve according to

$$dW(t) = \sum_{i=1}^{n} n_i(t) \left(\frac{dK_i(t)}{K_i(t)} - r(t)dt \right) W(t) + r(t)\, W(t)\, dt - C(t)\, dt. \tag{3.3}$$

To solve for its investment and consumption policies, the household maximizes (3.2) subject to (3.3). Merton (1969) shows that optimal consumption and investment policies satisfy

$$C(t) = \left[\frac{\rho}{1-\gamma} - \gamma \left(\frac{(\mu - r(t)\cdot\mathbf{1})' V^{-1} (\mu - r(t)\cdot\mathbf{1})}{2(1-\gamma)^2} + \frac{r(t)}{1-\gamma} \right) \right] W(t) \tag{3.4}$$

$$n(t) = \frac{1}{1-\gamma} V^{-1} (\mu - r(t)\cdot\mathbf{1}), \tag{3.5}$$

where μ is the $1 \times n$ vector of expected returns of investments in technologies, $\mathbf{1}$ is a vector of ones, V^{-1} is the inverse of the $n \times n$ variance–covariance matrix of returns of investments in technologies, and $n(t)$ is the vector of investment proportions.

As each household is the same, in equilibrium, $W(t) = K(t)$, and the sum of the investment proportions is one. Using equation 3.5, we can solve for the rate of interest. Premultiplying the equation on both sides by $n(t)'V$, where $n(t)'$ is the transpose of $n(t)$, we have

$$n(t)'Vn(t) = \frac{1}{1-\gamma} n(t)'(\mu - r(t)\cdot\mathbf{1}). \tag{3.6}$$

Using the fact that in equilibrium $n'1 = 1$, we can solve for $r(t)$:

$$r(t) = \mu_K(t) - (1-\gamma)\sigma_K^2(t), \tag{3.7}$$

where $\mu_K(t)$ is the expected output rate and $\sigma_K^2(t)$ is the variance of the output rate. Note that both $\mu_K(t)$ and $\sigma_K^2(t)$ are endogenously determined in this model. Equation 3.7 shows that the rate of interest is positively related to the expected output rate and negatively related to the variance of the output rate. This is because an increase in the expected output rate makes an investment in production more attractive relative to an investment in the risk-free bond for a constant interest rate, while the opposite is true if either relative risk aversion (i.e., $1-\gamma$) or the variance of the output rate increase.

3.2.2 Comparative Static Analysis of an Increase in Risk

We now compare the economy described in section 3.2.1 to one that is identical except that all the σ_{K_i}'s are multiplied by $\lambda > 1$. To simplify the notation, we omit the time variable t. Let r^*, μ_K^{*2}, and σ_K^{*2} be respectively the rate of interest, the expected output rate, and the variance of the output rate in the riskier economy. The interest rate equation can be written in terms of the exogenous variables to yield

$$r = \frac{1}{1-\gamma}[V^{-1}(\mu - r\cdot\mathbf{1})]'\mu - \frac{1}{1-\gamma}(\mu - r\cdot\mathbf{1})'V^{-1}(\mu - r\cdot\mathbf{1}). \tag{3.8}$$

Let $\mu'V^{-1}\mu = A$, $\mu'V^{-1}1 = 1'V^{-1}\mu = B$, and $1'V^{-1}1 = D$. Rewriting equation 3.8 using this notation, we get

$$\frac{1}{1-\gamma}(A - rB) - \frac{1}{1-\gamma}(A - 2rB + r^2D) - r = \frac{1}{1-\gamma}(rB - r^2D) - r$$
$$= r\left(\frac{B-(1-\gamma)-rD}{1-\gamma}\right) = 0. \tag{3.9}$$

Solving for r, we find that

$$r = \frac{B-(1-\gamma)}{D}. \tag{3.10}$$

It immediately follows that

$$r^* - r = \frac{(1-\gamma)-(1-\gamma)\lambda^2}{D} < 0, \tag{3.11}$$

so that the riskier economy has a lower rate of interest. This result is not surprising in light of our interest rate equation 3.7. In that equation, the interest rate is negatively related to the variance of output. It would not have been correct, however, to use that relation to infer that the riskier economy has a lower rate of interest. This is because a change in the variance of the returns of the production processes also brings about a change in the expected output rate. Hence, to find the effect of an increase in risk on the interest rate, one has to use a formula for the interest rate in terms of exogenous variables as we did here.

To compare the expected output rate in the two economies, we now write the expected output rate μ_K as a function of exogenous variables:

$$\mu_K = \frac{1}{1-\gamma}(A - rB) = \frac{1}{1-\gamma}\left(A - \frac{B^2 - (1-\gamma)B}{D}\right). \tag{3.12}$$

Hence, the difference between μ_K^* and μ_K is

$$\mu_K^* - \mu_K = \frac{1}{1-\gamma}\left(A - \frac{B^2}{D}\right)\left(\frac{1}{\lambda^2} - 1\right) < 0. \tag{3.13}$$

The inequality in equation 3.13 follows from the fact that $AD - B^2$ is always positive. Equation 3.13 states that the expected output rate is lower in the economy with more risk. When the returns of technologies have a higher variance, households choose a less risky mix of technologies. However, a mix of technologies that is less risky must also have a lower expected rate of return. Otherwise, the more risky mix of technologies is not efficient.

To compare consumption in the two economies, we can use equations 3.8 and 3.12 to rewrite consumption as

$$C = \left[\frac{\rho}{1-\gamma} - \frac{\gamma}{2(1-\gamma)}\left(\frac{A - rB}{1-\gamma} + r\right)\right] W. \tag{3.14}$$

Taking the difference between consumption in the more risky economy and consumption in the less risky economy, we get

$$C^*(t) - C(t) = \frac{\gamma}{2(1-\gamma)}\left(\frac{A - rB}{1-\gamma} + r - \frac{A(1/\lambda^2)}{1-\lambda} + \frac{r^*B(1/\lambda^2)}{1-\gamma} - r^*\right) W. \tag{3.15}$$

This quantity is negative if γ is negative and positive otherwise. Since there seems to be a widespread belief that individuals are more risk averse than if they had a logarithmic utility function, γ is likely to be negative so that consumption is negatively related to risk.

Finally, we solve for the relation between risk and investment. In this model, saving is equal to investment, so that planned investment is $\mu_K K - C$, that is, expected output minus consumption. Solving for the difference between planned investment in the riskier economy and the less risky economy, we get

$$(\mu_K^* K - C^*) - (\mu_K K - C) = (\mu_K^* - \mu_K)K + \frac{1}{2}\frac{\gamma}{(1-\gamma)}(\mu_K - \mu_K^*)K$$
$$+ \frac{1}{2}\frac{\gamma}{(1-\gamma)}(r - r^*)K. \tag{3.16}$$

By inspection, if γ is negative, all the terms in equation 3.16 are negative so that investment falls as the variance of the returns of investments in technologies increases.

3.2.3 A General Perspective

In section 3.2.2, we showed in a simple stochastic growth model that a proportional increase in the variance of the return of all technologies brings about a decrease in the rate of interest, the expected output rate and, if households have a coefficient of relative risk aversion in excess of one, a decrease in consumption and planned investment. It is easy to think of many ways in which this model could be extended. However, from the perspective of this chapter, the most interesting extension would be one that introduces government policy.

Stulz and Wasserfallen (1985) explore a related model. In that model, most of the results are derived under the assumption that households have a logarithmic utility function, which is a more restrictive assumption than the one used here. However, in that model, households hold real balances and the money stock changes stochastically. Changes in the money stock are brought about by purchases of the commodity by the government, so that no transfers are made to households. Such a model can be used to study the effects of an increase in the variance of the policy variable, that is, government purchases of the commodity.[4] It turns out that an increase in the variance of the money stock leads to the same results as those of an increase in the variance of the returns of the technologies described in section 3.2.2, at least when the expected rate of change of the price of money (i.e., the inverse of the price level) is maintained constant and when changes in the price of money do not covary with the returns of technologies. To understand this, note that the key to the results of section 3.2.2 is that, for given investments in technologies, an increase in the variance of the returns of the technologies increases the variance of changes in wealth without changing the mean rate of return of invested wealth. This makes households worse off and forces them to adjust their investment and consumption policies. In the Stulz and Wasserfallen (1985) model, an increase in the variance of the rate of change of the price of money increases the variance of changes in wealth for given real balances and portfolio choice so that households choose to invest more in less risky technologies. In that model, consumption decreases even with a logarithmic utility function because the increase in the variance of the rate of change of the price of money increases the nominal rate of interest and hence decreases real wealth through a real balance effect.

3.3 Mean-Variance Models

In this section, we address the issue of when a change in the risk of an asset increases its expected return relative to the rate of interest in the model of section 3.2 and other models of the same class. In the model of section 3.2, the expected returns on risky investments are technologically given while the fractions of aggregate wealth invested in the various technologies and the rate of interest are endogenously determined. Most of the research in finance takes the expected returns on risky assets to be endogenously determined and considers the asset supplies and the rate of interest to be exogenously given. However, for the analysis in the remainder of this chapter, it is of little importance whether expected returns on risky assets or the rate of interest are taken as given, because the analysis focuses on the difference between an asset's expected return and the rate of interest, that is, on the asset's risk premium.

3.3.1 Nondiversifiable Risks

In section 3.2, an increase in the variance of the return of all technologies increases the variance of invested wealth, that is, $\sigma_K^2(t)$. From the interest rate equation 3.7, an increase in the variance of the return of invested wealth is associated with an increase in the risk premium for risky assets. This suggests that a change in the risk of a subset of assets will increase the risk premium on that subset of assets only if it increases the variance of the return of invested wealth. This can be seen immediately by premultiplying the asset demands by V to get

$$(1-\gamma)\,Vn = \mu - r\cdot\mathbf{1}. \tag{3.17}$$

For the ith asset, equation 3.17 implies that

$$(1-\gamma)\sigma_{I_i,W} = \mu_i - r, \tag{3.18}$$

where $\sigma_{I_i,W} = \text{Cov}(dI_i/I_i,\, dW/W)(1/dt)$ and I_i is the price of the ith asset. Equation 3.18 holds irrespective of whether expected returns for risky assets or the supplies of risky assets are exogenously given, provided that asset demands are proportional to $V^{-1}(\mu - r\cdot\mathbf{1})$ as in equation 3.5. We will see in section 3.4 that, in general, asset demands are not given by an equation similar to equation 3.5 when asset supplies, expected returns of risky assets, the rate of interest, or the variance–covariance matrix of asset returns change stochastically over time.

Equation 3.18 means that asset i's risk premium is a linear function of the covariance of its return with the return to invested wealth. Hence, in this model, a change in an asset's risk changes its risk premium only insofar as it changes the covariance of the asset's return with the growth rate of invested wealth. Other changes in the risk of an asset do not affect the variance of the return of invested wealth and hence are called diversifiable. It immediately follows from equation 3.18 that in this model an asset's risk premium is not linearly related to the variance of its return. For instance, if $\sigma_{I_i, W}$ is negative, asset i's risk premium falls as the variance of its return increases. Furthermore, asset j could have a higher return variance than asset i while asset i has a higher risk premium than asset j. Consequently, asset return variances provide no information about how the expected return of a risky asset differs from another.

If one assumes that the expected rates of return on risky assets are endogenously given, one must take asset supplies as exogenously given. In this case, equation 3.18 can be rewritten so that it no longer depends directly on preferences. Let n^* be the vector of asset supplies, where n_i^* is the supply of asset i as a fraction of invested wealth. In equilibrium, since all households are the same, it must be the case that $n = n^*$, so that we can replace n by n^* in equation 3.17 to get

$$(1-\gamma)\, Vn^* = \frac{\mu_W - r}{\sigma_W^2}, \tag{3.19}$$

where μ_W is the expected return and σ_W^2 is the variance of the return of invested wealth. Using equation 3.19 to replace $(1-\gamma)$ in equation 3.18, we obtain

$$\sigma_{I_i, W}\frac{\mu_W - r}{\sigma_W^2} = \mu_i - r. \tag{3.20}$$

Equation 3.20 is the capital asset pricing model (CAPM) of Sharpe (1965) and Lintner (1965). In that model, equation 3.20 is usually written as

$$\mu_i - \mathrm{r} = \beta_i(\mu_W - r), \tag{3.20$'$}$$

where β_i is equal to $\sigma_{I_i, W}/\sigma_W^2$. If the CAPM holds, one can rank risk premia on risky assets by ranking the β coefficients of these risky assets. With the CAPM, the ratio of the risk premia of two risky assets is equal to the ratio of their β coefficients and depends on no other measure of risk.[5]

3.3.2 Some Problems in Measuring β Coefficients

We now have a measure of the priced risk of a risky asset that is correct under some assumptions. Put succinctly, sufficient conditions for equation 3.20′ to hold for general utility functions are that (1) capital markets are perfect (no taxes, no transaction costs, etc.), (2) trading is continuous, and (3) asset prices are lognormally distributed. We now turn to the issue of how to use empirically this measure of risk and of how useful it is to explain the cross-sectional variation in asset returns. In this section, we discuss the problems that arise in estimating β coefficients, while in section 3.3.3 we review some empirical tests of the capital asset pricing model.

To estimate β coefficients, one needs to compute the covariance of the return of a risky asset with the return of invested wealth. In the CAPM, the concept of invested wealth includes every risky asset in which investors put their money, so that invested wealth is not observable by those who compute estimates of β coefficients. While one can think of many possible proxies for invested wealth, there is no way to know how good these various proxies are. It would be convenient if a proxy that takes into account the returns of more assets than another would be a better proxy, but no theoretical reason can be found for such a result to hold. It would also be useful if proxies that are similar would always yield similar rankings of β coefficients. However, one can produce examples in which two similar proxies imply very different rankings of β coefficients among a set of securities. The most positive result one finds in the literature can be summarized as follows.[6] If the variance and mean of the returns of two proxies are similar and if the returns of the two proxies are highly correlated, the β coefficients of risky assets will not be very different with the two proxies. Since most proxies used in empirical research have highly correlated returns and do not differ much in mean-variance space, this means that, provided one is not overly concerned with the ranking of β coefficients, the β coefficients of a risky asset is not too sensitive to the proxy used for invested wealth.

Once one has identified a proxy for invested wealth, one must obtain data for the returns of the security whose β coefficient one seeks to estimate. This task is not difficult for securities that are frequently traded on organized exchanges. For such securities, one will generally have available a transaction price for a time near the closing time of the exchange. Hence, if one uses an index of stock prices as a proxy for invested wealth, the time series of the proxy and of the transaction prices for securities are concurrent. However, for other assets, the data available present some problems. For infrequently traded common stocks, for instance, the last price recorded might be a transaction price from the middle of the day. For such a common stock, the calendar time of the observed returns is not the same as the calendar time of the returns for the proxy. Furthermore, the observed price may result from a transaction at the bid or ask price of a market maker, which incorporates some elements of transaction costs and has different time-series properties from the "true" price. In summary, one is often likely to observe returns that differ, not always randomly, from the returns one would like to use but cannot. Financial economists have derived various methods to reduce the importance of that problem, but most of them were conceived for applications to common stocks.[7] One must therefore be careful when applying them to other assets.

In the CAPM, the β coefficient that is relevant for the pricing of risky assets is prospective; that is, it is the one that is expected to prevail over the next period. Hence, to obtain an estimate for that coefficient, one needs a model of how it evolves over time. The standard approach in finance is to assume the returns-generating process for the asset to be priced and that the proxy for invested wealth is constant over some period of time. When returns are sampled monthly, researchers typically assume that the joint distribution of returns for the asset and the proxy is constant for five years, while shorter periods of time are used when returns are sampled daily.[8] With such an assumption, the sample covariance is an unbiased predictor of the future covariance. While such an assumption is not devoid of justification, it is becoming increasingly clear that it can lead to misleading results.

To understand why more sophisticated models of the returns—generating process are often useful, consider a levered firm whose value fell over the recent past. Shareholder equity has therefore decreased in value. To make our point easier to understand, we assume that (1) the debt is risk-free and (2) the distribution of the growth rate of the value of the firm (i.e., the value of the debt plus the value of equity) is constant. An unexpected 1% increase in the value of the firm increases the value of equity by more than 1%, since the value of equity is only a fraction of the value of the firm. The lower the value of equity, the higher the percentage increase in the value of equity caused by a 1% increase in the value of the firm. Hence, if the β coefficient of equity is positive, it increases as the value of equity falls because equity becomes more sensitive to changes in the value of the firm. As the value of a firm's equity changes over time, its value should be useful information in estimating the firm's β coefficient.[9]

Even if all the problems just described are solved to satisfaction, it is not clear that one is likely to obtain an estimate for the β coefficient of an individual asset that is very useful. This is because, for individual assets, there is always substantial uncertainty about one's estimate of the β coefficient. To wit, using monthly returns from July 1963 to June 1968, Fama (1976) finds an estimate for the β coefficient of IBM of 0.67. However, the conditional standard error for the estimator of the β coefficient is 0.1331. If one assumes a diffuse prior, Fama (1976) shows that the posterior probability that the β coefficient of IBM belongs outside the interval 0.585 to 0.764 is 0.5. While one gets a much more precise estimate of β coefficients when one estimates the β coefficient of a portfolio of risky assets, it is often not practical to use portfolios. For instance, in macroeconomic applications, one might be interested in the risk of a particular currency rather than in the risk of a basket of currencies.

3.3.3 Tests of the CAPM

How useful is the β coefficient to explain the cross-sectional distribution of asset returns? To find an answer to that question, it is necessary to review the empirical evidence on the CAPM. A standard approach to testing the CAPM consists of regressing estimates of the expected excess returns of securities, that is, expected risk premia, on a constant and on the estimated β coefficients of these securities:

$$\mu_i - r = \gamma_0 + \gamma_1 \beta_i, \tag{3.21}$$

where μ_i is one's estimate of the expected return of security i and β_i is an estimate of the security's β coefficient. The hypotheses tested are that $\gamma_0 = 1$ and $\gamma_1 = \mu_W - r$, where μ_W is one's estimate of the expected return of invested wealth. Considerable ingenuity has been devoted to such tests. Usually these tests are conducted with portfolios of risky assets to have more precise estimates of the β coefficients. Initially tests were conducted in two stages, the first stage being the β estimation period, while the second stage tested equation 3.21.[10] More recently, tests have been conducted in one stage using a multivariate regression framework.[11]

It is generally the case that when equation 3.21 is tested, γ_0 turns out to be greater than zero while γ_1 is smaller than the sample mean of the excess return of the market portfolio. However, in most studies, the relation between expected returns and β coefficients is linear when portfolios are formed according to the β coefficients of the individual securities. Furthermore, it is generally the case that when the β coefficient is the selection criterion for portfolios, the variance of the returns of portfolios plays no role in explaining the cross-sectional variation of asset returns. While some studies have found a role for the variance of portfolio returns, it is generally the case that the variance plays a role because it is related to the estimation error in β coefficients.[12] When estimates of β coefficients become more precise, the variance of portfolio returns generally loses explanatory power. Interestingly, inference about the CAPM does not seem to depend much on the proxy chosen. Figure 3–1 shows the regression line for a test of equation 3.21 in one of the most well-known empirical studies of the CAPM.

Roll (1977) conjectured that using β coefficients of individual securities to form portfolios to test the CAPM may average out within portfolios factors that affect expected returns of risky assets. Roll's conjecture turned out to be

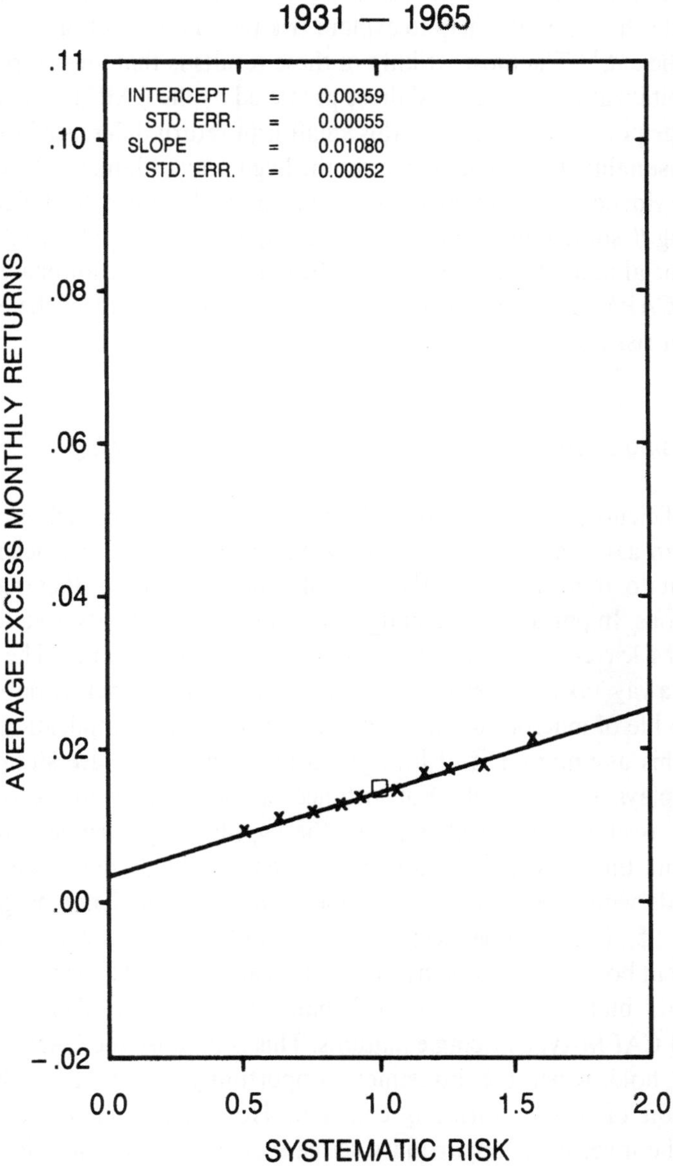

Figure 3–1. Average excess monthly returns versus systematic risk for the 35-year period 1931–1965 for each of ten portfolios (denoted by X) and the market portfolio (denoted by □). *Source:* F. Black (1972), *Journal of Business,* **45**.

correct as the body of research on testing asset pricing models grew. Countless studies have shown that firm size, price–earnings ratio, long-run dividend yield, and other variables help to explain risk premia in addition to estimates of β coefficient.[13] The most striking of these results is that annual returns of small capitalization firms exceed those predicted by the CAPM by at least ten percentage points. Furthermore, this small-firm return differential exhibits a sharp seasonality: most of it accrues in the beginning of January. While there is some evidence that part of the firm-size anomaly is due to difficulties in estimating β, something else must also be responsible for it.[14] If one believes that financial markets are reasonably efficient, the firm-size anomaly implies that the CAPM does not capture all sources of risk that affect the expected returns of risky assets.

3.3.4 Using β Coefficients in Macroeconomics: A Warning

Beta coefficients are unambiguously better measures of the priced risk of risky assets than asset return variances. However, when using β coefficients, it is important to remember that the CAPM relies on some rather restrictive assumptions. In particular, the budget equation of households used to derive the CAPM leaves no role for macroeconomic policy variables. The CAPM assumes away taxes, government bonds, money, and other variables that make the life of macroeconomists interesting. For many applications of the CAPM this assumption is of little importance, but there are situations in which it plays a crucial role. For instance, suppose one wants to study the effect on asset returns of changes in the supply of government bonds.[15] Clearly, in the presence of government bonds the budget equation of households would be different and asset demands would not be given by equation 3.5. Even if one decides to be bold and simply assumes that government bonds are part of invested wealth and nothing else changes in the households' budget equation, asset demands are likely to differ from those that yield CAPM-type pricing equations. This is because the CAPM is most likely to hold when the investment opportunity set, that is, the joint distribution of asset returns, is constant. However, when asset supplies change, the investment opportunity set cannot be constant and, in general, other factors affect an asset's expected return besides its β coefficient, as will be discussed in the next section.

Macroeconomists often use CAPM-like approaches but choose as their market portfolio an extremely small subset of risky assets. For instance, some authors have computed the risk of a currency as being the covariance of the return of a bond denominated in that currency with the return of a portfolio of bonds denominated in various currencies. It should be clear that such approaches have to be viewed with skepticism. There is no reason to suspect that invested wealth should be highly correlated with the return of such a portfolio. Furthermore, it is hard to see how the use of such a portfolio could otherwise be motivated unless one is willing to assume that each bond's return is uncorrelated with the return to invested wealth.

3.4 A More General Approach

In section 3.3, we derived a model of asset pricing in which an asset's expected excess return depends only on its β coefficient. This model failed to explain some empirical regularities. In this section, we relax some of the assumptions of the CAPM and show that the more general model is better able to explain the cross-sectional variation of expected asset returns.

3.4.1 A Multiple β Model

From a macroeconomic perspective, the most disturbing assumption of the CAPM is surely the assumption that the investment opportunity set is non-stochastic unless investors are myopic. This assumption precludes policy changes that have real effects. For instance, it does not allow for changes in asset supplies brought about by changes in government policies. To see better the implications of this assumption, suppose that each household has the same wealth and maximizes the following utility function:

$$E_t \int_t^{\infty} e^{-\rho(u(C(\tau))\tau)} u(C(\tau))d\tau. \tag{3.22}$$

We therefore let the households' rate of time preference and relative risk aversion change stochastically over time.[16] To allow for changes in the investment opportunity set, suppose now that the joint distribution of changes in the exogenous variables depends on a $1 \times n$ vector of state variables S. The state variables are assumed to follow jointly a Markov diffusion process. We can characterize the portfolio demands in terms of partial derivatives of the indirect utility function of wealth of the households, which we write as $J(W, S, t)$ and define as follows:

$$J(W,S,t) = \max_{\{\dot{c}(\tau),\, n(\tau)\}} E_t \int_t^{\infty} e^{-\rho(u(C(\tau))\tau)} u(C(\tau))d\tau. \tag{3.23}$$

Solving for the portfolio demands yields

$$n = \frac{-J_W}{J_{WW}W} V^{-1}(\mu - r \cdot \mathbf{1}) + \sum_{i=1}^{S} \frac{-J_{WS_i}}{J_{WW}W} V^{-1} V_{S_i}, \tag{3.24}$$

where J_W, J_{WW}, and J_{WS_i} are, respectively, the first partial derivative of the function J with respect to W, and the partial derivative of J_W with respect to W and with respect to the ith state variable. Furthermore, V_{S_i} is the vector of local covariances of risky asset returns with changes in the ith state variable. Note that the first term in the asset demands is proportional to the asset demands in section 3.2. Hence, for the CAPM to hold, the last S terms must be equal to zero. This happens either when (1) $J_{WS_i} = 0, i = 1, \ldots, S$, or when (2) $V_{S_i} = 0, i = 1, \ldots, S$.[17] For condition 1 to hold, households must be myopic, which implies that they have a logarithmic utility function. For condition 2 to hold, changes in state variables have to be uncorrelated with asset returns.

To understand the asset demands in this section, note that they differ from the asset demands used in sections 3.2 and 3.3 by terms that depend on derivatives of the marginal utility of wealth with respect to state variables. Hence, the asset demands in this section differ only because the marginal utility of wealth depends on state variables other than the level of wealth. The asset demands given by equation 3.23 hold under fairly general assumptions irrespective of whether asset supplies or expected returns are taken to be exogenous. For concreteness, suppose that the ith state variable is the expected growth rate of the money supply. An increase in that state variable can affect the marginal utility of wealth for all sorts of reasons. Consider the case in which the marginal utility of wealth increases as expected money growth increases for a given level of wealth, that is, $J_{WS_i} > 0$. One would expect sufficiently risk-averse households to hedge against the adverse effect of an unexpected increase in expected money growth on their lifetime expected utility.[18] They can do so by taking a long position in a portfolio whose return is highly correlated with unanticipated changes in expected money growth. However, by doing so, households drive down the expected returns on the assets that enter in positive amounts in that portfolio, that is, the assets whose returns are positively correlated with changes in expected inflation, compared to what they would be in a CAPM world. The desire of households to hedge against unanticipated changes in state variables therefore affects the expected returns of risky assets. Solving for equilibrium expected returns, we have

$$\mu_i - r = \beta_i^M(\mu_W - r) + \sum_{i=1}^{S} \beta_i^{S_i}(\mu_{S_i} - r), \tag{3.25}$$

where β_i^M is the theoretical multiple-regression coefficient from regressing the instantaneous return of asset i on the instantaneous return of invested wealth,

$\beta_i^{S_i}$ is the theoretical multiple-regression coefficient from regressing the instantaneous return of asset i on the instantaneous return of the portfolio that has the highest correlation with changes in state variable i among all possible portfolios, and μ_{S_i} is the expected return on that portfolio. Note that these theoretical regression coefficients may themselves be functions of the vector of state variables. If state variables play an important role in asset demands, it is clearly the case that they can lead to required expected returns on risky assets that differ substantially from those predicted by the CAPM. Because the model has no restrictions on the type of state variables that affect the expected returns of risky assets, it is compatible with a wide variety of general equilibrium models.

3.4.2 *Empirical Evidence on the Multiple-β Model*

The major new difficulty in testing the multiple-β model is that one has to find out what the relevant priced state variables are. A sensible approach is to see whether a particular set of state variables together with a proxy for invested wealth provide a better explanation for the cross-sectional variation of asset returns than invested wealth alone. The danger of such an approach is that it can transform a test of an asset pricing model into a fishing expedition. Macroeconomic models offer some intuition about which variables one would expect to be relevant. It would make sense for industrial production to be relevant for asset pricing because it provides information about the short-run prospects of the economy. In most macroeconomic approaches, both expected and unexpected inflation can affect the households' welfare. Finally, one would expect households to behave differently depending on the shape of the term structure of interest rates.

In the most notable study of the multiple-β model, Chan et al. (1985) find a role in asset pricing for all the possible state variables discussed in the previous paragraph plus two additional ones that seem a bit more surprising. These additional state variables are the rate of business formation and the yield difference between junk bonds and AAA bonds. They find that a positive covariance of an asset's return with the return of the market portfolio, industrial production growth, and the junk bond spread increases its expected return, while a positive covariance of the asset's return with the remaining state variables decreases its expected return. As the returns of small firms covary strongly with the junk bond spread, the multiple-β approach reduces sharply the abnormal returns of small firms observed in applications of the CAPM. In fact, while the abnormal returns of small firms do not disappear completely, they are no longer significant at conventional confidence levels.

Table 3–1 shows how the spread in sample returns between small and large firms is explained in the multiple-β model of Chan et al. (1985). The usefulness of the state variables approach in explaining the cross-sectional distribution of asset returns is obvious when one notices that the state variables explain a larger fraction of the sample return spread between small and large firms than does the risk premium of the CAPM.

While several papers have investigated the role of state variables in asset pricing models, none have provided results as striking as the Chan et al. (1985) study.[19] This is due in large part to the fact that financial economists only recently started to study empirically multiple-β asset pricing models. It is noteworthy, however, that studies of bond markets show that multiple-state variable models explain the term structure of interest rates better than single-state variable models. It would seem that this research could benefit heavily from using fully developed macroeconomic equilibrium models in which state variables are explicitly defined.

3.4.3 Multiple-β Models and Macroeconomics

While the empirical applications of the multiple-β model are promising, one has to be extremely careful when interpreting their results. The work of Chan et al. (1985) and Chen et al. (1986) shows that macroeconomic variables can help us understand the cross-sectional variation of asset returns. However, no explicit theoretical model is used to specify the relevant state variables. Hence, in their approaches, it may well be the case that, for instance, expected inflation matters in asset pricing because it is highly correlated with some unknown state variable. Therefore, one cannot use their results to forecast the effect on expected returns of a policy-induced change in the distribution of changes of expected inflation. Further research should focus on developing models that provide guidance for the choice of state variables.

3.5 A Fairly General Single-β Approach

In this section, we show that if the households' subjective rate of time preference is a constant, the asset pricing model of section 3.4 can be rewritten as a single-β model. However, in this case an asset's β coefficient is proportional to the covariance of the asset's return with consumption growth. The problems in estimating consumption β coefficients differ substantially from those in estimating invested wealth β coefficients. These problems are

Table 3–1. Average Monthly Component Contributions (%) of the Multiple-β Model, 1958–1977[a]

	Total return	EWNY	DEI	UITB	IP1SA	PREM	UTS	*Constant*	*Unexplained*
*P*1	1.513	0.661	−0.088	−0.025	0.160	0.304	−0.014	0.444	0.071
*P*2	1.248	0.674	−0.097	−0.033	0.034	0.342	−0.138	0.444	0.023
*P*3	1.265	0.635	0.024	−0.024	0.057	0.334	−0.144	0.444	−0.061
*P*4	1.153	0.599	−0.019	−0.090	0.037	0.235	−0.056	0.444	0.004
*P*5	1.155	0.630	0.037	−0.043	0.040	0.084	−0.054	0.444	0.019
*P*6	1.099	0.600	0.021	0.025	0.023	0.054	−0.096	0.444	0.028
*P*7	1.143	0.621	0.044	−0.002	0.050	0.072	−0.084	0.444	−0.002
*P*8	1.123	0.611	0.026	0.004	0.019	−0.009	0.003	0.444	0.026
*P*9	0.906	0.506	−0.035	0.047	−0.013	0.023	0.076	0.444	−0.141
*P*10	0.975	0.484	0.020	0.007	−0.009	0.060	0.044	0.444	0.046
*P*11	0.900	0.523	0.010	0.054	0.020	−0.073	−0.002	0.444	−0.075
*P*12	0.872	0.486	−0.030	0.053	−0.032	−0.151	0.062	0.444	0.040
*P*13	0.907	0.480	−0.007	−0.021	0.001	−0.135	0.044	0.444	0.058
*P*14	0.965	0.531	0.052	−0.034	−0.019	−0.143	0.014	0.444	0.121
*P*15	0.825	0.403	0.055	0.009	−0.063	−0.106	0.027	0.444	0.056
*P*16	0.751	0.389	0.005	0.002	−0.041	−0.136	0.049	0.444	0.038
*P*17	0.759	0.370	0.003	0.023	−0.070	−0.113	0.042	0.444	0.062
*P*18	0.624	0.410	0.073	−0.040	−0.081	−0.194	0.096	0.444	−0.083
*P*19	0.514	0.398	−0.038	−0.070	−0.044	−0.215	0.136	0.444	−0.097
*P*20	0.558	0.309	−0.000	−0.040	−0.044	−0.149	0.088	0.444	−0.049
*P*1 − *P*20	0.956	0.352	−0.088	0.015	0.204	0.453	−0.102	0	0.120
*Q*1 − *Q*5	0.687	0.270	−0.054	−0.010	0.132	0.471	−0.178	0	0.054

Source: Chan et al. (1985).

[a] *P*1, . . . , *P*20 are the 20 portfolios in ascending order of firm size. *P*1 − *P*20 is the difference between the top and the bottom portfolio. *Q*1 − *Q*5 is the difference between the top and bottom quintile. EWNY is the equally weighted NYSE index. IP1SA is the seasonally adjusted monthly growth rate of industrial production. DEI is the difference in expected inflation. UITB is the unexpected inflation. PREM is the difference in return between low-grade bonds and government bonds. UTS is the difference in return between long-term government bonds and T-bills.

discussed in the remainder of this section and the empirical evidence on the consumption-based asset pricing model is briefly reviewed.

3.5.1 The Consumption-Based Asset Pricing Model

We now assume that the household's subjective rate of time preference is constant, that is, in equation 3.23, $\rho(u(C(\tau))) = \rho$.[20] At the optimum, the gain in utility from consuming an additional unit of the commodity must be the same as the gain from investing an additional unit. Formally, we have, therefore,

$$U_C(C(W, S, t)) = J_W(W, S, t), \tag{3.26}$$

where $U_C(C(W, S, t))$ is the partial derivative of the instantaneous utility function with respect to consumption while $J_W(W, S, t)$ is the partial derivative of the indirect utility function of wealth with respect to wealth. Using equation 3.26, it immediately follows that

$$U_{CC}(C(W, S, t))C_W(W, S, t) = J_{WW}(W, S, t) \tag{3.27}$$

$$U_{CC}(C(W, S, t))C_S(W, S, t) = J_{WS}(W, S, t), \tag{3.28}$$

where $C_S(C(W, S, t))(C_W(W, S, t))$ is the vector of partial derivatives of the consumption expenditure function with respect to the state variables (wealth).

One can use equations 3.26–3.28 to eliminate the partial derivatives of the indirect utility function of wealth in the asset demand equations to obtain

$$n = \frac{-U_C}{(U_{CC}C_W W)} V^{-1}(\mu - r \cdot \mathbf{1}) + \sum_{i=1}^{S} \frac{-U_{CC}C_S}{U_{CC}C_W W} V^{-1}V_{S_i}, \tag{3.29}$$

where the time variable is omitted. Premultiplying equation 3.29 by $VC_W W/C$ and rearranging yields

$$\frac{1}{C}\left(VnC_W W + \sum_{i=1}^{S} C_{S_i} V_{S_i} W\right) = \frac{-U_C}{U_{CC}C} V^{-1}(\mu - r). \tag{3.30}$$

Breeden (1979) shows that the left side of equation 3.30 is $1/dt$ times the vector of local covariances of asset returns with consumption growth. Hence, for an individual asset, equation 3.30 can be rewritten as

$$T(\mu_i - r) = \frac{\sigma_{i,C}}{\sigma_C^2} = \beta_{i,C}, \tag{3.31}$$

where T is the households' relative risk tolerance $-U_C/U_{CC}C$, $\sigma_{i,C}$ is the local covariance of the return of asset i with consumption growth, and σ_C^2

is the local variance of consumption growth. $\beta_{i,C}$ is the consumption-β of the ith asset.

The consumption-based asset pricing model states that an asset's expected excess return is proportional to its consumption-β. To understand equation 3.31, note first that at the optimum a household's portfolio satisfies

$$E_t\left[\frac{U_C(C(W,S,t+\Delta t))}{U_C(C(W,S,t))}\left(\frac{I_i(t+\Delta t)}{I_i(t)}-\frac{I_j(t+\Delta t)}{I_j(t)}\right)\right]=0 \ \forall_{i,j}, \qquad (3.32)$$

where I_i is the price of the ith risky asset. If equation 3.32 does not hold for some risky asset, it should be possible for a household to increase its expected utility by rearranging its portfolio. Let $\Omega(t)$ be one plus the expected growth rate of marginal utility from t to $t+\Delta t$, that is, $\Omega(t)$ is equal to $E[U_C(C(W,S,t+\Delta t))/U_C(C(W,S,t))]$. With this new notation, equation 3.32 can be rewritten as

$$E_t\Omega(t)\left(E_t\frac{I_i(t+\Delta t)}{I_i(t)}-E_t\frac{I_j(t+\Delta t)}{I_j(t)}\right)=\operatorname{Cov}\left(\Omega(t),\frac{I_j(t+\Delta t)}{I_j(t)}\right)$$
$$-\operatorname{Cov}\left(\Omega(t),\frac{I_i(t+\Delta t)}{I_i(t)}\right). \qquad (3.33)$$

Hence, in this model, an asset's return is proportional to minus one times the covariance of its return with the growth rate of marginal utility. This is because a household values an asset that has high payoffs when marginal utility is high more than an asset that has high payoffs when marginal utility is low. Consequently, households require lower expected returns on assets whose returns covary negatively with marginal utility. In the limit of continuous time, however, $\Omega(t)$ is equal to $1+(U_{CC}/U_C)dC$ plus terms that are negligible when computing covariances. Substituting $1+(U_{CC}/U_C)\,dC$ for $\Omega(t)$ in equation 3.33 yields equation 3.31.[21]

An attractive feature of the consumption-based approach is that the coefficient of relative risk aversion can be eliminated from equation 3.31 by rewriting the equation in terms of the expected return of an *arbitrary* benchmark portfolio:

$$\mu_i-\mathrm{r}=\beta_{i,C}\frac{\mu_p-r}{\sigma_{p,C}}, \qquad (3.34)$$

where $\sigma_{p,C}$ is the local covariance of consumption growth with the rate of return of the benchmark portfolio and μ_p is the expected rate of return of the same portfolio. Since equation 3.34 does not depend directly on the parameters of the households' utility function, it can be tested if one observes asset returns and consumption.

It should be pointed out that equation 3.34 has two extremely attractive features for macroeconomists. First, it is compatible with most macroeconomic models. Hence, one does not have to choose a macroeconomic model to obtain an asset pricing equation. Second, equation 3.34 prices assets in terms of the covariance of their returns with a variable that has been studied considerably by macroeconomists. Hence, all of what macroeconomists know about consumption growth can be brought to bear to price risky assets.

3.5.2 Empirical Evidence

The consumption-based asset pricing model admits a stochastic investment opportunity set and can be tested even if one does not observe the return to invested wealth. Consumption data are published regularly, but not as frequently as asset price data. Nevertheless, it can be argued that one has an unbiased measure of consumption, while no such measure is available for the return to invested wealth.

Unfortunately, there are several problems with published measures of consumption that make it difficult to implement the consumption-based asset pricing model.[22] First, published measures of consumption are estimates of true consumption and hence include sampling error. Second, the measure of consumption suggested by the model is all-inclusive, while published measures of consumption report expenditures and neglect some consumption goods, for instance, leisure. Third, the model requires an estimate of instantaneous consumption growth whereas published measures of consumption provide the integral of consumption over a period of time. This summation reduces the variance of consumption and hence biases downward the estimates of consumption-β's. However, Breeden et al. (1986) show that for some assumptions about the distribution of consumption changes, this summation just multiplies β's computed with consumption growth by a scalar smaller than one, so that it has no significant effects on tests of the model.

The preceding paragraph makes clear that, even though consumption data are published, the data are such that one would not expect to measure consumption-β coefficients with much precision. It is important, however, not to believe that; therefore, the model with invested wealth β's is in some sense better. One can estimate the β of an asset with respect to some stock market index much more precisely than one can estimate the consumption-β of the same asset. Yet, the stock market index β may not be useful to price the risky asset while the consumption-β is. One way to improve estimates of consumption-β's is to substitute for consumption growth the rate of return of a portfolio whose return is highly correlated with consumption growth. With this approach, one can estimate "consumption" β's using daily data and hence, in principle, can estimate these β's with as much precision as one can estimate stock index β's.

Breeden et al. (1986) use this approach to test the consumption-based asset pricing model. Interestingly, the share of junk bonds in their portfolio that mimicks consumption growth is more than 0.5. This confirms the fact that the consumption-β and the multiple-β model do not differ in a substantial way. The two models should always yield the same results for asset pricing. Therefore, it is comforting that the junk bond premium, which plays an important role in empirical versions of the multiple-β model, also plays an important role in empirical versions of the consumption-based asset pricing model. An important problem with consumption-β's is that they depend on the state of the world. Hence, the model properly applies to conditional β's that are even harder to measure than the unconditional β's we have discussed so far in this section.[23] Breeden et al. (1986) test an unconditional version of the model. Using a multivariate approach, they show that the model works fairly well, even though they are able to reject it over the period 1929–1982. They show that the expected return on an asset whose consumption-β is zero is about the rate of interest and that the relation between expected excess returns and consumption-β's is close to being linear. Figure 3–2 shows their plots of sample average excess returns in relation to consumption-β's. It turns out that they are able to reject the model only because of the 1930s. The consumption data for the 1930s are not as good as for the later periods. At the same time, consumption is more volatile in the 1930s. Hence, the authors might reject the model because of poor data in the 1930s or because the 1930s increase the power of their tests.

At this point, the body of empirical work on testing the consumption based asset pricing model is growing quickly. However, much of this literature focuses on discrete-time versions of the model. Tests generally assume that the utility function has a specific functional form. Most tests assume that the utility function is a power utility function, so that households have constant relative risk aversion. If one replaces U_C in equation 3.33 with some nonlinear function of consumption, the expected return of risky assets does not depend on consumption alone; it is also a function of the parameters of the utility function. With a power utility function, equation 3.33 depends both on consumption and on the coefficient of relative risk aversion. One can then use the asset pricing equation to estimate the coefficient of relative risk aversion. If the model holds, one should get similar estimates for the coefficient of relative risk aversion using different assets. This approach makes stronger assumptions about preferences than the continuous-time version. However, it can be tested by making weaker distributional assumptions. Other ap-

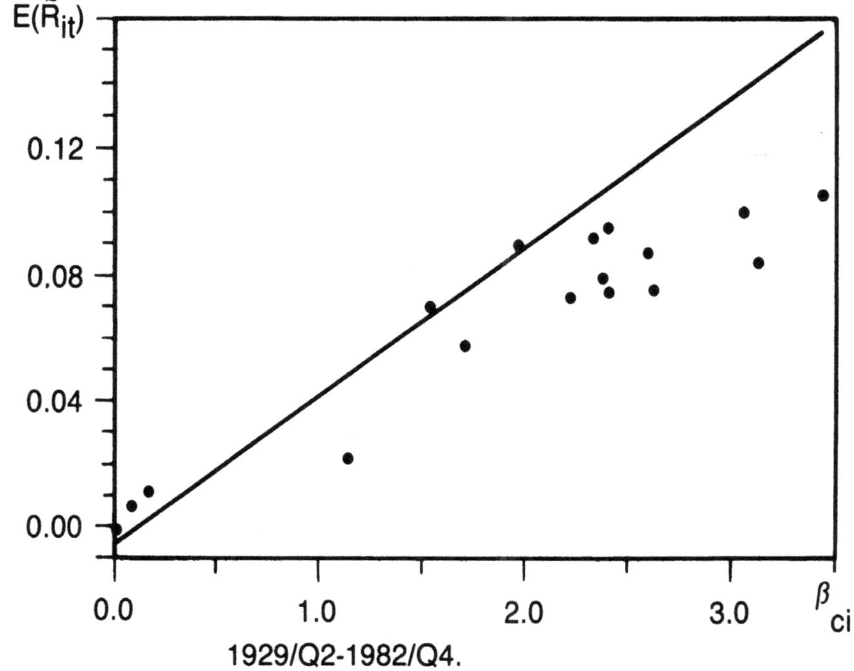

Figure 3–2. Average excess returns versus consumption β's. Scatter plots of parameter estimates with and without Consumption-Based Asset Pricing Model restriction. All data are annualized and in real terms, and consumption growth is adjusted to correct for summation bias. Seventeen assets (12 industry portfolios, 4 bond portfolios, and the CRSP Value-Weighted Index) are used. The intercept and slope of the solid straight line in each plot are determined by the maximum likelihood estimates for the expected return on the "zero-β" asset and premium for consumption-β risk, respectively (*not* the ordinary least-squares fit of the points). All points should fall on this line if the Consumption-Based Asset Pricing Model is true. The 17 points on each plot represent unrestricted estimates of expected return $E(\bar{R}_{it})$ and consumption beta, β_{ci}. (Note that the scale varies across the scatter plots.) *Sources:* D. T. Breeden et al. (1986), Research Paper No. 879, Graduate School of Business, Stanford University, Palo Alto, CA.

proaches to testing the model exploit the implications of the model if consumption-β coefficients stay constant through time. Some of the tests discussed in this paragraph tend to reject the model, but others do not.[24]

3.6 An Empirical Application

In sections 3.3–3.5 we discussed three different approaches to measuring risk. While two of these approaches were special cases of the multiple-β model discussed in section 3.4, empirical implementation of each of these risk measures has its own difficulties. If the three risk measures led to similar conclusions in most cases, one would be content with using invested wealth β coefficients, since these coefficients are the easiest to estimate. However, we saw that the invested wealth β coefficients of common stocks cannot account for the cross-sectional distribution of stock returns. In this section, we estimate the risk measures for bond and bill portfolios to see whether these measures produce different results for these portfolios and to find out whether one of these measures is more likely to explain the cross-sectional distribution of the returns of these portfolios. Because much attention has been devoted to the effect on interest rates of the change in the Federal Reserve Board's operating procedures in 1979, we also check whether the risk of bonds and bill portfolios changed at that time.

3.6.1 Data and Empirical Procedures

All of our data on bond and bill returns come from the University of Chicago Center for Research on Security Prices (CRSP) U.S. Government Bond File. We use monthly data from 1961 to 1985 on all securities in the file, except for those with special tax or call provisions. Using this data, we construct a sample of 13 constant maturity portfolios. Each portfolio consists of securities within a given maturity range, where maturity is measured at the beginning of the month. Maturity ranges were selected purposely to avoid having portfolios with missing observations. One-month increments are taken from one month up to a half year, three-month increments up to about a year, and one-year increments thereafter up to about six years. The last portfolio includes all securities with maturities of more than six years. Finer increments are used for shorter maturities because more short maturity securities are available than long maturity securities. The holding period return on a portfolio is computed as the arithmetic average of the holding period return of all the securities in a portfolio. Portfolios are rebalanced every month.

To estimate our risk measures, we run the following OLS regressions:

$$R_{jt} - R_{1t} = \alpha_j + \beta'_j R_{pt} + (\beta'_{jD} R_{pt}) D_t + \varepsilon_t \qquad j = 2, \ldots, 13,$$

where

R_{jt} is the holding period return on the jth portfolio;

R_{1t} is the holding period return on the portfolio with a maturity of more than one month but less than two months;

R_{pt} is a vector of returns or state variables;

D_t is a scalar dummy variable such that $D_t = 0$ from 1960, 1 to 1979, 9, and $D_t = 1$ from 1979, 10.

In such regressions, the elements of the vector β_j are estimates of our risk measures for the jth portfolio. For single-β-coefficient models, the vector β_j has only one element. In all cases, the standard errors of the estimates are adjusted for conditional heteroskedasticity with the method suggested by White (1980). It turns out that the adjustment has a significant effect on the standard errors of the estimates of β_{jD}, that is, the coefficients associated with the dummy variables.

We run three sets of regressions. In our choice of explanatory variables, we follow the existing literature. First, we assume that the CAPM holds and use the return on the value-weighted index of all New York Stock Exchange stocks, VWNY, as a proxy for the return of invested wealth. Second, we assume that the multiple-β model holds and use the same state variables as Chan et al. (1985). These variables are (1) VWNY, the excess return on the CRSP value-weighted index, as the proxy for the return to invested wealth; (2) UIP, the innovations of the industrial production index[25]; (3) DEI, the change of expected inflation; (4) UI, unanticipated inflation; (5) LTB, the excess return (over one-month T-bill) on long-term government bonds, that is, bonds with a maturity of 20 years, obtained from Ibbotson and Sinquefield (1985); and (6) PREM, the junk bond premium, defined as the return on noncallable, nonconvertible corporate bonds that are at best Moody BAA bonds minus the return on long-term government bonds, using Ibbotson (1979) supplemented by a sample constructed from the Bank and Quotation Records. All six variables are measured as changes or innovations contemporaneously with the holding period return on the bill and bond portfolios. To obtain expected inflation, we assume the Fisher equation and that the real rate of interest follows a random walk, and proceed as in Fama and Gibbons (1984).[26] Finally, to estimate consumption β coefficients, we use the innovations from an AR(1) model fitted to the log of real consumption of nondurables and services.[27] Except for the stock index VWNY, which is available through 1985, the data series for the variables end at around the end of 1983. The simple correlation coefficients among these variables are reported in table 3–2.

3.6.2 Risk Measures for Portfolios of Bills and Bonds

Table 3–3 shows the means and standard deviations of the portfolios for the period 1961,1 to 1979,9 and the period 1979,10 to 1985,12. It is immediately

Table 3–2. Simple Correlations among the Wealth Proxy, Consumption, and Other State Variables[a]

	VWNY	UCON	UIP	DEI	UI	PREM	LTB
			1960, 1 to 1979, 9				
VWNY	1.0						
UCON	0.280*	1.0					
UIP	0.105	0.058	1.0				
DEI	−0.109	−0.123	−0.186*	1.0			
UI	−0.215*	−0.297*	0.019	0.025	1.0		
PREM	0.129	0.127	0.004	−0.099	−0.151	1.0	
LTB	0.277*	0.027	−0.025	−0.003	−0.041	−0.562*	1.0
			After 1979, 9				
VWNY	1.0						
RCNS	0.135	1.0					
IP	0.009	0.326*	1.0				
DEI	−0.276*	−0.112*	−0.274	1.0			
UI	0.013	−0.071	0.231	−0.258	1.0		
PREM	−0.298	0.172	0.347*	−0.067	0.252	1.0	
LTB	0.435*	−0.396*	−0.301*	−0.083	−0.255	−0.905*	1.0

[a] VWNY is the excess return on the CRSP value-weighted index of New York Stock Exchange stocks. UCON is the innovation of the deflated per capita consumption of nondurables and services. UIP is the innovation of the industrial production index. DEI is the change of expected inflation. UI is the unanticipated inflation. PREM is the return on the junk bonds, corporate bonds with Moody rating of BAA and below, minus the return on the long-term government bonds. LTB is the excess return on the government bonds with maturity of about 20 years. Asterisks denote significance at the 0.05 level.

obvious that the standard deviation of the excess returns cannot explain the pattern of the sample mean excess returns. For both subperiods, standard deviations increase monotonically with maturity. However, in the first subperiod sample excess returns follow a humped pattern that peaks at a maturity of five months. Interestingly, sample excess returns are negative for maturities of nine months and more. In the second subperiod, returns increase monotonically for all maturities except for bonds with maturities of more than seven years. However, bonds with the longer maturities have positive sample excess returns.

Table 3–3. Descriptive Statistics of the Excess Returns on the Bill and Bond Portfolios[a]

		1961, 1–1979, 9		1979, 10–1985, 12	
	Maturity Range (months)	*Mean* ($\times 10^2$)	*Standard Deviation* ($\times 10^2$)	*Mean* ($\times 10^2$)	*Standard Deviation* ($\times 10^2$)
$r2$	$2 < T < 3$	0.0220	0.0425	0.0318	0.1261
$r3$	$3 < T < 4$	0.0202	0.0784	0.0415	0.2131
$r4$	$4 < T < 5$	0.0368	0.1102	0.0639	0.3012
$r5$	$5 < T < 6$	0.0458	0.1389	0.0692	0.4017
$r6$	$6 < T < 9$	0.0294	0.1944	0.0686	0.5729
$r7$	$9 < T < 12$	0.0248	0.3018	0.0766	0.8015
$r8$	$12 < T < 24$	0.0081	0.4567	0.1308	1.239
$r9$	$24 < T < 36$	−0.0063	0.6841	0.1414	1.808
$r10$	$36 < T < 48$	−0.0222	0.8421	0.1594	2.257
$r11$	$48 < T < 60$	−0.0432	0.9802	0.1544	2.493
$r12$	$60 < T < 72$	−0.0350	1.2003	0.1723	2.859
$r13$	$72 < T$	−0.0881	1.6535	0.1592	3.602

[a] Excess returns are defined as raw returns minus the return on the bill portfolio with maturity of more than one month but less than two months.

Table 3–4 describes the estimates of invested wealth β coefficients of the various portfolios. For the first subperiod, these estimated β coefficients increase monotonically with maturity. Furthermore, all the estimated β coefficients increase by an amount that is an increasing function of maturity in the second subperiod.[28] Hence, estimated β coefficients in the second subperiod are also monotonic in maturity. Therefore it follows that the CAPM cannot explain the pattern of the sample excess returns of these portfolios.

Table 3–5 shows the estimates of the β coefficients for the multiple-β model. In the first subperiod, expected inflation and long-term bond returns seem to be the most significant state variables. Interestingly, the estimated invested wealth β coefficients are negative and increase in absolute value up to a maturity of the 9–12 months and then fall to increase again with the longer maturities. The estimated long-term bond β coefficients for the long-term bond increase monotonically with maturity. In Chan et al. (1985), a positive expected inflation β coefficient and a positive long-term bond β coefficient decrease the expected return of a risky asset, so that the multiple-β model can

Table 3–4. Estimating the Capital Asset Pricing Model of Bill and Bond Returns[a]

$$r_{it} - r_{1t} = \alpha_i + \beta_i \text{VWNY}_t + \beta_{iD} \text{VWNY}_t D_t + \varepsilon_{it},$$
$$i = 2, \ldots, 13$$

1961, 1–1985, 12

	$\hat{\alpha}_i$ $(t(\hat{\alpha}_i))$	$\hat{\beta}_i$ $(t(\hat{\beta}_i))$	$\hat{\beta}_{iD}$ $(t(\hat{\beta}_{iD}))$
r2	0.023 (5.65)	0.111 (1.04)	0.305 (0.90)
r3	0.023 (3.29)	0.151 (0.64)	0.825 (1.39)
r4	0.040 (3.97)	0.370 (1.21)	1.341 (1.63)
r5	0.046 (3.55)	0.542 (1.58)	1.954 (1.86)
r6	0.029 (1.63)	1.149 (2.98)	3.260 (2.30)
r7	0.022 (0.88)	1.898 (3.03)	4.283 (2.18)
r8	0.014 (0.35)	3.165 (3.91)	7.025 (2.39)
r9	−0.008 (−0.14)	4.866 (4.68)	10.642 (2.62)
r10	−0.024 (−0.33)	5.760 (4.58)	13.287 (2.51)
r11	−0.049 (−0.62)	6.649 (4.46)	16.053 (2.89)
r12	−0.043 (−0.45)	6.368 (3.16)	18.824 (2.76)
r13	−0.108 (−0.87)	10.054 (3.82)	23.083 (2.66)

[a] Coefficients are scaled by 10^2. VWNY_t is the return of the value weighted CRSP index of all New York Stock Exchange stocks, in excess of r_{1t}, the return on bills with maturity of one to two months. D_t is a dummy variable with value equal to zero in 1961, 1–1979, 9 and equal to one in 1979, 10–1985, 12. T statistics are adjusted for conditional heteroskedasticity.

explain the pattern of sample excess returns for the first subperiod to some extent. It can be verified that in the second subperiod, the absolute value of the estimates of the expected inflation β coefficient increases monotonically. Furthermore, it would seem that the risk premium associated with the long-term bond spread changes sign, on the basis of the sample means. Consequently, the multiple-β model seems to have a fighting chance to explain the pattern of sample excess returns in the second subperiod also.

Table 3–6 shows the estimates of the consumption β coefficients. None of the estimates are significant at conventional levels. With one exception, the estimates increase monotonically with maturity. Hence, for the first subperiod, the consumption-based model does not improve on the CAPM. None of the changes in the estimated values of the consumption β's in the second subperiod are significant. Most of the changes are negative. Hence, the consumption-based model does not pick up a change in risk in 1979.

Table 3–5. Estimating a Multiple-β Model of Bill and Bond Portfolio Returns[a]
$r_{it} - r_{1t} = \alpha_i + \beta_i(\text{VWNY})\ \ \text{VWNY}_t + \beta_{iD}(\text{VWNY})\ \ \text{VWNY}_t D_t + \beta_i(\text{UIP})\ \ \text{UIP}_t + \beta_{iD}(\text{VIP})\ \text{UIP}_t D_t + \beta_i(\text{LTB})\ \text{LTB}_t + \beta_{iD}(\text{LTB})\ \text{LTB}_t D_t + \beta_i(\text{DEI})\ \text{DEI}_t + \beta_{iD}(\text{DEI})\ \text{DEI}_t D_t + \beta_i(\text{UI})\ \ \text{UI}_t + \beta_{iD}(\text{UI})\ \ \text{UI}_t D_t + \beta_i(\text{PREM})\ \ \text{PREM}_t + \beta_{iD}(\text{PREM})\ \ \text{PREM}_t D_t \quad i\,2, \ldots, 13$

1961, 1–1983, 11

	$\hat{\alpha}_i$	$\hat{\beta}_i$(VWNY)	$\hat{\beta}_{iD}$(VWNY)	$\hat{\beta}_i$(UIP)	$\hat{\beta}_{iD}$(UIP)	$\hat{\beta}_i$(LTB)	$\hat{\beta}_{iD}$(LTB)
r2	0.025	−0.009	0.168	−0.751	−0.005	0.882	−0.103
	(7.22)	(−0.09)	(0.51)	(−1.84)	(−0.004)	(1.75)	(−0.10)
r3	0.032	−0.182	0.444	−0.876	−1.769	2.045	1.053
	(6.21)	(−0.85)	(0.78)	(−1.10)	(−0.59)	(2.77)	(0.58)
r4	0.052	−0.124	0.708	−1.550	−2.338	3.019	1.533
	(7.897)	(−0.56)	(1.06)	(−1.74)	(−0.66)	(3.63)	(0.66)
r5	0.064	−0.132	0.870	−2.197	−4.765	4.080	4.339
	(8.52)	(−0.57)	(1.10)	(−2.27)	(−1.20)	(4.15)	(1.54)
r6	0.054	0.149	1.879	−3.501	−7.052	6.627	4.456
	(5.67)	(0.67)	(1.60)	(−3.40)	(−1.07)	(6.23)	(1.19)
r7	0.064	0.186	1.845	−4.817	−7.404	119.737	4.812
	(4.72)	(0.52)	(1.16)	(−3.05)	(−1.02)	(7.88)	(1.03)
r8	0.073	0.338	3.470	−4.88	−14.728	21.203	3.940
	(3.62)	(0.65)	(1.41)	(−1.86)	(−1.15)	(8.00)	(0.53)
r9	0.089	0.353	3.949	−5.426	−11.256	34.888	5.759
	(3.17)	(0.45)	(1.24)	(−1.62)	(−0.79)	(10.28)	(0.54)
r10	0.088	0.483	2.414	−4.589	−8.009	39.747	17.969
	(2.38)	(0.44)	(0.49)	(−0.91)	(−0.50)	(9.01)	(1.24)
r11	0.083	0.442	4.265	−7.803	−16.995	48.010	16.839
	(2.06)	(0.39)	(0.95)	(−1.37)	(−1.04)	(8.85)	(1.13)
r12	0.102	−0.747	4.209	−5.417	−13.327	54.011	16.230
	(2.16)	(−0.51)	(0.75)	(−0.89)	(−0.66)	(7.27)	(0.92)
r13	0.073	−0.704	2.584	1.674	−12.974	80.674	11.400
	(1.64)	(−0.51)	(0.42)	(0.29)	(−0.65)	(14.85)	(0.67)

[a] Coefficients are scaled by 10^2. VWNY is the excess return on the value weighted CRSP index of New York Exchange stocks. UIP is the innovation of the industrial production index. LTB is the excess return on the long term government bonds with maturity of about 20 years. DEI is the change of expected inflation. UI is the unanticipated inflation. PREM is the spread between the return on corporate bonds with Moody rating of Baa and below and long-term government bonds. D is the dummy variable with value equal to zero in 1961, 1–1979, 9 and equal to one in 1979, 10–1983, 11. T statistics are adjusted for conditional heteroskedaticity.

1961, 1–1983, 11

$\hat{\beta}_i$(DEI)	$\hat{\beta}_{iD}$(DEI)	$\hat{\beta}_i$(UI)	$\hat{\beta}_{iD}$(UI)	$\hat{\beta}_i$(PREM)	$\hat{\beta}_{iD}$(PREM)	H_0[b]
−26.58	−27.163	2.602	3.676	0.185	−0.281	0.109
(−3.33)	(−2.10)	(1.54)	(0.95)	(0.71)	(−0.51)	
−61.27	−20.151	2.437	6.334	0.530	0.075	0.057
(−3.95)	(−0.86)	(0.92)	(0.94)	(1.32)	(0.08)	
−96.15	−15.111	4.618	7.159	0.688	0.509	0.13
(−4.51)	(−0.48)	(1.24)	(0.81)	(1.61)	(0.04)	
−115.40	−27.050	4.283	4.147	0.656	1.613	0.001
(−5.78)	(−0.84)	(1.13)	(0.38)	(1.29)	(1.06)	
−139.59	−54.572	4.240	12.390	1.277	1.476	0.003
(−7.83)	(−1.32)	(0.88)	(0.81)	(2.44)	(0.74)	
−216.00	−49.542	9.529	4.413	2.544	1.404	0.063
(−7.74)	(−0.93)	(1.40)	(0.23)	(3.52)	(0.58)	
−213.30	−197.509	6.788	11.408	4.232	1.652	0.057
(−5.36)	(−2.39)	(0.69)	(0.41)	(3.31)	(0.40)	
−188.16	−327.970	−5.556	28.576	6.944	1.432	0.015
(−3.41)	(−2.84)	(−0.38)	(0.84)	(3.85)	(0.23)	
−178.15	−323.906	−11.620	10.603	5.929	6.966	0.036
(−2.49)	(−2.09)	(−0.73)	(0.25)	(2.69)	(0.84)	
−91.24	−365.963	−29.372	27.187	7.247	6.995	0.018
(−1.15)	(−2.37)	(−1.40)	(0.64)	(2.76)	(0.85)	
−333.44	−198.962	25.726	0.692	5.509	7.313	0.568
(−3.60)	(−1.10)	(0.96)	(0.01)	(1.52)	(0.75)	
−119.08	−350.749	−9.100	7.117	2.854	12.438	0.307
(−1.37)	(−1.96)	(−0.42)	(0.15)	(0.98)	(1.26)	

[b] H_0: β_{iD}(VWNY) = β_{iD}(UIP) = β_{iD}(LTB) = β_{iD}(DEI) = β_{iD}(UI) = β_{iD}(PREM) = 0. Reported numbers are p values.

However, the poor performance of this model may be due to measurement error in consumption rather than flaws in the model itself.

3.6.3 Did the Risk of Bill and Bond Portfolios Increase after 1979?

Mascaro and Meltzer (1983) argue that the change in the Federal Reserve operating procedures in 1979 increased the risk of bills and bonds and hence increased interest rates. In their analysis, they measure risk by the variance of unanticipated money growth and of velocity. Since they find no role for the variance of velocity, they come to the conclusion that the variance of unanticipated money growth is the major determinant of the risk premium of bonds.

In table 3–4, we see that the estimated invested wealth β coefficients increase substantially after 1979. While table 3–3 shows that the variance of the returns of our portfolios increases after 1979, it is interesting to note that the increase in the return variance does not entirely explain the increase of the estimated invested wealth β coefficients. The estimates of the invested wealth β coefficients increase partly because the correlation of the returns of the portfolios with the return of our proxy for invested wealth increases. This is documented in table 3–7. The estimated invested wealth β coefficients also increase dramatically in the second subperiod in table 3–5. However, with the multiple-β approach, the absolute value of the estimate of the expected inflation β increases also. Finally, for portfolios with longer maturities, the estimated long-term bond β coefficients increase also. Hence, the multiple-β model suggests a pervasive increase in the risk of bill and bond portfolios. Table 3–5 also reports the test result of the hypothesis that all the coefficients of all dummy variables are jointly equal to zero. The hypothesis is not rejected for the two portfolios with the longest maturity, which is not surprising because the long-term bond is one of the explanatory variables. For most of the shorter maturity portfolios, the hypothesis is rejected at 5% level. There appears to be strong evidence of a shift of risk characteristics between the two subperiods. As noted previously, no clear results emerge from the consumption-based model.

3.7 Concluding Remarks

Changes in the riskiness of households' investment opportunities that affect the expected return of risky assets have pervasive effects on the consumption

Table 3-6. Estimating the Consumption-Based Asset Pricing Model of Bill and Bond Returns[a]

$$r_{it} - r_{1t} = \alpha_i + \beta_i \text{UCON}_t + \beta_{iD} \text{UCON}_t \text{D}_t + \varepsilon_{it} \quad i = 2, \ldots, 13$$

1961, 1–1983, 12

	$\hat{\alpha}_i$ $t(\hat{\alpha}_i)$	$\hat{\beta}_i$ $t(\hat{\beta}_i)$	$\hat{\beta}_{iD}$ $t(\hat{\beta}_{iD})$
r2	0.022 (5.09)	−0.028 (−0.04)	0.079 (0.01)
r3	0.023 (2.99)	0.515 (0.40)	−6.870 (−0.66)
r4	0.039 (3.66)	0.804 (0.42)	−9.230 (−0.60)
r5	0.047 (3.31)	0.659 (0.29)	−7.899 (−0.38)
r6	0.030 (1.49)	2.829 (0.84)	−11.720 (−0.38)
r7	0.025 (0.88)	4.570 (0.87)	−11.844 (−0.25)
r8	0.014 (0.33)	7.562 (0.93)	−6.231 (−0.08)
r9	−0.005 (−0.08)	12.077 (1.12)	2.585 (0.02)
r10	−0.023 (−0.29)	10.444 (0.80)	4.795 (0.03)
r11	−0.046 (−0.52)	0.137 (0.89)	−7.708 (−0.05)
r12	−0.040 (−0.39)	2.790 (0.13)	4.933 (0.03)
r13	−0.104 (−0.77)	22.871 (0.86)	4.737 (0.02)

[a] Coefficients are scaled by 10^2. UCON_t is the innovation of the deflated per capital consumption of nondurables and services. D_t is a dummy variable with value equal to zero in 1961, 1–1979, 9 and equal to one in 1979, 10–1983, 12. T statistics are adjusted for conditional heteroskedasticity.

and investment policies of households. In this chapter, we discussed the theoretical and empirical properties of three measures of the riskiness of assets. We argued that invested wealth β coefficients are insufficient to explain the cross-sectional variation of expected returns of risky assets. However, multiple-β approaches promise to be more successful. As macroeconomic models provide candidates for state variables that affect expected returns, it would seem that part of financial economics that deals with asset pricing will be inextricably linked with macroeconomics.

Table 3–7. Simple Correlations between Excess Returns on the Bill and Bond Portfolios and the Wealth Proxy, Consumption, and Other State Variables[a]

Excess return	VWNY	UCON	UIP	DEI	UI	PREM	LTB
				1960, 1 to 1979, 9			
*r*2	0.113	−0.002	−0.138	0.154	−0.067	−0.120	0.368*
*r*3	0.085	0.027	−0.100	0.168	−0.158	−0.114	0.396*
*r*4	0.145*	0.030	−0.118	0.069	−0.172	−0.148*	0.467*
*r*5	0.166*	0.019	−0.133*	0.097	−0.184	−0.212*	0.552*
*r*6	0.252*	0.060	−0.143*	0.065	−0.198	−0.190*	0.592*
*r*7	0.268*	0.063	−0.129	0.018	−0.185	−0.195*	0.641*
*r*8	0.296*	0.069	−0.092	−0.003	−0.160	−0.234*	0.711*
*r*9	0.303*	0.074	−0.074	−0.021	−0.161	−0.244*	0.743*
*r*10	0.292*	0.052	−0.056	−0.028	−0.145	−0.303*	0.757*
*r*11	0.289*	0.058	−0.077	−0.047	−0.149	−0.303*	0.763*
*r*12	0.226*	0.009	−0.054	−0.033	−0.070	−0.377*	0.784*
*r*13	0.258*	0.058	−0.017	0.002	−0.070	−0.495*	0.923*

After 1979, 9

r2	0.133	0.018	−0.287*	0.010	−0.152	−0.545*	0.601*
r3	0.192	−0.060	−0.334*	−0.034	−0.150	−0.573*	0.688*
r4	0.242*	−0.057	−0.348*	−0.037	−0.174	−0.635*	0.745*
r5	0.270*	−0.029	−0.382*	−0.025	−0.227	−0.649*	0.780*
r6	0.355*	−0.020	−0.375*	−0.083	−0.202	−0.663*	0.787*
r7	0.359*	0.003	−0.375*	−0.048	−0.248	−0.708*	0.830*
r8	0.371*	0.034	−0.379*	−0.054	−0.249	−0.707*	0.834*
r9	0.378*	0.057	−0.345*	−0.048	−0.255	−0.756*	0.886*
r10	0.371*	0.054	−0.315*	−0.056	−0.264	−0.751*	0.890*
r11	0.396*	0.036	−0.339*	−0.064	−0.264	−0.773*	0.916*
r12	0.387*	0.038	−0.320*	−0.063	−0.239	−0.779*	0.912*
r13	0.388*	0.054	−0.304*	−0.071	−0.261	−0.814*	0.944*

[a] Excess returns are defined as raw returns minus returns on r_1, the bill portfolio with maturity more than one month but less than two months. VWNY is the excess return on the CRSP value-weighted index of New York Stock Exchange stocks. UCON is the innovation of the deflated per capital consumption of nondurables and services. UIP is the innovation of the industrial production index. DEI is the change of expected inflation. UI is the unanticipated inflation. PREM is the return on the junk bonds, corporate bonds with Moody rating of BAA and below, minus the return on the long term government bonds. LTB is the excess return on the government bonds with maturity of about 20 years. Asterisks denote significance at the 0.05 level.

Notes

1. See Brunner and Meltzer (1984, p. 1).

2. See, for instance, Kydland and Prescott (1982), Long and Plosser (1983), King and Plosser (1984).

3. Fischer (1975) provides a short but useful introduction to the continuous-time techniques used in finance. However, this paper can be understood without any knowledge of these techniques, since we mainly discuss rather than derive results. The model used here is discussed extensively in Cox et al. (1985). They also provide references to the continuous-time literature in finance.

4. Note that the relevant variance is the one of the households' predictive distribution over the growth of the policy variable. This variance may change even though the variance of the "true" distribution of the policy variable does not change because, for instance, of uncertainty about the policy regime. See Stulz (1986b).

5. Black (1972) shows that when there is no risk-free asset, r is replaced in equation 3.20′ with the expected return of asset z such that $\beta_z = 0$.

6. Roll (1977) discusses extensively the problems that arise because the rate of return of invested wealth is not observable. See Green (1986) for the result summarized here.

7. See Scholes and Williams (1977) for an early discussion of these issues.

8. For a discussion of these methodological issues, see Fama (1976, Chapter 4).

9. See Chan (1985).

10. The most widely cited early studies are those of Black et al. (1972) and Fama and MacBeth (1973).

11. See Gibbons (1982), Stambaugh (1982), and Shanken (1985).

12. See Miller and Scholes (1972). Tinic and West (1986) find a role for the variance using the methodology of Fama and MacBeth (1973).

13. See Schwert (1983) for a review of this evidence.

14. See Roll (1981), Chan (1985), and Chan and Chen (1986) for evidence that problems in estimating β partly explain the size anomaly.

15. See Frankel (1986).

16. Merton (1973) developed a multiple-β model under the assumption of a constant subjective rate of time preference. Bergman (1985) shows that the model holds with an expected utility function of lifetime consumption like the one in equation 3.22.

17. These conditions are presented in Merton (1973). For related conditions in a discrete-time model, see Fama (1970). See also Constantinides (1980).

18. See Stulz (1986a) for a model that studies the effect of changes in expected money growth on asset demands and expected asset returns.

19. See also Chen et al. (1986).

20. Bergman (1985) shows that the consumption-based model does not hold when ρ depends on current consumption.

21. Grossman and Shiller (1982) derived the consumption-based asset pricing model as the limit in continuous-time of equation 3.32.

22. See Grossman et al. (1985) and Breeden et al. (1986).

23. Grossman and Shiller (1982) show that the unconditional version of the model can be tested.

24. See Hansen and Singleton (1983), Dunn and Singleton (1986), and Mark (1985) for rejections. Wheatley (1985) and Marsh (1981) are unable to reject.

25. The AR(1) model run on the industrial production index is $\mathrm{IP}_t = 0.00202\ (0.0005) + 0.5002\ (0.057)\ \mathrm{IP}_{t-1} + a_t$ for 1961,1–1979,9 and $\mathrm{IP}_t = 0.00028\ (0.25) + 0.7162\ (0.097)\ \mathrm{IP}_{t-1} + a_t$ for

1979,10–1984,3, where IP_t is the change in the log of the seasonally adjusted industrial production index from $t-1$ to t. Standard errors of estimates are in parentheses.

26. We assume that the Fama and Gibbons estimates, estimated for 1953–1977, hold for our sample period.

27. The AR(1) model run on the consumption series is $RCON_t = 0.00258$ (0.0003) $-$ 0.273 (0.064) $RCON_{t-1} + a_t$ for 1961,1–1979,9 and $RCON_t = 0.00138$ (0.0005) $-$ 0.236 (0.138) $RCON_{t-1} + a_t$ for 1979,10–1983,12, where $RCON_t$ is the change in the log of the deflated per capita consumption of nondurables and services from $t-1$ to t. Standard errors of estimates are in parentheses.

28. The intercept α is zero if the CAPM holds. Therefore, regressions are also run without the intercept. The slope coefficients are essentially the same whether there is an intercept or not.

References

Bergman, Y. Z. (1985), "Time Preference and the Capital Asset Pricing Model," *Journal of Financial Economics*, **14**, 145–160.

Black, F. (1972), "Capital Market Equilibrium with Restricted Borrowing," *Journal of Business*, **45**, 444–454.

Black, F., M. Jensen, and M. Scholes (1972), "The Capital Asset Pricing Model: Some Empirical Findings," in M. Jensen (Ed.), *Studies in the Theory of Capital Markets*, Praeger, New York, pp. 79–121.

Breeden, D. T. (1979), "An Intertemporal Asset Pricing Model with Stochastic Consumption and Investment Opportunities," *Journal of Financial Economics*, **7**, 265–296.

Breeden, D. T., M. R. Gibbons, and R. H. Litzenberger (1986), "Empirical Tests of the Consumption-Oriented CAPM," Research Paper No. 879, Graduate School of Business, Stanford University, Palo Alto, CA.

Brunner, K. and A. Meltzer (1984), "Introduction," in K. Brunner and A. Meltzer (Eds.), *Essays on Macroeconomic Implications of Financial and Labor Markets and Political Processes, Carnegie-Rochester Conference Series on Public Policy*, Vol. 21, pp. 1–13.

Chan, K. C. (1985), "Market Value Changes and Time-Varying Risk," Ph.D. dissertation, University of Chicago.

Chan, K. C. and N.-F. Chen (1986), "Estimation Errors of Stock Betas and the Role of Firm Size as an Instrumental Variable for Risk," University of Chicago CRSP Working Paper No. 179.

Chan, K. C., N.-F. Chen, and D. Hsieh (1985), "An Exploratory Investigation of the Firm Size Effect," *Journal of Financial Economics*, **14**, 451–472.

Chen, N.-F., R. Roll, and S. Ross (1986), "Economic Forces and the Stock Market," *Journal of Business*, **59**, 383–404.

Constantinides, G. M. (1980), "Admissible Uncertainty in the Intertemporal Asset Pricing Model," *Journal of Financial Economics*, **8**, 71–86.

Cox, J., J. Ingersoll, and S. A. Ross (1985), "An Intertemporal General Equilibrium Model of Asset Prices," *Econometrica*, **53**, 363–384.

Dunn, K. and K. Singleton (1986). "Modeling the Term Structure of Interest Rates under Nonseparable Utility and Durability of Goods," *Journal of Financial Economics*, **17**, xxx–xxx.

Fama, E. F. (1970), "Multiperiod Consumption-Investment Decision," *American Economic Review* **60**, 163–174.

——— (1976), *Foundations of Finance*, Basic Books, New York.

Fama, E. F. and M. R. Gibbons (1984), "A Comparison of Inflation Forecasts," *Journal of Monetary Economics*, **13**, 327–348.

Fama, E. F. and J. MacBeth (1973), "Risk, Return and Equilibrium: Empirical Tests," *Journal of Political Economy*, **81**, 607–636.

Fischer, S. (1975), "The Demand for Index Bonds," *Journal of Political Economy*, **83**, 509–534.

Frankel, J. (1986), "Portfolio Crowding-Out Empirically Estimated," *Quarterly Journal of Economics*, **100** (Supplement), 1041–1066.

Gibbons, M. (1982), "Multivariate Tests of Financial Models: A New Approach," *Journal of Financial Economics*, **10**, 3–27.

Green, R. C. (1986), "Benchmark Portfolio Inefficiency and Deviations from the Security Market Line," *Journal of Finance*, **41**, 295–312.

Grossman, S. J., A. Melino, and R. J. Shiller (1985), "Estimating the Continuous-Time Consumption-Based Asset Pricing Model," NBER Working Paper No. 1643, Cambridge, MA.

Grossman, S. J. and R. J. Shiller (1982), "Consumption Correlatedness and Risk Measurement in Economies with Non-traded Assets and Heterogeneous Information," *Journal of Financial Economics*, **10**, 195–210.

Hansen, L. and K. Singleton (1983), "Stochastic Consumption Risk, Risk Aversion, and the Temporal Behavior of Asset Returns," *Journal of Political Economy*, **91**, 249–265.

Ibbotson, R. (1979), "The Corporate Bond Market: Structure and Returns," unpublished manuscript, University of Chicago.

Ibbotson, R. and R. Sinquefield (1985), *Stocks, Bonds, Bills and Inflation: The Past and the Future*, The Financial Analysts Research Foundation, University of Virginia, Charlottesville.

King, R. G. and Plosser, C. I. (1984), "The Behavior of Money, Credit, and Prices in a Real Business Cycle," *American Economic Review*, **74**, 363–380.

Kydland, F. and E. C. Prescott (1982), "Time to Build and the Persistence of Unemployment," *Econometrica*, **50**, 1345–1370.

Lintner, J. (1965), "The Valuation of Risk Assets and the Selection of Risky Investments in Stock Portfolios and Capital Budgets," *Review of Economics and Statistics*, **47**, 13–37.

Mark, N. (1985), "On Time-Varying Risk Premia in the Foreign Exchange Market: An Econometric Analysis," *Journal of Monetary Economics*, **9**, 383–406.

Marsh, T. A. (1981), "Intertemporal Capital Asset Pricing Model and the Term Structure of Interest Rates," Ph.D. dissertation, University of Chicago.

Mascaro, A. and Meltzer, A. H. (1983), "Long and Short-Term Interest Rates in a Risky World," *Journal of Monetary Economics*, **12**, 485–518.

Merton, R. C. (1969), "Lifetime Portfolio Selection under Uncertainty: The Continuous-Time Case," *Review of Economics and Statistics*, **51**, 247–257.

——— (1973), "An Intertemporal Asset Pricing Model," *Econometrica*, **41**, 867–887.

Miller, M. H. and M. S. Scholes (1972), "Rates of Return in Relation to Risk: A Reexamination of Some Recent Findings," in M. C. Jensen (Ed.), *Studies in the Theory of Capital Markets*, Praeger, New York.

Roll, R. (1977), "A Critique of the Asset Pricing Theory's Tests, I. On Past and Potential Testability of the Theory," *Journal of Financial Economics*, **4**, 129–176.

——— (1981), "A Possible Explanation of the Small Firm Effects," *Journal of Finance*, **36**, 879–888.

Scholes, M. R. and J. Williams (1977), "Estimating Betas from Nonsynchronous Data," *Journal of Financial Economics*, **5**, 309–328.

Schwert, G. W. (1983), "Size and Stock Returns, and Other Empirical Regularities," *Journal of Financial Economics*, **12**, 3–12.

Shanken, J. (1985), "Multivariate Tests of the Zero-Beta CAPM," *Journal of Financial Economics*, **14**, 327–348.

Sharpe, W. F. (1984), "Capital Asset Prices: A Theory of Market Equilibrium under Conditions of Risk," *Journal of Finance*, **19**, 425–442.

Stambaugh, R. F. (1982), "On the Exclusion of Assets from Tests of the Two-Parameter Model: A Sensitivity Analysis," *Journal of Financial Economics*, **10**, 237–268.

Stulz, R. M. (1986a), "Asset Pricing and Expected Inflation," *Journal of Finance*, **41**, 209–223.

——— (1986b), "Interest Rates and Monetary Policy Uncertainty," *Journal of Monetary Economics*, **17**, 331–347.

Stulz, R. M. and W. Wasserfallen (1985), "Macroeconomic Time-Series, Business Cycles and Macroeconomic Policies," *Carnegie-Rochester Conference on Public Policy*, **22**, 9–54.

Tinic, S. and R. R. West (1986), "Risk, Return and Equilibrium: A Revisit," *Journal of Political Economy*, **94**, 126–147.

Wheatley, S. (1985), "Some Tests of International Equity Markets Integration," Ph.D. dissertation, University of Rochester, Rochester, NY.

White, H. (1980), "A Heteroskedasticity-Consistent Covariance Matrix Estimator and a Direct Test for Heteroskedasticity," *Econometrica*, **48**, 817–838.

Commentary by Arnold Zellner

The Chan and Stulz chapter is a stimulating and valuable contribution to the analysis of the problem of how risk and uncertainty may affect economies. In the successful tradition of financial economics, their chapter includes both theoretical and empirical results. In their theoretical analyses, they show in the context of a simple stochastic growth model that in theory (1) risk matters and (2) a "riskier" economy has a lower interest rate, lower investment, in general, and lower consumption given that $\gamma < 0$, where γ is the parameter in their constant relative risk-aversion utility function, $U(C) = C^{\gamma}/\gamma$. These are valuable theoretical results illustrating the importance of taking account of risk in macroeconomic models. They then proceed to consider the theoretical motivation for three different measures of risk in the financial economic literature, the mean-variance single-β approach, the multiple-β approach, and the consumption-β approach, and consider the extent to which these approaches have been successful in explaining asset returns, both in past studies

Research financed by the National Science Foundation and by income from the H. G. B. Alexander Endowment Fund. Graduate School of Business, University of Chicago.

and in their current study of returns on Treasury bonds of differing maturities following the 1979 change in the Fed's operating procedures. They find the multiple-β approach most satisfactory of the three in explaining asset returns but state that

> We show that measures of risk that are widely used in finance may not be useful to macroeconomists, because macroeconomists are generally concerned about the effects on risk of policy changes that have no role in models used by financial economists. We argue that the lesson from the empirical evidence most relevant for macroeconomists is that the most popular approach, the mean-variance approach, fails to adequately explain differences in expected returns among risky assets. (p. 80).

Also, in connection with the multiple-β approach, unobserved state variables enter the analysis and as the authors state,

> No explicit theoretical model is used to specify the relevant state variables. . . . One cannot therefore use [the results of such models] to forecast the effect on expected returns of a policy-induced change in the distribution of changes of expected inflation. Further research should focus on developing models that provide guidance for the choice of state variables. (p. 96).

In my opinion, this is sound advice and may encourage macroeconomists to develop better stochastic models of the term structure of interest rates that may validate the authors' choice of state variables employed in their empirical analysis of bond returns.

Of course, it may be somewhat naive on the part of macroeconomists to expect that financial economists' risk measures would be satisfactory for direct use in macroeconomics. These risk measures were developed for a specific range of problems, models, and applications, usually portfolio choice problems in which macro policy changes are not considered. Indeed the clever stochastic growth model employed by the authors is formulated as a dynamic, stochastic portfolio problem, solved using a particular utility function and under other simplifying assumptions. As the authors indicate, they have investigated an elaborated version of the model in which households hold real balances and the money stock changes stochastically. In a similarly constructive vein, let me suggest the following points for further theoretical investigation.

1. In their stochastic growth model, it is assumed that optimizing agents know the values of the parameters, for example, μ, the vector of mean returns and V, the covariance matrix of returns. It is well known in the portfolio analysis literature (see, e.g., Zellner and Chetty (1965), Brown (1976, 1978), Bawa et al. (1979), and Jorion (1983, 1985)) that solutions to portfolio

problems are different when values of μ and V have to be learned or estimated from past data. Similarly in the stochastic growth model portfolio problem, solutions will be different when economic agents have to learn about values of parameters from their data. Also, just as anticipated and unanticipated changes in variables such as income and money have differing impacts on economic behavior, it is to be expected that anticipated and unanticipated changes in variances and covariances will have different impacts on behavior. See Merton (1980) for an attempt to estimate the direct effect of return variance on expected market excess return. Unpublished empirical analyses of Merton's problem by some of my students using measures of anticipated and unanticipated variances of returns yielded the result that the former exerted a small positive effect and the latter a large negative effect on the mean market excess return.

2. In defining a "riskier" economy, the authors used changes in standard deviations (or equivalently changes in variances) $\sigma^*_{K_i} = \lambda\sigma_{K_i}$ with $\lambda > 1$. Note that if $V^* = \lambda^2 V$ is considered, such a change preserves correlations, $\rho^*_{ij} = \lambda^2 v_{ij}/\lambda^2\sqrt{v_{ii}v_{ij}} = v_{ij}\sqrt{v_{ii}v_{ij}} = \rho_{ij}$, where v_{ij} is a typical element of V. It would be interesting to consider other possible changes, say from V to a diagonal covariance matrix or from V to various types of patterned covariance matrices, say $\sigma^2_K(I + \rho\mathbf{11}')$, a form in which all correlations are the same. Various forms of the covariance matrix can represent the return structures of various types of economies and it is interesting to assess the consequences of changes from one structure of production to another. Perhaps classifying economies with respect to forms of their associated covariance matrices would be useful.

3. The growth model employed in the chapter utilizes a production process, given in equation 3.1, of a particular form with constant parameters μ_{K_i} and σ_{K_i}. Omitting the stochastic term, this function is $(1/K_i)dK_i/dt = \mu_i$; that is, the proportionate rate of output is a constant, μ_i. Other forms of this relation, for example, $(1/K_i)dK_i/dt = \mu_i(1 - K_i/\phi_i)$, with $\phi_i > 0$, that yield a logistic function solution would be interesting to consider as would elaborations of their diffusion equation 3.1 to allow μ_{K_i} and σ_{K_i} to depend on $K_i(t)$ and possibly other state variables. Elaboration of their diffusion equation in this way would bring it into a form similar to equations in catastrophy theory, which permit large, abrupt changes in solutions (see. e.g., Cobb et al. (1983)). Finally, as noted in the production literature (see, e.g., Zellner et al. (1966). Just and Pope (1978, 1979), and Rossi (1983)) controlled changes in inputs can often systematically affect the variability of production processes. In the present problem, assuming that $\sigma_{K_i} = \sigma_{K_i}(K_i)$ would allow the value of the standard deviation of the production process to be affected by the choice of a

value for K_i. Whether the authors' analyses can be extended to incorporate these and other possible modifications is an interesting research issue.

4. As an alternative to using a stochastic macroeconomic model to define a country's risk, it may be worthwhile to consider market appraisals of countries' risk as has been done by Daniel Kohler of the Rand Corporation. He discovered that many countries' bonds are traded in an international market located in Switzerland. Using data relating to transactions in this market he was able to classify countries with respect to risk class. It would be interesting to compare Kohler's results on risk measurement and country classification with the results of other approaches.

To return to the basic problem of how to introduce risk into macroeconomic models, as the authors' quotation above indicates, macroeconomists are generally concerned about the effects on risk of policy changes. They also write that, "The Lucas critique has convinced many [macroeconomists] of the necessity of building their models on the actions of optimizing households" (p. 1). While this is true, use of optimizing models of households and firms alone does not adequately treat the problems raised by the Lucas critique. If policy changes unexpectedly, the optimizing behavior of households and firms will be changed and models based on past optimizing behavior will generally be vitally affected (see, e.g., Dufour (1979) for the effects of tax policy changes on the stability of investment function parameters). There is a problem of modeling such possible policy changes and the risk associated with them.

One possible approach to this problem that has been suggested in the literature is to employ stochastic, time-varying parameter models that *may* adapt quickly to various unexpected policy changes (see, e.g., Swamy et al. (1986a,b)). Until such models have a firm theoretical basis, this approach is just a mechanical one, which, however, *may* yield satisfactory forecasts.

Another approach would involve attempting to define various models incorporating various types of possible policy changes and associating prior probabilities with each model. As information arrives on the variables of the models, the prior probabilities on each of the models incorporating various policy mixes can be updated and used to solve the optimizing problems of economic agents. Thus in addition to risk associated with stochastic error terms and parameters with unknown values, risk associated with uncertain forms of policy and models would be reflected in optimizing behavior. See Geisel (1975) for consideration of the methodology of computing posterior probabilities on alternative models and an application of it to two alternative simple Keynesian and Quantity Theory macroeconomic models. Also, Baxter (1985) has computed posterior probabilities period by period to measure the degree of the public's confidence in two South American monetary reforms. The probabilities on various models and on the possible success of certain public policies represent important elements of risk affecting the behavior of individuals. And, of course, such probabilities can be used by economic agents in solving portfolio and other optimization problems. For some related analyses, see Grossman (1975) and Boyer and Kihlstrom (1984).

The practical problems with the approach described in the previous paragraph should not be minimized. However, economic agents and analysts probably take account of possible changes in policy regimes in an intuitive or informal fashion. Often indications of a possible policy regime change, say a change in tax structure are revealed in committee hearings, for example. As such information is obtained economic agents probably alter their behavior to take account of possible structural policy changes. Certainly economic modelers investigate different assumed policy scenarios in simulation experiments, and so on. The quantification of such considerations appears to be possible (see, e.g., Peck and Richels (1987)). Quantification of the risk associated with a set of possible scenarios and associated models for each seems possible. At the very least, the predictive covariance matrices associated with outcomes for various scenarios or possible sets of scenarios can be evaluated. For example, if $p_1(\mathbf{y}|D_1)$ and $p_2(\mathbf{y}|D_2)$ are the predictive pdfs for a vector of outcomes $\mathbf{y}$ under scenarios 1 and 2, with D_i, $i = 1, 2$, the conditioning information in scenario i, and P and $1 - P$ are the probabilities associated with the two scenarios, $p(\mathbf{y}|D_1, D_2) = Pp_1(\mathbf{y}|D_1) + (1 - P)p_2(\mathbf{y}|D_2)$ is the predictive pdf for $\mathbf{y}$ taking account of scenario uncertainty. The covariance matrices of $p(\mathbf{y}|D_1)$, $V(\mathbf{y}|D_1)$, of $p(\mathbf{y}|D_2)$, $V(\mathbf{y}|D_2)$, and of $p(\mathbf{y}|D_1, D_2)$, $V(y|D_1, D_2)$ can be computed and compared. If $\mathbf{y}$ is a vector of returns, as in the authors' model, $p_1(\mathbf{y}|D_1)$ might be associated with one possible structure of production, $p_2(\mathbf{y}|D_2)$ that associated with another, and P and $1 - P$ the probabilities associated with the first and the second production structures, respectively. Note that contrary to many current analyses that assume production technologies are completely known, the present example allows for possible uncertainty regarding the forms of production relations. Similar uncertainty probably exists with respect to alternative monetary policy rules. By use of probabilities in this way, a formalization of the thought processes of economic agents and analysts in their attempts to deal with various kinds of Lucas-type policy uncertainties is obtained. Whether this approach is fruitful or not can only be determined by the extent to which it provides better understanding and predictions of the behavior of agents faced with the risks associated with possible policy changes.

As regards the authors' empirical analysis, I found the results intriguing. That the standard deviation of excess returns cannot explain the pattern of the sample mean excess returns is an indication that the standard deviation is an inadequate measure of risk. It would be interesting to model the monthly sample standard deviations of excess returns on individual bonds or the logarithms of these sample standard deviations using ARIMA models to separate anticipated and unanticipated changes in standard deviations and check to see whether unanticipated changes of standard deviations can possibly explain the pattern of the sample mean excess returns.

Further, with respect to the results for the single-β model, if the multiple-β model is appropriate, then some variables have been left out of the single-β model and this fact, as is well known, can lead to biased coefficient estimates and the White correction for conditional heteroskedasticity, which "has a significant effect on the standard errors" (p. 104), is then not appropriate. The finding that "the CAPM cannot explain the pattern of the sample excess returns" (p. 106) is still interesting. However, note that the mean excess returns for the longer maturities in table 3–3 have rather large associated standard errors, which raises some questions about what is the exact pattern of mean excess returns as a function of maturity. In table 3–5, the estimation results for the multiple-β model are presented. The p values for the hypothesis H_0 that all β_{iD} parameters are equal to zero are not interpreted as well as might be desired (see, e.g., Zellner (1984, p. 288ff)) and the authors' guarded conclusions "that the multiple-β model can explain the pattern of sample excess returns for the first subperiod to some extent" (pp. 106–107) and that it "seems to have a fighting chance to explain the pattern of sample excess returns in the second subperiod also" (p. 107) indicate the tentative nature of the results. Finally, that the "consumption-based model does not improve on the CAPM" and "does not pick up a change in risk in 1979" (p. 107) suggests to me that the authors' results will spur additional research on this very intriguing empirical problem.

In closing let me again congratulate the authors for their useful and interesting research contribution.

References

Bawa, V. S., S. J. Brown, and R. W. Klein (1979), *Estimation Risk and Optimal Portfolio Choice*, North-Holland, Amsterdam.

Baxter, M. (1985), "The Role of Expectations in Stabilization Policy," *Journal of Monetary Economics*, **15**, 343–362.

Boyer, M. and R. E. Kihlstrom (Eds.) (1984), *Bayesian Models in Economic Theory*, North-Holland, Amsterdam.

Brown, S. (1976), "*Optimal Portfolio Choice under Uncertainty*," Ph.D. dissertation, Graduate School of Business, University of Chicago.

——— (1978). "The Portfolio Choice Problem: Comparison of Certainty Equivalence and Optimal Bayes Portfolios," *Communications in Statistics*, **8**, 321–334.

Cobb, L., P. Koppstein, and N. H. Chen (1983), "Estimation and Moment Recursion Relations for Multimodal Distributions of the Exponential Family," *Journal of the American Statistical Association*, **78**, 124–130.

Dufour, J. M. (1979), "*Methods for Specification Errors Analysis with Macroeconomic Applications.*" Ph.D. dissertation, Department of Economics, University of Chicago.

Geisel, M. S. (1975), "Bayesian Comparisons of Simple Macroeconomic Models," in S. E. Fienberg and A. Zellner (Eds.), *Studies in Bayesian Econometrics and Statistics*, North-Holland, Amsterdam.

Grossman, S. (1975), "Rational Expectations and the Econometric Modeling of Markets Subject to Uncertainty: A Bayesian Approach," *Journal of Econometrics*, **3**, 255–272.

Jorion, P. (1983), "*Portfolio Analysis of International Equity Investments,*" Ph.D. dissertation, Graduate School of Business, University of Chicago.

——— (1985), "International Portfolio Diversification with Estimation Risk," *Journal of Business*, **58**, 259–278.

Just, R. and R. Pope (1978), "Stochastic Specification of Production Functions and Economic Implications," *Journal of Econometrics*, **7**, 67–86.

——— (1979), "Production Function Estimation and Related Risk Considerations," *American Journal of Agricultural Economics*, **61**, 276–284.

Merton, R. (1980), "On Estimating the Expected Return on the Market," *Journal of Financial Economics*, **8**, 323–361.

Peck, S. C. and R. G. Richels (1987), "The Value of Information to the Acidic Deposition Debates," *Journal of Business and Economic Statistics*, **5**, 205–210.

Rossi, P. E. (1983), "*Specification and Analysis of Production Models,*" Ph.D. Dissertation, Graduate School of Business, University of Chicago.

Swamy, P. A. V. B. and J. R. Barth (1986b), "Random Coefficients," Special Studies Paper 190, Federal Reserve Board, Washington, DC.

Swamy, P. A. V. B., A. B. Kennickell, and P. von zur Muehlen (1986a), "Forecasting Money Demand with Econometric Models," Special Studies Paper 196, Federal Reserve Board, Washington, DC.

Zellner, A. (1984), *Basic Issues in Econometrics*, University of Chicago Press.

Zellner, A. and V. K. Chetty (1965), "Prediction and Decision Problems in Regression Models from the Bayesian Point of View," *Journal of the American Statistical Association*, **60**, 608–616.

Zellner, A., J. Kmenta, and J. Drèze (1966), "Specification and Estimation of Cobb-Douglas Production Function Models," *Econometrica*, **34**, 784–795.

4 MANAGEMENT VERSUS ECONOMIC CONDITIONS AS CONTRIBUTORS TO THE RECENT INCREASE IN BANK FAILURES

Richard W. Nelson

The number of commercial bank failures varied within a narrow and low range between 1943 and 1974. The highest number of failures during that period was 9, in 5 of the 32 years during this interval; the lowest number was 1. The number of failures has risen and become much more volatile since 1974, varying between 5 and 17 from 1975 to 1981 and then rising sharply to 34 in 1982, 45 in 1983, 78 in 1984, 118 in 1985, and 145 in 1986.[1] In relative terms, the failure rate has increased from negligible levels to 1% of the number of commercial banks operating in the United States. A 1% failure rate remains low relative to experience in other industries. Nonetheless, the increase in the number of failures is a dramatic development and as such merits an explanation.

This chapter attempts to develop some insight into the causes of the recent increase in bank failures. Has, for instance, the increase in failures resulted from an increase in risk in the banking system? If so, did bankers consciously take on greater risk or did it catch up with them unknowingly? What has been the impact of macroeconomic instability? The answers to these questions have important implications for public policy. For instance, reforming the incentives for risk bearing implicit in our current Federal deposit insurance system will have little impact on failures resulting from unstable economic conditions or unanticipated risk taking.

Our analysis proceeds as follows. Section 4.1 develops a conceptual model of the failure process. Sections 4.2 and 4.3 consider the role of macroeconomic instability and management decisions within that model, in relation to recent developments in each area. Section 4.4 presents an empirical model of bank failures to investigate the magnitude of these effects. Section 4.5 summarizes our conclusions.

4.1 The Conceptual Model

A bank fails when the government agency that chartered it declares it insolvent, generally on a determination that its net worth has become negative.[2, 3] The risk of failure, then, is the likelihood that a bank's net worth will become negative over some period of time. Similarly, the riskiness of the banking system can be viewed in terms of the expected number of failures over a period of time.[4]

4.1.1 Sources of Uncertainty

Uncertainty in banking can be traced to the existence of stochastic events that affect banks' profits and, consequently, their net worth.[5] Ex ante, each of these events is defined by a set of possible outcomes and the associated likelihoods of their occurring. Combinations of outcomes of all possible events then define states of nature within which banks operate.

The standard classifications of risk in banking may be thought of as categorizations of the set of stochastic events that affect the profits of banks. Borrowers can default on their legal obligations to a bank, introducing a stochastic element in the return on assets. The possibility that the present value of these payments plus proceeds from sale of collateral received by the bank upon default may be less than the present value of contractual obligations constitutes credit risk. Withdrawals by depositors, receipts from sale of assets or new borrowing, and loan take downs are also stochastic events and together introduce liquidity risk—the possibility that the bank will have to sell illiquid assets at fire-sale prices and, at the extreme, be unable to make obligated payments.

Variations in market interest rates are also stochastic in character and may cause interest payments to rise or fall more sharply than interest receipts, posing interest rate risk. Demand for particular banking services or the operating costs associated with their production also are stochastic events, and variations in the outcomes pose operating risks to the bank. Finally, use of a bank's resources by employees for personal gain, at the expense of shareholders, may also be viewed as a stochastic event creating risk of fraud.

In turn, some of the events enumerated above are themselves affected by a set of secondary events. Thus, a borrower's ability to make payments to a bank usually is linked to sales of products or services, prices, wage payments, or other events affecting the borrower's net worth. Movements in interest rates depend on inflation, technological opportunities, time preferences, central bank policy, and other factors that affect the demand for and supply of loanable funds. Withdrawals from deposit accounts depend on events affecting depositor's cash flows as well as confidence in the bank and/or banking system. Demand for products depends on tastes, which may change, and competitors' moves. Costs depend on labor contracts not yet written. And even fraud may be related to financial pressures on employees.

Events occur and after some time the outcomes become known. Ex post, the bank's profits are a deterministic function of these outcomes.[6] Certain outcomes, or states of nature, imply losses (negative profits) greater or equal to the bank's equity at the beginning of the period, and thus failure. Ex ante, the state of nature under which a bank will operate is unknown and failure is itself a stochastic event. The risk or likelihood of failure can be derived from the likelihood of the various states of nature, their effects on profits, and the initial level of equity capital. Actual failure then results from the interaction of the bank's riskiness ex ante and the states of nature that actually occur.

Extension to the banking system implies that the riskiness of banks collectively and events interact to determine the actual number of failures. However, individual banks are likely to vary in the source of their exposure, that is, in the particular states of nature to which they are vulnerable, even if their overall riskiness is the same. Banks may also differ in their overall riskiness.

The analysis to this point suggests two very different mechanisms for generating an increase in the actual number of failures in the banking system. First, there may be an increase in the riskiness of the banking system, reflecting decreases in equity capital, increases in the likelihood of relatively adverse states of nature, or adverse shifts in the relation between particular states of nature and profits. Increases in risk would be expected to increase the average number of failures over a period of time, with the increase continuing as long as the fundamental causes of the increased risk remain in effect. The variability of the number of failures might also increase.

The second mechanism for generating an increase in bank failures is simply bad luck, or an adverse draw from the set of possible states of nature. Because the number of failures in the banking system is a stochastic process, the number of failures would be expected to vary over time even if the riskiness of banks were constant. The occurrence of events or states of nature systematically affecting a significant group of banks could result in a sharp increase in the number of failures. Importantly, the resulting increase in bank failures would persist over an extended period of time if the events generating them are similarly persistent or if there are lags in the process of restoring capital to beginning-of-the-period levels when depleted by losses short of those causing failure.

4.1.2 The Role of Management

Management sets policies that affect the relation between a bank's profits and the state of nature under which it operates. Credit decisions determine the parties that are contractually obligated to make payments to the bank. Because the fortunes of individual borrowers differ under a given state of nature, credit decisions affect the relationship between the state of nature and profits.

Bank management can choose to hold low-risk financial assets, at the extreme U.S. government securities, or it may choose portfolios of varying degrees of risky assets. In the process of making credit decisions, bank managers also determine the extent of collateral and diversification in the banks' portfolios. In general, diversification can reduce portfolio risk if the returns on individual loans are less than perfectly positively correlated. In terms of our model, diversification may be thought of relative to the external events that define alternative states of nature. Importantly, a portfolio may be diversified against some events but not others.

Bank managers also have tools to control the liquidity risk and interest rate sensitivity of their banks. Their choices with regard to these tools affect the sensitivity of the bank's profits to variations in the bank's cash flow and to variations in interest rates. Managers also enter into labor contracts, commit their banks to serving particular markets, and make a host of decisions that affect the operating risk of their banks.

Bank managers can react to environmental changes so as to neutralize their impact on risk. Alternatively, they can play a proactive role, initiating policies that affect risk. In either case, they are expected to choose policies that maximize shareholder welfare, considering both risk and return. Their choices, consequently, are influenced by the risk aversion of investors and by market incentives to bear risk. As long as managers are choosing optimally, a rise in the number of failures reflecting increased riskiness of banks would result only from decreased risk aversion on the part of investors or increased incentives for bearing risk. Opportunities and incentives for bearing risk, however, are likely to differ in different geographic and product markets, causing individual bank managements to differ in the amount of exposure that they seek.

Whether it is possible or rational for bank management to seek to insulate their banks altogether from the risk of failure is an empirical question that we shall return to in subsequent sections of this chapter. One aspect of this issue, however, relates to management abilities and requires further conceptual development.

4.1.3 Imperfect Management

Risk in banking may also develop unconsciously, and thus be independent of market incentives for risk bearing. Such nonoptimal behavior could result from inaccurate identification of the relation between states of the world and profits (e.g., inaccurate credit or duration analysis or imperfect diversification), failure to identify events as relevant or outcomes as possible (e.g., inaccurate identification of the range over which interest rates might vary), or simply from imperfect control over a decentralized decision process (e.g., lack of control over credit decisions made by individual loan officers or positions taken by foreign exchange traders).

All management is imperfect in the sense of being susceptible to error in analysis or judgment. However, management is not homogenous in this regard. Individuals comprising management differ in ability and training. Further, exactly what constitutes good management is not known and may vary with circumstances. Thus, the process of selecting management is itself an exercise in decision making under uncertainty and is constrained by scarcity of individuals with desired characteristics.

The preceding discussion suggests that banks are likely to be imperfectly managed. Management "quality" is likely to vary on a continuum between "good" (i.e., able to define and implement optimal policies) and "bad," somewhere at the lower end of the spectrum. As a result, risks will vary systematically over banks with differences in management quality. These differences are likely to persist over time, but may vary with elements of the external environment. The overall riskiness of the banking system may also vary over time as the result of general trends in management quality or the environmental conditions with which managers must deal.

Imperfect management implies that analyses of bank risk and banking failures must extend beyond consideration of incentives or even current management philosophies. For instance, even a "don't bet the bank" philosophy may not insulate a bank against the possibility of failure if it is imperfectly implemented. Systematic weaknesses in management across banks could also expose the banking system to risk of large numbers of failures. And a rise in the number of failures could result from an industry-wide decline in the quality of management as well as from increased incentives for bearing risk or bad luck.

4.1.4 Learning

At the same time that events affect a bank's profits and its failure or survival, events bring new information to the attention of its managers. Learning thus becomes an important element in the model and introduces a potential for dynamic, managerial responses.

One such response would seek to eliminate mistakes that are evident, with hindsight based on new information. A banker who had unknowingly taken on greater risk than desired, say by inadequate attention to internal controls, can be expected to seek to reduce that risk over time, perhaps by strengthening the management control system. Whether such a dynamic response is actually successful in reducing the overall risk of the bank depends on the speed of adjustment to new information and the rate at which new errors are introduced. The latter again reflects the banking environment.

Over the shorter run, the environment seems likely to remain relatively stable and learning seems likely to be successful. Thus, a wave of bank failures reflecting management errors would likely be self-correcting. However, rapidly changing external conditions would be expected to be associated with systematic discovery or introduction of new errors, implying relatively high failure rates. As a result of these influences, bank failures seem unlikely to be stable over time, but rather to occur in cycles of length reflecting the extent of change and managements' ability to learn from actual experience.

4.1.5 Summary

Our conceptual model can be summarized simply in the following terms. Bankers operate in a world where stochastic events affect their profits and the likelihood of survival or failure. They choose policies based on their likely effects on bank profits, considering the range of possible outcomes and their likelihood. In general, bankers decide rationally to bear a positive amount of risk. They may also make mistakes, and as a result assume more risk than they intend. Ex ante, the environment and policies adopted by bank management together determine the riskiness of a bank and the riskiness of the banking system. Ex post, events occur and the bank's profits are determined. The result may be failure of a bank or a number of banks. Over time, failure brings new information on risks, learning occurs, and bankers who survive adjust their policies accordingly. With this model in mind, we turn now to the recent environment as a possible contributor to recent bank failures.

4.2 Macroeconomic Instability and Recent Bank Failures

The 1970s and 1980s have been characterized by greater macroeconomic instability than had occurred during the 1950s and 1960s. Recessions occurred at a rate of one per three years from 1970 to 1982, compared to one per five years from 1945 to 1970.[7] Economic activity declined in 26% of the months during the 1970–1982 period, compared to 16% during the earlier period. And the unemployment rate rose to higher peaks — 6.0% in December 1970, 8.9% in May 1975, 7.6% in May 1980, and 10.8% in December 1982; unemployment averaged 6.8% of the work force between 1971 and 1982, compared to 4.5% between 1945 and 1970.[8] Thus, recessions both rose in frequency in the 1970s and early 1980s and had a more severe impact on the economy than they did during the previous two decades.

Recessions involve declining real (inflation-adjusted) sales, production, and incomes that adversely affect the net worth and liquidity of individuals and firms that have borrowed from commercial banks. They also generally are accompanied by declines in interest rates and inflation and downward shifts in the demand for loans by both individuals and businesses. The most direct effect on commercial banks is an increase in loan delinquencies or charge-offs, both of which reduce bank profits.

Recessions have been a persistent feature of the U.S. economy, but their timing, severity, industry and geographic impacts, and other specific characteristics have differed significantly, making each unique and stochastic from the point of view of bank management. Because recessions are not uniformly felt throughout the economy, bank management can use diversification to limit risk. It remains true, however, that recessions by their very definition have systematic effects on economic agents, and thus that the possibilities for diversification are inherently limited. The more pervasive and the deeper the recession, the less are the opportunities for effective diversification of risks.

The severity of a recession's impact on individual banks is likely to vary with their sectoral and geographic specialization and the characteristics of the recession. Banks assuming relatively great credit risk are likely to be affected especially severely. In practice, differences in the exposure of individual banks to the effects of recession may be marked, but all remain vulnerable to failure under a sufficiently adverse macroeconomic climate.

The second major area of macroeconomic instability is in the area of prices. The rate of inflation rose secularly, from around $1-1\frac{1}{2}\%$ per year in the mid 1960s to 12–13% in 1980–1981, and then subsequently declined to under 3% in 1986.[9] Within the upward tend, the rate of inflation also was highly volatile, in part reflecting the severity of the recessions of 1973–1975 and that of 1980. The reversal in secular trend from accelerating inflation to disinflation was unprecedented in the post-World War II era.

Commodity prices, particularly of energy-related and agricultural products, rose much more rapidly than the general price level during the 1970s and then actually declined in the 1980s. The price of crude petroleum, for instance, increased eightfold between 1970 and 1981, and then fell by 22% through 1985 and by an additional 56% in 1986. Agricultural prices increased almost two and one-half times between 1970 and early 1984, and subsequently fell 13% by late 1986. Declines were much greater in individual agricultural products. The price of wheat, for instance, fell by 10% in 1985 and an additional 23% in 1986. The price of corn fell by 23% in 1985, and by 41% in 1986. These declines in commodity prices were unprecedented in their magnitude over the post-World War II period.

It can be argued that anticipated price movements have no effects on real profits and incomes, provided that markets adjust perfectly to them. Unanticipated price movements, however, redistribute profits and incomes from losers to winners.[10] The losers are more likely to default on their bank debt, whereas winners find themselves in a stronger financial position. Most of the benefits of inflation are likely to go to holders of equity, whereas limited liability limits the extent to which they share in the losses. Thus, it may be expected that unanticipated price movements will have a net negative effect on banks and other holders of debt.[11]

In theory, unanticipated increases or decreases in prices could create losses for banks. Price declines, however, are potentially more serious since they reduce the value of collateral at the same time that they increase the likelihood of default. Thus, banks are likely to avoid potential losses upon default by taking possession of and selling collateral if prices are stable or rising, but to lose even on secured loans if prices are falling. This effect also suggests an interaction between price movements and recessions with regard to the impact on banks, with recessions having particularly severe effects when prices are falling.

The effects of macroeconomic instability and falling prices on bank failures have been well recognized in the historical literature.[12] Bremmer (1935) described the first two decades of the twentieth century as "an era of banking prosperity" and attributed this fact to "a gradual and steady upward swing of the price level, with the result that collateral held by the banks and the net worth of the unsecured borrowers constantly increased in value."[13] Gambs (1977) studied the impact of the level of economic activity and the condition of agriculture on bank failures during the 1922–1932 period. Based on regression analysis of observations by states, he concluded that weakness in overall economic activity and in agriculture both were associated with increases in bank failures. Benston (1973) traces the banking difficulties of the 1930s to the "decline of the money supply that began about March 1929" and the resulting squeeze on liquidity.[14] He concludes that "the Great Depression was like a plague that destroyed the weakest, but those who succumbed need not have done so had the financial situation been that which they *had every right to expect* [emphasis added] would prevail."[15,16]

More recently, bank failures rose in all but one of the five recessions between 1945 and 1970; the average number of failures during years in which economic activity was at a trough of the business cycle was 7.8, compared to 4.4 during other years.[17] Between 1971 and 1982, bank failures averaged 19 per year at troughs of the business cycle, compared with 7.4 during other years. Further, the sharper effect of recession on failures after 1970 coincided with increasing severity of recessions during that period.

Economic instability then provides a plausible explanation for a significant rise in bank failure in the 1970s and 1980s, and especially in 1981 and following years. Although the recession came to an end in November 1982, unemployment remained high by historical standards in 1983, 1984, 1985, and 1986. The underutilization of economic capacity through 1986 suggests that many borrowers continued to be affected by the recession well after the trough of the business cycle. The reversal from accelerating inflation to disinflation came in 1982, coinciding with the recent upturn in bank failures, and disinflation has continued through 1986. The declines in oil and agricultural prices accelerated even while the economy was recovering.[18] And actual bank failures have been relatively concentrated among agricultural banks. About one-quarter of all banks have one-quarter or more of their loans related to agriculture; these banks, however, accounted for about one-half of the failures during 1985.[19]

4.3 The Influence of Management

Analyses of bank failure have also typically identified management as a major cause. For example, Sinkey (1979) concludes that "except for periods of structural imbalance due to overbanking and severe economic depression, the major cause of problem and failed institutions, weak and/or dishonest bank managers and/or directors, basically has remained unchanged."[20] Most authors have also been quick to point out that banks that are poorly managed tend to fail during periods of stress, and thus management and economic conditions are related.[21]

Students of previous waves of bank failures also have concluded that the quality of management has varied over time. Thus, Bremmer argues forcefully that easy banking during the first two decades of the twentieth century and free policies in chartering banks led to the "admission to the banking fraternity of thousands of incompetent individuals" and ultimately contributed to the ensuing debacle in the 1920s and 1930s.[22]

Similar arguments can be made about the role of management in the recent wave of bank failures. In a world of perfect bank management and conservative "don't bet the bank" philosophies, it can be argued that only very severe economic events would be expected to have any influence on failures. In fact, however, bank management is imperfect, reflecting imperfections in the supply and selection of managerial talent, and poor management is likely to continue to be a cause of bank failures. Recent economic instability may not have been so severe as to threaten the best managed banks, but was sufficient to make errors very costly. And as in the 1900s and 1910s, bankers lived relatively easy lives during the 1950s and 1960s, and may have forgotten the lessons learned during the Great Depression. Similarly, chartering of new banks increased greatly, although not to levels experienced during the early 1900s.

Recent theoretical studies have hypothesized a second source of management influence, characterized not by inept management but rather driven by market incentives. Summarizing one such approach, Benston et al. (1986) state that the "key change [in recent times] is the increased incentive toward risk taking that has resulted from related increases in deposit insurance and decreases in equity capital."[23] Chan et al. (1986) identify a decrease in "information reusability" as an alternative factor that has increased incentives for banks to take risks. Finally, changes in the structure of the economy also may have introduced new incentives for risk taking among commercial banks.

Inexperience, increases in deposit insurance coverage, decreases in information reusuability, and structural changes in the economy all provide plausible reasons to suspect that banks have become riskier in recent years. Unfortunately, how bankers have responded to these changes is difficult to document. The actual failure record provides little help since it is likely to reflect the impact of increased economic instability as well as of management policies.

4.3.1 Balance Sheet Trends

To the extent that balance sheet trends reflect bank risk, banks with balance sheets exhibiting relatively great risk would be expected to have relatively high likelihoods of failure. A number of authors have presented evidence supporting this view.[24] These studies, however, are of limited use in explaining the recent rise in failures because they leave unanswered the issues of what triggers the failure of vulnerable banks (e.g., economic instability) and whether banks have in recent years become systematically more risky, or more vulnerable to failure under adversity.

Table 4–1 presents some trends in the aggregate balance sheet of the banking industry since World War II, using data as of the end-of-year prior to the peak of each business cycle over this period. This analysis provides information on trends in the vulnerability of the banking system to the ensuing recession.

The major trend in the assets of the banking system over this period was the sharp decline in the ratio of riskless assets to total assets. Combined, U.S. government securities and cash and due from banks represented about two-thirds of the total assets of the banking system in 1948, but had declined to about one-fifth of total assets by 1980. The decline, which resulted from declines in both components of the numerator, occurred primarily in the 1950s and 1960s and probably reflected changes in the structure of the economy and in the technology of cash management. In particular, government borrowing needs were low and private borrowing needs were high as the economy shifted from a wartime to a peacetime basis, and it is not surprising that the banking system was affected. The ratio of government securities to total assets, for instance, declined to levels that had characterized the banking system prior to the war.[25]

Bank management could have chosen to offset the increased portfolio risk by increasing equity capital. Equity capital rose relative to total assets of the banking system during this period, but not sufficiently fast to prevent a decline in the ratio of equity capital to risk assets between 1948 and 1973, from 21% to 7%. This decline came to an end in 1973, but, in contrast to the decline in riskless assets, took the banking system to substantially lower ratios than had existed earlier in the twentieth century.

Figures for individual banks, also summarized in table 4–1, show that the aggregate trends in the ratio of equity to risk assets reflect broadly based behavior on the part of banks, not just the behavior of the largest banks. In 1956, there were only 406 commercial banks with ratios of equity to risk assets under 10%. This figure increased sharply through 1973, when it reached 6049. Since 1973, however, the number of banks with equity to risk asset ratios under 10% and thus with relatively high risk, has actually fallen.

Table 4–1. Balance Sheet Trends of Commercial Banks 1948–1980

	12/48	12/52	12/56	12/59	12/69	12/73	12/79	12/80
Ratios to total assets								
U.S. government securities	44.6	34.4	26.9	24.0	11.5	9.3	8.3	8.8
Cash & due from banks	24.1	22.9	22.4	20.2	16.0	12.6	11.6	11.0
Riskless assets	68.7	57.3	49.3	44.2	27.4	22.0	19.8	19.9
Equity/risk assets	20.6	16.7	14.8	14.3	9.3	7.4	7.3	7.3
Number of banks with equity/risk assets								
Under 10%			406	527	3434	6049	5710	4632
10–15%			3645	4198	6163	5550	6061	6590
15–20%			3965	3974	2199	1295	1739	2171
Over 20%			5149	4415	1692	1082	854	1042
Foreign branch assets as % of total					7.3	13.7	19.4	20.4

Composition of domestic risk assets (%)								
Municipal securities	10.8	13.0	11.7	12.4	15.6	15.0	12.3	12.4
Other securities	7.6	5.5	3.1	2.6	0.6	1.0	1.4	1.3
Federal funds	NA	NA	NA	NA	2.6	5.6	5.7	6.0
Other loans (gross)								
Nonfarm real estate	17.6	18.5	19.3	19.4	17.5	17.9	21.9	21.7
Securities loans	4.2	4.1	3.9	3.6	2.6	1.9	1.2	1.1
To farmers	5.1	6.2	5.0	4.9	3.8	3.6	3.7	3.4
To business	37.5	33.7	35.7	34.7	33.3	31.7	27.8	28.1
To individuals	11.7	15.1	17.1	17.7	16.7	15.9	17.4	15.5
Other	2.0	1.9	2.4	2.0	2.0	2.0	1.8	1.9
Other assets	3.4	3.1	3.3	3.7	5.3	5.4	9.3	11.2

Source: FDIC, *Annual Report*, various dates.

The fact that banks have been operating with lower ratios of equity capital to risk assets in the 1970s and 1980s is consistent with the increased failure rate that has occurred. However, it is not possible on this analysis alone to decompose the decline in equity capital into components reflecting inexperience, deposit insurance, or the structure of the economy. The decline in capital ratios did follow the creation of the FDIC, albeit with a lag. However, the strengthening of capital ratios since 1973 does suggest that whatever the cause, management influence has not increased risk since that time.

Changes in the composition of risk assets of banks also are shown in table 4–1. The rise in assets booked in foreign branches was very sharp. Some of this growth reflected loans to less-developed countries, many of which were not paying interest in the early 1980s and, under current circumstances, appear to involve relatively great risk of default. Loans to less-developed countries, and foreign loans in general, however, affect primarily a small number of large, multinational banks. Within the domestic office portfolio, there were increases in municipal securities, federal funds, nonfarm real estate loans, loans to individuals, and in other assets, with decreases in other securities, loans secured by securities, loans to farmers, and other loans to financial and nonfinancial businesses. The risk implications of these trends are not all clear without more detailed information than is available.[26]

Reported balance sheet information, of course, hides much detail on the quality of individual loans and investments and concentrations at individual banks. A lowering of credit standards within categories of loans, a reduction in resources spent on credit analysis, or lax management controls might be expected to affect credit quality generally, over all categories of loans. Large banks also have come to depend heavily on liability management as a source of funds and technique for managing liquidity, and have expanded their involvement in off-balance sheet banking. These practices constitute additional potential sources of risk that are not reviewed here.

4.4 Evidence from the Historical Record of Bank Failures

Increased risk taking by bank management and economic instability both provide plausible explanations for the recent rise in banking failures. In this section, we seek evidence on the relative impact of these influences by estimating an empirical model of bank failures.[27] Our sample consists of yearly observations over the 1896–1985 period. Such a lengthy period has the advantage of providing a broad range of experience, including periods when economic instability has been comparable to or greater than that of recent years. It has the disadvantage of encompassing structural changes that also may have affected failures, which are difficult to adjust for in an empirical analysis.

The establishment of the Federal Reserve in 1914 was one such event. The Federal Reserve was created in response to recurring banking crises in the late 1800s and early 1900s. It was given the power of lender of last resort to stabilize the banking system. To the extent that earlier failures had resulted from systematic liquidity crises and that the Federal Reserve acted effectively as lender of last resort, failures would be expected to be lower, ceteris paribus, after 1914 than prior to that date. However, the Federal Reserve did not act forcefully during the 1930s, and the full effect of its establishment probably came after that time.

To estimate the effect of liquidity crises on bank failures, we introduce a variable equal to the percentage decline in the assets of the banking system, truncated at 0 when assets are increasing. This measure shows serious liquidity crises in 1921 and in 1931–1934, when annual contractions in the assets of the banking system ranged from 8% to 22%. Smaller contractions occurred in 1908, 1938, and 1947.[28] We expect failures to be higher in years of banking contraction, because of the effect on financial asset prices, and interpret this variable as reflecting at least in part the effectiveness of the Federal Reserve in dealing with potential liquidity crises.

The establishment of the FDIC in 1933 was a second structural event with profound implications for the banking system. The FDIC has served in a role as receiver in failures of insured banks, and has intervened in bank failures by providing financial support for arranged mergers, as well as by paying depositors directly. One result was to change the process (and definition) of bank failures. Prior to 1933, banks were considered to have failed when they suspended payment on deposits; after 1933 banks failed when they became "problems" resolved with financial assistance by the FDIC. Currently, most failing banks are merged into healthy banks rather than liquidated, and there are fewer suspensions than failures. However, the number of suspensions probably overstated failures prior to the establishmemt of the FDIC since some suspended banks did eventually reopen.

Deposit insurance also had a fundamental effect on the riskiness of the banking system. By removing incentives for runs on banks by insured depositors, FDIC deposit insurance may be argued to have reduced liquidity risk in banking.[29] This suggests a lower incidence of failures among banks that are fundamentally sound but might be forced to liquidate assets at "fire-sale" prices. As previously discussed, FDIC insurance also has increased incentives for bankers to take on risk, especially with the substantial increases in insurance coverage; the regulatory agencies may not have been effective in limiting that risk through examination and regulation. To the extent that they are measurable, additional risks assumed by banks after establishment of the FDIC will be picked up by other variables. However, some of the increase in risk is likely to be unmeasurable.

We include a dummy variable equal to 1 from 1896–1933 and zero from 1934–1985 to account for effects of Federal deposit insurance not otherwise measurable. The change in the definition of bank failures after 1933 and the favorable effect of the FDIC on liquidity suggest a positive coefficient on this variable. However, this conceivably could be outweighed by the indirect effect of increased incentives to bear risk.

Information on bank portfolios available over the entire sample period is limited but does include aggregate data for cash assets, U.S. government securities, all other assets, and equity capital. We use these data to construct a ratio of equity to risk assets, defined as total assets less cash assets and U.S. government securities, which we interpret as a measure of management influence on risk. We expect a negative coefficient on this variable.

We use the rate of unemployment as our principal measure of economic activity. Increases in unemployment imply sharp reductions in income for many individuals who are bank customers, and reduced ability to repay loans to banks. More generally, increases in unemployment are associated with downturns in economic activity in which sales of business concerns fall off unexpectedly. Importantly, unemployment remains high during initial stages of economic recoveries, reflecting continued hard times for individuals and business until the economy again reaches capacity. We expect the unemployment rate to be positively related to bank failures.

Our final variables measure changes in fuel and farm prices. Because theory suggests that systematic decreases and increases in prices could both cause a rise in failures, and the magnitude of the effects could differ depending on the direction of the change in prices, we separate each variable into two components—percentage price increases (truncated at zero when prices decline) and percentage price decreases (truncated at zero when prices increase). The denominator used in calculating the percentage change is a moving average of the previous three years. We expect declines in prices to be negatively related to bank failures and to have more important effects than price increases.

Both the number of failures and the impact of other factors are likely to be proportional to the number of banks in existence. Accordingly, we use as our dependent variable the proportion rather than the number of banks that fail in a given year. The means, standard deviations, and sources of the data are shown in table 4–2.

In addition to the basic model covering the entire sample period, we ran three additional regressions over subperiods. Model B includes years from

Table 4–2. Variables Used in the Model

	Mean	*Standard Deviation*
Failure rate[a]	0.0110	0.0399
Equity of risk assets[b]	0.1900	0.0799
Unemployment rate	0.0696	0.0506
Farm price increase[c]	0.0956	0.1426
Farm price decrease	−0.0368	0.0870
Fuel price increase	0.0996	0.1623
Fuel price decrease	−0.0219	0.0287
Asset contraction	−0.0063	0.0287

Sources: (1) For the number of failures: for 1890–1920, Bremer (1935, pp. 34–35); for 1921–1933, Bremer (1935, p. 42); for 1934–1985, FDIC, *Annual Report*, 1985. Bremer's data include data on failures of private banks, which were numerous in the early part of the twentieth century. In 1933, failures exclude banks that suspended payments during the bank holiday and later reopened. Data reported by the FDIC include mutual savings banks; failures of mutual savings banks were rare prior to 1980 and were omitted where they could be identified. (2) For the number of private banks for 1896–1940, Board of Governors of the Federal Reserve System, *Banking Studies*, p. 418 (as of June 30). For the number of incoporated banks: for 1896–1924, *Banking Studies*, p. 418 (as of June 30); for 1925–1970, Board of Governors of the Federal Reserve System, *Banking and Monetary Statistics* (as of December 31); and 1971–1985, Board of Governors of the Federal Reserve System, *Annual Statistical Digest*, various dates (as of December 31). (3) For assets and equity capital, Board of Governors of the Federal Reserve System, *All Bank Statistics: 1896–1955; Banking and Monetary Statistics; Annual Statistical Digest*, various dates. (4) For the unemployment rate and prices, U.S. Bureau of the Census, *Historical Statistics of the United States, from Colonial Times to 1970; Statistical Abstract of the United States,* various dates; Council of Economic Advisers, *Economic Report of the President*, 1986.

[a] The failure rate is the number of failures divided by the number of commercial banks.

[b] Risk assets are calculated as total assets minus cash assets and U.S. government securities.

1950 to 1985. There were no serious liquidity crises during this period and the asset contraction variable is omitted. Data on unemployment have been gathered consistently over this period, removing the possible structural change suggested by Romer (1986).[30] The disadvantage of this sample is that it does not contain the same range of experience with regard to economic instability and price movements as does the full sample period. Model C includes earlier years, from 1896 to 1949. Finally, Model D includes only the years from 1914 to 1949. Because initial estimates using ordinary least squares showed signs of marginal, first-order serial correlation, the model was reestimated with the Cochrane-Orcutt adjustment. The estimated coefficients and their standard errors are shown in table 4–3.

The signs and significance of the coefficients show reasonable stability over the various regressions. They are generally consistent with expectations based on both the economic instability and managerial influence hypotheses.

Table 4–3. Regression Results[a]

	Regression			
	(A) 1896–1985	(B) 1950–1985	(C) 1896–1949	(D) 1915–1949
Constant	0.0066	0.0003	0.0401	−0.0460
	(0.0076)	(0.0006)	(0.0263)	(0.0757)
Dummy: 1896–1934 = 1	0.0142**		0.0131	0.0320*
	(0.0053)		(0.0085)	(0.0188)
Equity-risk assets	−0.0699**	−0.0135**	−0.1607**	0.1185
	(0.0314)	(0.0054)	(0.0726)	(0.2418)
Unemployment rate	0.1510**	0.0310**	0.1836**	0.1562
	(0.0454)	(0.0112)	(0.0706)	(0.0956)
Farm price increase	0.0008	0.0007	−0.0060	−0.0160
	(0.0154)	(0.0017)	(0.0287)	(0.0406)
Farm price decrease	0.0697	−0.0125**	0.1002	0.1362
	(0.0428)	(0.0059)	(0.0666)	(0.0938)
Fuel price increase	−0.0241	−0.0019*	−0.0457	−0.0365
	(0.0146)	(0.0010)	(0.0391)	(0.0555)
Fuel price decrease	−0.0665	−0.0586**	−0.0359	−0.0887
	(0.0739)	(0.0153)	(0.1148)	(0.1778)
Asset contraction	−0.7669*		−0.7720**	−0.7751**
	(0.1083)		(0.1524)	(0.1994)
R^2	0.705	0.549	0.650	0.633
DW	2.106	1.174	2.393	2.394
r	−0.373	0.426	−0.286	−0.292
constant/$(1-r)$	0.0048	0.0006	0.0312	−0.0356

[a] Standard errors in parentheses.
* Statistically significantly different from zero at the 10% level.
** Statistically significantly different from zero at the 5% level.

However, the magnitudes of some of the coefficients differed considerably over the regression equations, suggesting structural change that was not incorporated in the model. We shall focus here on the results for the most recent period (column B of table 4–3), given our interest in recent bank failures.

In the regression equation for the recent sample period, the unemployment rate, farm price decreases, oil price decreases, and the ratio of equity capital to risk assets all have coefficients that are statistically significant at the 95% level of confidence and the expected signs. The magnitude of the coefficient of unemployment implies an increase of 4.6 failures per one percentage point increase in unemploymnet at a base of 15,000 banks—about the current level. Decreases in farm and fuel prices have effects equal to 1.9 and 8.8 failures, respectively, per one percentage point decrease. The magnitude of the coefficient on the ratio of equity capital to risk assets implies an increase of 2.0 failures per one percentage point decrease in the capital ratio, again on a base of 15,000 banks.

The regressions for the full sample period also suggest that the liquidity crises of 1908, 1921, 1931–1934, and 1938 had major effects on bank failures during those times. In addition, the creation of the FDIC appears to have had a significant structural effect, decreasing the number of failures by 212 banks per year on a base of 15,000 banks.

At its peak in 1982 and 1983, the unemployment rate rose to almost 10% on an annual basis. Assuming that a 5% unemployment rate is consistent with full employment, our estimates suggest that the recession caused an increase in failures of 23 banks in these years. The decrease in fuel prices contributed an additional 30–35 bank failures during 1984 and 1985, and farm prices contributed an additional 14 failures in 1985. Together, these factors explain a significant percentage but not all of the rise in failures, as shown in table 4–4.[31]

Our estimates, then, provide an explanation of a large part of the recent increase in failures. Their failure to explain recent failures fully probably reflects the use of an aggregate price index for farm products rather than indices for individual commodity prices. As previously noted, prices of corn and wheat, for example, fell much more sharply than did the aggregate index, and the actual failure rate has been relatively high among banks specializing in farm lending.

4.5 Conclusions

On purely theoretical grounds, there are reasons to suspect that management and economic instability both have contributed to the recent increase in bank

Table 4–4. Estimated Contributions to Recent Bank Failures

	1981	1982	1983	1984	1985
Unemployment above 5%	12	22	21	12	10
Fuel price decrease	0	0	0	35	34
Farm price decrease	0	5	1	0	15
Total[a]	17	31	27	52	64
Total failures	10	34	45	78	118
Memorandum:					
Number of banks	14,882	14,963	15,023	15,133	15,233

[a] Note that this total is not the equation's estimate of the number of failures, but rather the increase in failures that would result from the factors noted.

failures. Our empirical estimates, based on the failure record since 1896, support a significant role for both factors.

Ultimately, management is "responsible" for all bank failures in the sense that different decisions could have prevented failure regardless of the course of external events. In general, however, it is not optimal for banks to seek complete insulation against failure, either from the shareholder's perspective of from that of public policy. Further, banks are, in practice, imperfectly managed, reflecting the limited supply of managerial talent and the environmental conditions under which management comes of age. The fact that there has been a systematic relation between economic instability and failures, then, says either that bank managers have always been willing to "bet the bank" or that there has been some proportion of ineffective managers in the industry.

As to the future, our results suggest that the number of bank failures will decline from recent levels, even under current management policies, provided that economic conditions improve. The timing of such declines depends on the course of the economy and trends in prices. Recent experience may have convinced bankers to return to more conservative management policies, providing an additional avenue of change. Closer scrutiny by shareholders and directors may also have improved management quality, in some cases by bringing in new managers. Tighter regulation of bank equity capital may also hold potential to reduce risk in the banking system. However, even the most stringent proposals that have been discussed would be insufficient to increase equity ratios to the levels of the 1950s, and would leave other elements contributing to risk in place. In sum, both economic conditions and the dynamic responses of the banking system point in the direction of fewer banking failures in the years ahead. The number of failures seems likely to remain above the levels of the 1950s and 1960s, even in "good times," but to be manageable by the bank regulatory agencies. In any case, it is questionable whether a return to a 1950s banking system would be very desirable on grounds of economic efficiency.

Notes

1. Figures on bank failures are as reported by the Federal Deposit Insurance Corporation. Included in the total for 1986 are seven "open-bank" assistance transactions. These transactions were rare prior to 1985, but appear to have been treated inconsistently in the bank failure figures. For example, Continental Illinois is not considered to have failed in the official statistics for 1984. The number of failures of commercial and savings banks for 1985 and prior years are reported in the 1985 *Annual Report* of the FDIC. The number of failures of savings banks was determined, where possible, from the *Annual Reports* of various years and subtracted from the total. The number of failures for 1986 is as reported by staff of the FDIC as of early 1987.

2. Prior to 1933, there were cases in which banks "suspended" payment and later reopened. Such suspensions generally reflect liquidity problems and do not fall within the definition of bank failure considered in this chapter, although they clearly do constitute a broader type of failure. However, we would want to include failures of private banks, of which there were many at the beginning of the twentieth century. These banks operate as partnerships, without bank charters, and thus failure does not involve action by a chartering agency. It is also true that the chartering agency has some flexibility in defining insolvency, particularly with regard to the distinction between market or book values. Under some circumstances, the FDIC also can provide assistance to banks that otherwise would have failed. The latter fall within our concept of failures, whatever they are called in official pronouncements.

3. Failure of course, may be precipitated by a run on the bank, which forces it to sell assets at "fire-sale" prices, causing losses that in turn impair net worth. The proceeds from the sale of illiquid assets depend on the speed with which those assets must be liquidated. Thus "runs" on banks, for whatever reason, may create capital losses that would not have occurred otherwise, possibly causing insolvency. See Benston et al. (1986). Whether such a situation actually occurs depends on the availability of a lender who is willing to provide credit to the bank based on a longer-term appraisal of the value of its assets. Such a lender could emerge from the private sector in time of crisis. History prior to the creation of the Federal Reserve shows that such lenders did, indeed, emerge, although less than perfectly. In present context, the Federal Reserve is expected to fill this role as the lender of last resort.

4. One practical definition would be the expected number of failures as a ratio to the total number of banks in the system. Another would be the proportion of deposits or assets in failing banks.

5. New issues of equity may also be treated as a stochastic event affecting net worth within the framework developed in this chapter. Banks with low or negative net worth, however, generally are thought to be unable to raise new equity funds.

6. Uncertainty may not be eliminated even ex post if there is pure noise (unrelated to events) in the relations, or if the relations are understood imperfectly or the outcomes are measured imperfectly.

7. The years 1945, 1970, and 1982 were all troughs of economic cycles, as dated by the National Bureau of Economic Research.

8. Because the "natural" rate of unemployment is thought to have increased during the 1970s, unemployment figures probably overstate the severity of recent recessions.

9. Figures reported are for the consumer price index.

10. Unanticipated inflation may also reduce efficiency generally by increasing risk of economic activity.

11. This situation would be different were U.S. banks permitted to invest in equities. This is one of many examples of risk-increasing regulation.

12. These effects are to be distinguished from the effects of changes in financial asset prices. Increases in interest rates, for instance, imply declines in the market value of long-term loans or bonds, both of which are held in the portfolios of commercial banks. The sharp rise in interest rates between 1979 and 1981, not discussed in the text, is another element of instability with significant potential effects on banks. This rise was directly responsible for bankruptcy (whether recognized or not) of most thrift institutions during this period. For an interesting discussion of a historical precedent during the free banking era, see Rolnick and Weber (1984). They conclude that for the most part, "banks failed when economic times turned bad and the values of their portfolios declined" (p. 290).

13. Bremmer (1935, p. 37).

14. Benston (1973, p. 32).

15. Benston (1973, p. 32).

16. In discussing the Banking Crisis of 1930, White (1984) concludes that "many [banks] were barely solvent. For them, the worst possible situation was the coincidence of difficult times for their local clients with a relatively tight national monetary policy" (see p. 137).

17. The difference in the averages for these periods is statistically significant at high level of confidence.

18. For discussions of the agricultural crisis, see Drabenstott and Duncan (1985), Keplinger et al. (1985), and Melichar (1986).

19. Sixty-two of the 118 commercial banks that failed in 1985 were agricultural banks, that is, had at least one-quarter of their loans related to agriculture. The number of failing agricultural banks was 25 in 1984 and 7 in each of the two preceding years. See Federal Deposit Insurance Corporation, *Annual Report*, 1985, p. 26.

20. Sinkey (1979, p. 19).

21. See, for example, Benston (1973, p. 32).

22. Bremmer (1935, p. 39).

23. Benston et al. (1986, p. 22). See also Kane (1985).

24. See Short et al. (1985), for instance, for a microeconomic analysis of balance sheet behavior on bank failures.

25. Interestingly, the declines in the ratio of U.S. government securities to assets after 1945 brought the banking system back to the situation at the beginning of the century. Declines to 1960 had carried the ratio back to 23%, about the same as during the Great Depression. By 1970, the ratio had fallen to 9%, slightly above the levels of the Great Depression. Declines continued through 1985, when the ratio reached 3% — about the same as in the early years of the century.

26. Data on the actual default experience are very little help in evaluating creditworthiness since they reflect the effects of economic instability as well as of credit policies.

27. See Bovenzi and Nejezchleb (1985) for a previous study.

28. Total assets of the banking system declined during parts of 1946 and 1947 as a result of the Federal debt retirement program after World War II. The decline was not accompanied by any contraction of loans to or deposits of businesses and individuals, and thus did not reflect a liquidity crisis. See FDIC, *Annual Report*, 1946, p. 46.

29. This effect is similar to that of the Federal Reserve's lender of last resort.

30. Romer (1986) presents evidence that economic statistics prior to World War II, including the unemployment rate, systematically exaggerate the extent of macroeconomic instability owing to errors in estimation. She concludes, however, that better estimates still would leave the Great Depression as a period of unusually great instability in between periods of roughly comparable instability.

31. The level of failures during "good" economic times can be estimated by evaluating the regression equation at full employment and stable prices, and the current level of equity-risk assets. Using estimates from the more recent sample period, 5% unemployment, and the current level of equity-risk assets, the model suggests a "good times" level of five failures per year in 1985. However, a 5% confidence interval would imply plus or minus 24 failures around this level. Also, the equation forecasts negative levels of failures in the 1950s. These facts suggest that our model needs additional refinement to make it useful in forecasting the level at which failures are likely to settle when economic conditions become more stable. The high level of statistical significance of the estimated coefficients nonetheless suggests that variations in the independent variables have played a significant role in causing the recent rise in bank failures, and that failures will decrease if these variables return to previous levels.

References

Benston, G. J. (1973), *Bank Examination*, New York University, Graduate School of Business Administration, Institute of Finance, as the Bulletin, Nos. 89–90.

Benston, G. J., R. A. Eisenbeis, P. M, Horvitz, E. J. Kane, and G. Kaufman (1986), *Perspectives on Safe and Sound Banking*, MIT Press, Cambridge, MA.

Blair, R. D. and A. A. Heggestad (1978), "Bank Portfolio Regulation and the Probability of Bank Failure: A Note," *Journal of Money, Credit, and Banking*, February.

Board of Governors of the Federal Reserve System (1941), *Banking Studies*, Washington, DC.

Bovenzi, J. and L. Nejezchleb (1985), "Bank Failures: Why Are There So Many?" *Issues in Bank Regulation*, Winter.

Bremer, C. D. (1935), *American Bank Failures*, Columbia Univ. Press, New York.

Cates, D. C. (1985), "Management Discipline: The True Bulwark Against Banking Crisis," *Issues in Bank Regulation*, Winter.

Chan, Yuk-Shee, S. Greenbaum, and A. Thakor (1986), "Information Reusability, Competition and Bank Asset Quality," *Journal of Banking and Finance*, June.

Drabenstott, M. and Duncan (1985), "Farm Credit Problems: The Policy Choices", *Economic Review*, Federal Reserve Bank of Kansas City, March.

Federal Deposit Insurance Corporation, *Annual Report* (various dates).

Federal Reserve Bank of Richmond (1965), "Recent Bank Failures — Why?" *Monthly Review*, September, pp. 2–5.

Gambs, C. M. (1977), "Bank Failures: An Historical Perspective," *Monthly Review*, Federal Reserve Bank of Kansas City, June, pp. 10–20.

Gilbert, R. A. (1975), "Bank Failures and Public Policy," *Review*, Federal Reserve Bank of St. Louis, November.

——— (1985), "Recent Changes in Handling Bank Failures and Their Effects on the Banking Industry," Federal Reserve Bank of St. Louis, *Review*, June/July.

Kane, E. J. (1985); *The Gathering Crisis in Federal Deposit Insurance*, MIT Press, Cambridge, MA.

Keplinger, K., G. Wilson, S. Johnson, and D. Whitehead (1985), "Agricultural Banks in the Southeast: How Are They Faring?" *Economic Review*, Federal Reserve Bank of Atlanta, May.

Maisel, S. J. (Ed.) (1981), *Risk and Capital Adequacy in Commercial Banks*, University of Chicago Press, Chicago.

Melichar, E. (1986), "Agricultural Banks Under Stress," *Federal Reserve Bulletin*, July.

Rolnick, A. J. and W. E. Weber (1984), "The Causes of Free Bank Failures: A Detailed Examination," *Journal of Monetary Economics*, November.

Romer, C. (1986), "Spurious Volatility in Historical Unemployment Data," *Journal of Political Economy*, February.

Rose, P. S. and W. L. Scott (1978), "Risk in Commercial Banking: Evidence from Postwar Failures," *Southern Economic Journal*, July.

Short, E. D., G. P. O'Driscoll, Jr. and F. D. Berger (1985), "Recent Bank Failures, Determinants and Consequences," *Bank Structure and Competition*, Federal Reserve Bank of Chicago.

Sinkey, J. F. Jr. (1979), *Problem and Failed Institutions in the Commercial Banking Industry*, JAI Press, Greenwich, CT.

White, E. N. (1984), "A Reinterpretation of the Banking Crisis of 1930," *Journal of Economic History*, March.

Commentary by George G. Kaufman

In his chapter, Richard Nelson attempts to identify the causes of commercial bank failures. This is obviously a very important public policy topic in today's environment of the largest number of bank failures since the Great Depression, and represents an area where our knowledge is not what it should be. Nelson divides the potential causes of bank failures into two broad classifications: (1) internal management (which he refers to as ex ante) and (2) external market factors or states of nature (which he refers to as ex post). To test his hypotheses empirically, Nelson constructs a regression model with eight independent variables, although it is likely that there is some degree of collinearity among these variables and thus some double counting.

The results are quite satisfactory—the R^2s values range from 55 to 71%, depending on the sample period, the Durbin-Watsons are mostly not bad, and the significant coefficients have the expected signs. The estimates show that the failure rate is higher, the lower the equity-risk assets ratio (the management variable), the higher unemployment, the greater asset contraction (as a proxy for liquidity problems), and, in the post-World War II period, the sharper declines in agricultural and energy prices. There is also a dummy variable for the introduction of the Federal Deposit Insurance Corporation in 1934, which shows the failure rate to be lower afterward.

Although satisfactory, the results are not overly surprising. This study parallels work being done by, among others, Arnold Kling at the Board of Governors, Lynn Nejezchleb and his colleagues at the FDIC, and Bert Ely for the CATO Institute. Ely's work focuses on the importance of the sharp declines in farm prices and income as major contributors to the bank failures of the 1920s. Similar to these other studies, Nelson's shows that individual banks fail for basically the same reasons we know that nonbank firms fail. Nelson also shows by simulation that if the economy were to do better, the bank failure rate would decline. Thus, individual banks do not appear to be very "special," particularly with respect to the basic reasons for their failures.

My comments are mostly on what Nelson's chapter did not do and what I hope his next work will do. The really interesting and important issue for the ongoing public policy debate is not so much the reasons for individual bank failures but whether such failures can trigger nationwide (systemic) contagion of other banks, the financial system, and the economy as a whole. (Regional contagion is a different, less severe problem, and is to be expected if the states of nature are common to these banks.) The likelihood of national contagion is the major reason for considering banks unique and in need of special regulation for safety. Because Nelson does not allow for mutual interaction between bank failure and the states of nature, the chapter provides little evidence on this question one way or the other.

Nelson concludes that external market forces are a more important contributor to the bank failure rate than internal management. But recent evidence strongly suggests that the two are not independent of each other. The extant structure of federal deposit insurance affects management/owner incentives in a way that increases the possibility of bank failure, particularly in recent years. Federal deposit insurance is a two-sided sword that cuts both ways. On the one side, it has stabilized the banking system as a whole and ended the threat of nationwide contagion by effectively eliminating the incentive of depositors to run on the system as a whole by withdrawing currency from all banks and thereby starting multiple contractions in money and credit that can tumble financially sound as well as unsound banks. (Regional contagion results only in a game of musical banks where the withdrawn funds are redeposited at perceived safer banks outside the region.) On the other side, federal deposit insurance has increased individual bank risk exposure (as reflected in Nelson's capital to risk asset ratio) and therefore has increased the probabilities of bank failures by:

1. Reducing the intensity of market discipline exerted on the bank by depositors as a result of insurance per se, that is, by introducing moral hazard;

2. Mispricing the premiums by not scaling them to the insured bank's risk exposure and thus increasing the bank's reward for risk taking; and

3. Delaying the closure of economically insolvent institutions and permitting them to continue to operate on a cash-flow basis, or what used to be known in the pre-FDIC days as a Ponzi scheme.

The interaction of the same degree of external instability (same states of nature) and the greater internal risk exposure has worked to increase the number of bank failures.[1]

To curtail the incentive for additional risk taking, the bank regulatory agencies have relied primarily on restrictive regulation that limits the activities in which banks can engage. But these restrictions have reduced competition and efficiency. Alternatively, it is possible to reduce the incentive for risk taking through the market mechanism by dealing directly with each of the three sources of risk incentive as follows:

1. Depositor monitoring and discipline can be intensified by reducing the maximum dollar insurance coverage per account from $100,000 to, say, $40,000, the limit before it was increased in 1980 as part of the Depository Institutions Deregulation and Monetary Control Act (DIDMCA). At minimum, some more intensive depositor monitoring can be achieved by not increasing the maximum coverage above $100,000 either de jure or de facto.

2. The higher profit from risk taking can be reduced by charging higher insurance premiums on such ventures to offset the bank's ability to obtain insured funding at a riskless or near riskless rate, and

3. Market discipline by shareholders could be increased by declaring economically insolvent banks legally insolvent more quickly and forcing earlier recapitalization, sale, merger, or, as a last resort, liquidation. Such action would increase the cost of failure to shareholders/managers and not permit them to obtain free second chances to regain profitability on other peoples' funds, including those of the FDIC. Moreover, this would reduce the cost of failure to depositors and the FDIC. If the institution is closed precisely at the point when the market value of its net worth declines to zero — the definition of economic insolvency — there would be no losses to uninsured depositors or the deposit insurance agency. Since there would be no losses, except from fraud and insufficient monitoring, insurance premiums would be required only to cover the agency's operating expenses and thus would be able to be reduced substantially. This is not an insignificant politically appealing factor.

Any study of recent bank failures needs to address the question of why the rate of bank failures has increased so much more sharply since 1980 than both before World War II and in the post war period and is predictable from models such as Nelson's. The answer lies, in part, in the greater regional and sectional disparities in recent years that are averaged out in the aggregate national data; in part, in accelerated entry both by commercial banks into the traditional market areas of other banks and by nonbank firms into the traditional product areas of commercial banks, that has increased the number of competitors and thereby the intensity of competition (greater entry and competition by definition implies greater exit); and, in part, in the increased opportunity of bank managers/owners to place larger bets. The latter occurred for three interrelated reasons:

1. The increases in de jure insurance coverage from $40,000 to $100,000 in 1980 and in de facto coverage at a high probability to all deposits following the Continental Illinois Bank crisis in 1984 have significantly reduced the quantity and quality of depositor discipline.

2. The dramatic advances in computer and telecommunication technology in recent years have permitted the almost costless and instantaneous transfer of funds across large distances.

3. The removal of Regulation Q ceiling on time and savings deposits starting in the late 1970s has permitted risk-prone banks to bid without restriction with or without broker assistance for funds country-wide, if not world-wide, and to expand in size multifold almost overnight.[2] (Previously these banks had been restructured for funds pretty much to their nearby geographical areas, which did not permit as easy rapid growth.)

How is it that, after I have argued that federal deposit insurance encourages risk taking, Nelson's regression estimates show that the rate of bank failures decreased significantly after the introduction of the FDIC in 1934? I believe that the contradiction reflects primarily misspecification error. The bank failure rate has varied greatly from decade to decade within Nelson's sample period 1896 to 1985. The annual failure rate was about 1/2% through 1919, jumped to near 2% in the 1920s, skyrocketed to above 15% from 1930 through 1933, fell sharply again to almost 0% from 1934 through 1983, and has climbed to near 1% since 1984.[3] Thus, the pre-FDIC period is dominated by the high failure rate in the relatively brief 14-year period from 1920 through 1933. (The failure rate was also low from the end of the Civil War through 1896.) Although high, the failure rate in the 1920s was primarily limited to very small agricultural banks in primarily agricultural states. Thus, the FDIC dummy variable is in large measure picking up independent effects not specified elsewhere in the model and not the introduction of federal deposit insurance. The FDIC variable may be expected to be weaker for a longer sample period. Indeed, even within Nelson's period there is evidence of this. The FDIC dummy coefficient is statistically significant at the 10% level in Nelson's column D in table 4–3, which covers the period 1915–1949, but becomes insignificant when the period is extended back to 1896 in column C. It would be interesting to see what the coefficient would be had Nelson specified a dummy variable for the establishment of the Federal Reserve in 1914 rather than the FDIC! I suspect that it may indicate an increase in the number of failures, certainly immediately afterward. Would this prove that Milton Friedman has been right all along?

Moreover, the failure rate after the introduction of federal deposit insurance has, in part, been lower than before because of a change in the effective definition of bank failure. Before the FDIC, economically insolvent banks generally failed when a shortage of liquidity made them unable to meet deposit withdrawals.[4] After the FDIC, many of these banks were able to avoid immediate failure and to survive for considerable time and possibly even regain solvency by acquiring the necessary liquidity to meet deposit demands through attracting de jure or de facto federally insured funds. If failure were defined on a market value basis in both periods, the difference in rates would not be as stark. Indeed, for savings and loan associations, the failure rate may be higher after the establishment of the FSLIC than before!

My remaining points are quite simple. All Treasury securities should not be classified as riskless for the capital to risky asset ratio. Longer-term treasuries carry significant interest rate risk. At least in the old days, bank asset contraction occurs primarily during economic downturns and is likely to be collinear with unemployment and prices. Particularly for the 1920s and 1980s, regional and sectional data should be specified to supplement the national economic data. Last, Nelson's discussion of the differences between the actual and predicted failure rate whets the appetite and he should show, at minimum, a plot of the residuals.

In sum, this is an interesting chapter that rightfully serves as a necessary lead-in to the important public policy questions of today, such as:

- Are bank failures more important than the failure of other firms of comparable size?
- Are bank failures contagious on a nationwide basis?
- How strong are the adverse risk-taking incentives under federal deposit insurance?

- What kinds of bank management/ownership are particularly susceptible to these incentives?
- What can be done to prevent commercial banks and the FDIC from slipping into the quicksand that has entrapped the savings and loan associations and the FSLIC to a tune of almost $30 billion eventually payable by the U.S. Treasury and the taxpayer?

Notes

1. E. J. Kane (1985), *The Gathering Crisis in Federal Deposit Insurance*, MIT Press, Cambridge, MA; J. Benston et al. (1986), *Perspectives on Safe and Sound Banking*, MIT Press, Cambridge, MA.
2. Financial Corporation of America (American Savings) exploded in size from $200 million in 1978 to $34 billion in 1984, before management was changed by FSLIC. This growth rate is not that unique, particularly among currently troubled savings and loan associations in the southwest.
3. Benston et al., Chapter 2.
4. G. Kaufman (1986), "Banking Risk in Historical Perspective," *Staff Memorandum* 86–3 (Federal Reserve Bank of Chicago), August.

III RISK: AN INTERNATIONAL OVERVIEW

5 EMPIRICAL ASSESSMENT OF FOREIGN CURRENCY RISK PREMIUMS

Richard Meese

Empirical investigation into the nature and significance of exchange rate risk premiums has evolved from naive studies of the time-series properties of spot and forward exchange rates to sophisticated tests of agents' first-order conditions for expected utility maximization. Modern empirical work recognizes that any test concerning the behavior of exchange rate risk premiums is necessarily a joint hypothesis test of an equilibrium model of exchange risk and return, an assumption about expectations formation, and a set of auxiliary statistical assumptions under which formal inference proceeds. The evolution in theoretical and econometric sophistication over the past 15 years is the subject of this review. Fortunately, the task of reviewing the risk premium literature has been greatly simplified by the recent publication of a number of related survey papers.[1] In particular, this review makes considerable use of Hodrick's (1987) recent monograph, *The Empirical Evidence on the Efficiency of Forward and Future Foreign Exchange Markets.*

The author gratefully acknowledges research support from the Institute of Business and Economic Research, the Schaubaucher Fellowship, and the Berkeley Program in Finance. Joe Mattey, Maurey Obstfeld, and Andy Rose provided comments on an earlier draft.

The existence (or lack) of risk premiums in foreign exchange markets can have sharp policy implications. In some models sterilized intervention — the sale or purchase of domestic government securities for foreign government securities by the monetary authority so as to leave the monetary base unchanged — will have a direct effect on the spot exchange rate and other macroeconomic variables only when investors view domestic and foreign currency government bonds as imperfect substitutes in their portfolios.[2] It is common practice to equate the perfect substitutability of domestic and foreign assets null hypothesis and the unbiased forward rate hypothesis. The relationship between substitutability and unbiased forward rates is treated in more detail below. However, even if domestic and foreign bonds are viewed as perfect substitutes, sterilized intervention might signal information about future policy that rational agents will incorporate in current decision making. Mussa (1981) provides an analysis of this alternative channel for policy to effect exchange rates.

Following convention, we define the exchange rate risk premium or excess return as

$$P(t)=(f(t,N)-E[s(t+N)|I(t)])/s(t), \tag{5.1}$$

where $s(t+N)$ is the period $t+N$ spot rate (dollars per foreign currency units), $f(t,N)$ is the period t forward rate for delivery in period $t+N$, and $E(\cdot I(t))$ denotes expectation conditional on time t information.[3] In section 5.1, theoretical models for the unobservable risk premium (5.1) are reviewed. Some review of theoretical models of asset pricing is required to interpret the empirical work that is reviewed in section 5.2. The roles of expectation formation and the auxiliary statistical assumptions required to conduct inference are highlighted throughout the section 5.2 discussion of risk premium empirical work. The chapter concludes with suggestions for future research, section 5.3.

5.1 Theoretical Models of Exchange Rate Risk Premiums

A useful dichotomy of the modern asset market approach to exchange rate determination is to separate models with a macroeconomic foundation from those rooted in modern finance theory. The portfolio balance approach, which includes flexible and sticky price monetary exchange rate models as special cases, is an important member of the former group. While the portfolio balance models were not originally couched in terms of explicit utility-maximizing behavior, they can be rationalized on this ground under plausible assumptions.[4] The salient feature of the portfolio balance models is a set of postulated asset demand equations where rates of return and price variables are endogenous, and asset supplies are policy determined (and usually exogenous). In the empirical portfolio balance models of Frankel (1979b), Dooley and Isard (1982), and Danker et al. (1985) the risk premium can be expressed as a function of the outstanding stocks of foreign and domestic securities and wealth. In contrast, Obstfeld's (1983) portfolio balance model is driven by a political risk premium instead of an exchange rate risk premium, since the forward premium is the proxy for the expected change in the exchange rate. In this case political risk (the possibility of changes in tax codes, capital controls, default, and the like) is hypothesized to explain international portfolio diversification. While these four papers do not constitute an exhaustive list of empirical portfolio balance models, they provide a reasonable characterization of the approach.[5]

Finance-oriented models of exchange rate determination generally treat rate of return and price variables as exogenous, and focus on optimal asset demands. While the postulated asset demand equations of the portfolio balance approach are replaced by asset demands derived from micro foundations, the general equilibrium solution for rates of return and prices is lost. Optimal asset demands are derived contingent on particular stochastic specifications for prices and interest rates. Fortunately, this is an active research area, and the recent papers by Stulz (1981, 1982), Svensson (1985), Cox et al. (1985), and Froot (1986), among others, attempt to blend the optimizing approach with an explicit characterization of the factors on which prices and rate of return processes ultimately depend. The need to do so was given considerable force by the Lucas (1976) critique; asset demand equations derived from expected utility maximization are generally policy regime dependent when arbitrary asset supply and macroeconomic factor processes are postulated.

In the rest of this section attention is focused on the theoretical relation between forward and expected future spot exchange rates. Since the portfolio balance models and the class of international asset pricing models pioneered by Solnik (1974)[6] lead to conclusions about the forward rate—expected future spot rate relation that are qualitatively similar, there is some latitude in the choice of the model used to derive equilibrium asset prices. The following discussion makes use of the Lucas (1982) model as described by Hodrick and Srivastava (1984) and Hodrick (1987). While this model relies on some very restrictive assumptions, it provides considerable insight into the nature of the exchange rate risk premium (1). In this type of individual utility maximization model the equilibrium price of an asset is found by equating the foregone marginal utility from purchasing an asset to the conditional expectation of the present discounted value of the marginal utility of return from holding the asset. To price a nominal forward exchange, contract money is introduced into the real asset pricing model by the restriction that agents purchase a country's idiosyncratic endowment with that country's money. Arbitrage ensures that the N-period forward price of foreign exchange be equal to the expected present value of a known return $R(t, N)$ at time t of investing in a nominally risk-free discount bill with payoff in period $t + N$, multiplied by the spot rate that will prevail at $t + N$. The asset pricing model provides the interpretation of the discount factor as the intertemporal marginal rate of substitution (Richard and Sundaresan, 1981) between period t and $t + N$ dollars, $Q(t + N, N)$, where, for convenience, a U.S. perspective has been adopted. Thus, the forward rate can be written as

$$f(t, N) = E[Q(t + N, N) * s(t + N) * R(t, N)|I(t)]. \tag{5.2}$$

Using the definition of conditional covariance (5.2) may be rewritten as

$$f(t, N) = E[s(t + N)|I(t)] + \text{Cov}[Q(t + N, N) * R(t, N), s(t + N)|I(t)], \tag{5.3}$$

where $\text{Cov}(\cdot, \cdot I(t))$ denotes covariance conditional on the information set $I(t)$, and the derivation of (5.3) makes use of the first-order condition for utility maximization $E[Q(t + N, N) * R(t, N)|I(t)] = 1$. The second term on the right side of (5.3) has the interpretation of a risk premium, but it is useful to transform (5.3) into an equation consistent with the definition of the risk premium given in equation 5.1. This can be done by dividing both sides of (5.3) by the current spot rate. For conceptual purposes, it may be helpful to introduce a benchmark return, $R^B(t + N, N)$, defined explicitly in Hansen and Hodrick (1983) or Hodrick (1987). It is then possible to rewrite (5.3) as a conditional capital asset pricing equation (CAPM):

$$\begin{aligned} &E[(s(t + N) - f(t, N))/s(t)|I(t)] \\ &= B(t) * E[R^B(t + N, N) - R(t, N)|I(t)], \end{aligned}$$

where

$$B(t) = \frac{\text{Cov}[(s(t + N) - f(t, N))/s(t), R^B(t + N, N)|I(t)]}{\text{Var}[R^B(t + N, N)|I(t)]} \tag{5.4}$$

and $\text{Var}[\cdot|I(t)]$ denotes conditional variance.

It is worth noting that in our discussion of international asset pricing, (1) nothing requires the spot exchange rate to follow a random walk process, and (2) the existence of a risk premium is completely consistent with market efficiency and rational expectations, since the forward rate incorporates all available information but differs from the expected future spot rate. The forward rate will be an unbiased predictor of the future spot rate only when the second term on the left side of (5.3) is zero. This can arise when agents face uncertain returns from holding forward contracts that are uncorrelated with the uncertain returns of all other assets or with agents' consumption opportunities. Risk neutrality is not sufficient to produce the unbiased forward rate hypothesis in this class of intertemporal asset pricing model since it ensures only that the marginal rate of substitution of money (dollars) is not a function of consumption. In this case $Q(t + N, N)$ simplifies to the product of a discount factor times the ratio of the purchasing power of money in periods t and $t + N$. Risk neutrality guarantees that expected real profit is zero; there will still be a nominal expected profit on a forward foreign exchange position. The argument that maximization of an expected utility function of real arguments does not give rise to the unbiased forward rate hypothesis that was used to resolve Siegel's (1972) paradox.[7] The paradox, an implication of Jensen's inequality, says that if the forward rate is an unbiased predictor of the future spot rate then the same hypothesis cannot be true for exchange rates quoted in reciprocal terms.

At the risk of becoming pedantic, this section is concluded with an attempt to provide some intuition for the overview of the international asset pricing paradigm outlined above.[8] Consider a domestic individual who holds a long position in a foreign currency, that is, a forward purchase of foreign exchange. There is risk associated with this position because the future spot rate is unknown. The individual holding the long position may require compensation from the holder of the short position, that is, expected profits, if dollar denominated losses from going long tend to be realized when dollars are dear. In this example, the holder of the short position is willing to accept a position with expected loss because holding this position produces profit in the complement of the states of nature that produce profits for the holder of the long position. If the buyer of the forward foreign currency receives profits in "good" times and loss in "bad" times, then the seller receives the opposite payoff: profit in times when it is needed and losses when it can be most afforded. Thus the seller of forward foreign currency can be thought of as purchasing insurance from the buyer.

5.2 Empirical Tests of Exchange Market Risk Premiums

The theoretical asset pricing model of section 5.1 yields $f(t,n) = E[Q(t + N, N) * s(t + N) * R(t, N)|I(t)]$. If the variables in this expression for the forward rate are jointly lognormally distributed with constant (across time) conditional convariances, then

$$\ln[f(t, N)] = \text{constant} + E\{\ln[s(t + N)|I(t)]\}, \qquad (5.5)$$

where ln denotes natural logarithm. With the additional assumption of rational expectations (5.5) can be written as a regression equation:

$$\ln[s(t+N)] = a_0 + a_1 * \ln[f(t,N)] + e_1(t+N), \tag{5.6}$$

where the disturbance term (or expectations error) $e_1(t+N)$ is orthogonal to $\ln[f(t,N)]$, and $a_1 = 1$ under the composite null of (1) the asset pricing model of section 5.1, (2) jointly lognormally distributed variables with constant conditional covariances, and (3) rational expectations. In some of the published empirical work, the additional restriction $a_0 = 0$ is also imposed (incorrectly) as part of the joint null. Henceforth we will refer to this joint test as the unbiased forward rate hypothesis. Because $s(t)$ and $f(t,N)$ are in the period t information set, (5.5) also implies regression equations of the form

$$\ln[s(t+N)/s(t)] = b_0 + b_1 * \ln[f(t,N)/s(t)] + e_2(t+N), \tag{5.7a}$$

with $b_1 = 1$ under the null, and

$$\ln[s(t+N)/f(t,N)] = c_0 + c_i * X(t) + e_3(t+N), \tag{5.7b}$$

where $c_0 = a_0$, $c_i = 0$ for all variables $X(t)$ in the information set $I(t)$, and $e_3(t+N) = e_1(t+N)$ under the composite null hypothesis.

The striking result from the extant empirical research on the unbiased forward rate hypothesis is that studies based on (5.6) tend to support, while empirical papers based on (5.7a) of (5.7b) soundly reject the null. To understand this empirical anomaly it will prove useful to summarize some "stylized facts" that characterize the empirical behavior of forward and spot exchange rates:

1. The sample variance of the natural logarithm of the spot exchange rate calculated over any subinterval of the modern floating rate period is essentially equal to the sample variance of the natural logarithm of the forward exchange rate. The sample correlation coefficient between the logarithms of contemporaneous spot and forward rates of any maturity (1, 2, 3, 6, or 12 months) is near unity for any subinterval of the modern floating rate period. The comovement in contemporary spot and forward rate changes is noted by Mussa (1979, p. 14), while evidence of the near equality of sample variances and of the unit correlation between the logarithm of the levels of spot and forward rates is provided below.

2. The univariate autoregressive representations of the logarithms of the levels of spot and forward rates of any maturity have smallest root indistinguishable from unity.[9] Meese and Singleton (1982) conduct a formal test of this hypothesis for spot and three-month forward rates, but the unit root

regularity has been noted by other researchers; see Poole (1967), Giddy and Dufey (1975), Mussa (1979), and Meese and Rogoff (1983a, b), among others.

The sample means, variances, and contemporaneous spot and forward rate correlation coefficients, calculated over the period December 1977 through April 1986, are presented in table 5–1. The sample statistics are calculated using daily exchange rate observations from the Interactive Data Corporation foreign exchange data base. The evidence for empirical regularity (1.) is striking, but begs the question of why we should be interested in sample second moments when regularity (2.) suggests that the logarithms of the levels of spot and forward exchange rate do not possess finite unconditional population variances. The answer is that by themselves, these two empirical regularities explain the contradictory results from tests of the unbiased

Table 5–1. Sample First and Second Moments of the Logarithms of Spot and Forward Exchange Rates: December 1977 through April 1986 (Daily Observations)

			$\ln(f(t, N)$		$ln(s(t+N))$		
Currency	*N*	*Sample Size*	*Mean*	*Var.*	*Mean*	*Var.*	*Corr.*
Australian dollar	1	2048	−0.0151	0.0330	−0.0149	0.0321	0.9927
	3	2046	−0.0182	0.0346	−0.0148	0.0322	0.9989
	12	NA					
British pound	1	2123	0.5528	0.0446	0.5525	0.0446	0.9998
	3	2124	0.5518	0.0448	0.5525	0.0445	0.9992
	12	2114	0.5507	0.0447	0.5532	0.0446	0.9954
Canadian dollar	1	NA					
	3	2071	−0.2057	0.0045	−0.2058	0.0041	0.9685
	12	2043	−0.2079	0.0048	−0.2058	0.0041	0.9859
German mark	1	2114	−0.8261	0.0321	−0.8308	0.0320	0.9999
	3	2116	−0.8186	0.0324	−0.8309	0.0320	0.9996
	12	2110	−0.7884	0.0337	−0.8308	0.0320	0.9953
Japanese yen	1	2113	−5.421	0.0086	−5.426	0.0085	0.9993
	3	2110	−5.414	0.0088	−5.426	0.0085	0.9956
	12	2096	−5.380	0.0095	−5.426	0.0085	0.9692
Swiss franc	1	2120	−0.6761	0.0219	−0.6833	0.0215	0.9994
	3	2122	−0.6651	0.0226	−0.6834	0.0215	0.9986
	12	2045	−0.6181	0.0264	−0.6815	0.0219	0.9883

NA: Not available..

forward rate hypothesis based on formulations (5.6) and (5.7a, b). The explanation is simplified by the assumption that the sampling interval is the same as the forward contract length, $N = 1$.[10] Empirical regularity (1.) suggests that the slope coefficient from a regression of contemporaneous $\ln[s(t)]$ and $\ln[f(t, N = 1)]$ (or the reverse regression) will be one because the sample regression coefficient is equal to sample correlation coefficient when both variables have the same sample variance. That the estimate of a_1 in (5.6) is also going to be close to one can be shown through reference to cointegration.[11] Consider the following stochastic model for spot and forward rates that is completely consistent with regularities (1., 2.):

$$\ln[s(t)] - d * \ln[f(t, N = 1)] = e_4(t) \tag{5.8a}$$

$$\ln[s(t)] - \ln[s(t-1)] = e_5(t), \tag{5.8b}$$

where the process $[e_4(t), e_5(t)]$ has zero mean, covariance matrix $V = \{v(i,j)\}$ for $i, j = 4, 5$, and can be serially correlated. To be consistent with our stylized facts d must be near one.[12] Rearranging (5.8), we can obtain an expression for the future spot aligned with its corresponding forward rate.

$$\ln[s(t+1)] = d * \ln[f(t, N = 1)] + e_4(t) + e_5(t+1). \tag{5.9}$$

Equation 5.9 is not a legitimate regression equation. Since the regressor is correlated with the composite disturbance. However, when there exists a common stochastic trend (unit root) in the $\ln[s(t+1)]$ and $\ln[f(t, N+1)]$ processes, the ordinary least-squares estimator of d in (5.9) converges to d at such a rapid rate that the simultaneous equations bias can be ignored.[14] Because of the (near) unit root in spot and forward rates, the (near) equality of their sample variances, and their (near) unit sample correlation coefficient, we are guaranteed a finding of a_1 equal to d equal to a number close to one when estimating regression models of the form (5.6). In the jargon of cointegration, $s(t+1)$ and $f(t, N = 1)$ are CI(1, 0) with cointegrating constant near one.

Meese and Singleton (1982) conduct a formal test for a unit root in the $\ln[s(t+N)/f(t, N)]$ process for the Swiss franc, Canadian dollar, and the German mark using three-month forward contracts and weekly data, January 1976 to July 1981. They provide evidence against the null hypothesis of a unit root. A new way of interpreting this result is to say that $\ln[s(t+N)]$ and $\ln[f(t, N)]$ are cointegrated with a cointegrating constant of one. Much of the early empirical work on the relation between the levels of spot and forward rates can be reinterpreted as attempts to estimate the cointegrating constant. For example, take Tryon's (1979) empirical results for regressions of the form (5.6) using the British pound, French franc, Swiss franc, Italian lira, German mark, and Japanese yen relative to the dollar over the period March

1973 to December 1978. In Tryon (1979, Table 1) estimates of a_1 in (5.6) range from 0.843 to 0.992 with Durbin-Watson statistics (imputed from the residual first-order autocorrelation coefficients) that range from 0.928 to 1.518. We can thus infer, using Engle and Granger (1987, Table II), that the disturbance is stationary or equivalently, that $s(t+1)$ and $f(t, N = 1)$, are cointegrated with a cointegrating constant in the neighborhood of one.

If we consider the unbiased forward rate regression (5.7b) in light of representation (5.9), it should be clear that the forecast error $\ln(s(t+1)/f(t, N \doteq 1))$ can be serially correlated, so our empirical regularities (1., 2.) do not necessarily suggest that c_i will be close to zero when $X(t)$ contains lagged values of the dependent variable. Also, the unbiased forward rate regression (5.7a) can be interpreted as a regression of $e_5(t)$ on $[-e_4(t)]$ of (5.8a, b) when $d = 1$. Again our empirical regularities (1., 2.) do not necessarily suggest that b_1 will be equal to one, since the covariance of the $[e_4(t), e_5(t)]$ process is not restricted by regularities (1., 2.).

While the recent development of the properties of estimators in cointegrated systems now provides an explanation of the near unit coefficient in regressions of the form (5.6), earlier researchers acknowledged the fact that a unit root in the spot and forward rate processes would invalidate standard asymptotic distribution theory for tests of $a_1 = 1$ in (5.6). With this type of consideration in mind, Geweke and Feige (1979), Tryon (1979), and Hansen and Hodrick (1980) were careful to test the unbiased forward rate (UBFR) hypothesis using an implication of the relation that was more likely to accord with the requirements of the large sample distribution theory. Their tests, based on variants of (5.7a, b), and a number of subsequent papers,[14] have established beyond all reasonable doubt that the composite unbiased forward rate hypothesis is statistically inconsistent with the data. The strongest evidence against the null obtains when $X(t)$ is chosen to include lagged values of the regressand in (5.7) or lagged values of the dependent variable for related currencies. Last, it is important to remember that the results of these studies must always be interpreted in light of the usual 'peso problem" caveat: the possibility that expectations about some event—which may or may not occur outside the sample period—affect variables within the sample period.[15]

5.2.1 *Empirical Significance of Exchange Market Risk Premiums*

The profession has reacted to the statistical rejection of the UBFR hypothesis in roughly four ways. The first reaction is one of skepticism based on either the peso problem, the lack of small sample distribution theory for the sophisticated econometric artillery that has been aimed at the null hypothesis,[16] or the possibility that uncertainty caused by government policy creates temporary periods of skewness in the distribution of future exchange returns. In addition, less restrictive models of the risk premium have thus far met with limited empirical success. Since elegant finance models have not produced successful empirical accounts of time-varying risk premiums, the skeptics argue that there is scant economic evidence against the UBFR hypothesis.

A second reaction to the statistical rejection of the UBFR hypothesis is characterized by a more scientific assessment of its economic significance. Using a single-period utility maximization model (see note 4) Frankel (1986) argues that the risk premium cannot by itself explain the significant autocorrelation in forward rate prediction errors (nonzero c_i in (5.7b) when $X(t)$ includes lagged values of the dependent variable). In the simple two-asset (dollars and pounds) version of Frankel's (1986) one-period model we can express a function of the risk premium (5.1), $s(t) * P(t)$, as

$$\ln[f(t, N = 1)] - E\{\ln[s(t+1)] | I(t)\} = \text{constant} + p * \text{Var}\{[i(t) - i(t)^*] | I(t)\} * Y(t), \qquad (5.10)$$

where p is the coefficient of relative risk aversion, $[i(t) - i(t)^*]$ is the U.S. minus U.K. interest differential (excess asset return), and $Y(t)$ is the proportion of dollar assets in the investor's portfolio. If we assume the conditional variance of the excess asset return is constant and equal to u, (5.10) implies that the variance of the risk premium is equal to $(p * u)^2$ times the variance of $Y(t)$. Frankel (1986) uses $p = 2$, estimates u to be 0.01 per annum, and deduces that the standard error of the risk premium is roughtly 2% of the standard error of $Y(t)$. In addition, Frankel (1986) uses the implications of mean-variance optimization to deduce the value of the regression coefficient on a single lag value of the dependent variable in a regression of the form (5.7b), and concludes that the variance of the risk premium is much too small to account for the observed values of this regression coefficient. The argument is quite convincing if one accepts the maintained hypothesis that the conditional variance of the excess asset return is constant. Giovannini and Jorion (1986) and table 5–2 below provide evident against the conditional homoskedasticity of returns assumption. The best out-of-sample forecasting model for second moments of exchange returns presented in table 5–2 appears to be simple exponential smoothing, an ARIMA(0, 1, 1) model.[17] These results imply that time variation in u is sufficient to explain the observed values of the regression coefficient on a lagged forecast error in (5.7b). Finally, Frankel's (1986) model is a special case of the theoretical asset pricing model considered in section 5.1: the multiperiod utility maximization problem reduces to the single-period problem when preferences are logarithmic or asset returns are intertemporally independent.

Fama (1984), Hodrick and Srivastava (1986), and Cumby (1986) provide different assessments of the economic significance of the statistical rejection of the UBFR hypothesis. The authors of the first two papers construct a lower bound on the variance of the risk premium using the identity,

$$[f(t, N) - s(t)]/s(t) = E\{[s(t+N) - s(t)]/s(t) \mid I(t)\} + P(t), \tag{5.11}$$

or using uppercase letters to simplify notation.

$$F(t, N) = E[S(t+N) \mid I(t)] + P(t). \tag{5.11'}$$

Table 5–2A. Exchange Rate Return Second Moments: Monthly Exchange Returns Calculated from Daily Observations over the Period December 1977 through April 1986[a]

	Maximum Values					
Australian dollar	36.24					
British pound	0.94	45.23				
Canadian dollar	0.81	0.85	14.80			
German mark	0.93	0.96	0.82	49.87		
Japanese yen	0.93	0.93	0.77	0.96	23.78	
Swiss franc	0.93	0.94	0.83	0.99	0.95	42.28
	Minimum Values					
Australian dollar	1.70					
British pound	−0.46	2.42				
Canadian dollar	−0.46	−0.63	0.76			
German mark	−0.63	−0.42	−0.72	2.72		
Japanese yen	−0.34	−0.65	−0.72	−0.21	2.74	
Swiss franc	−0.47	−0.37	−0.65	−0.20	−0.04	3.02
	Average Values					
Australian dollar	6.69					
British pound	0.34	10.91				
Canadian dollar	0.19	0.25	4.03			
German mark	0.37	0.60	0.26	11.06		
Japanese yen	0.42	0.43	0.22	0.62	9.89	
Swiss franc	0.38	0.58	0.27	0.81	0.63	13.07

[a] Monthly return standard deviations run down the diagonal, and monthly correlations are displayed off the diagonal. A daily rate of return is defined as $[s(t) - s(t-1)]/s(t-1)$ for t in the same month. All monthly return standard devaiations are expressed as annual percentages and are calculated as if daily returns within a month constitute a random sample.

Table 5–2B. Root Mean Square Prediction Errors for Time Series Models of Return Standard Deviation[a]

Horizon (month)	*(1) Random Walk*	*(2) Exponential Smoothing*	*(3) Constant Only*	*(4) Univariate Autoregression*
		Australian Dollar		
1	10.27	7.60	9.23	8.10
12	11.00	8.99	10.43	12.33
		Canadian Dollar		
1	2.08	1.96	2.02	1.96
12	2.78	2.45	2.10	2.19
		British Pound		
1	7.31	5.77	6.40	6.07
12	8.64	7.02	7.40	8.86
		German Mark		
1	7.72	5.63	6.28	6.07
12	7.35	6.77	7.21	7.14
		Japanese Yen		
1	5.93	4.42	4.53	4.73
12	6.30	5.49	5.00	5.09
		Swiss Franc		
1	9.15	6.75	6.64	6.61
12	9.57	7.22	7.38	7.30

[a] All models were initially estimated over the first 50 observations. Prediction errors are calculated using rolling regression over the final 50 observations. The time-series models are (1) a random walk without drift, (2) simple exponential smoothing, an ARIMA (0, 1, 1), (3) the (10%) trimmed sample mean, and (4) an unconstrained univariate autoregression with lag length estimated by Akaike's AIC.

Equation 5.11 implies that the variance of the forward premium $F(t, N)$ equals the variance of the risk premium plus two times the covariance of $E[S(t+N)|I(t)]$ and $P(t)$. Equation 5.11 also implies

$$\begin{aligned}\mathrm{Cov}[F(t, N), S(t+N)] = {} & \mathrm{Cov}\{E[S(t+N)|I(t)], S(t+N)\} \\ & + \mathrm{Cov}\{P(t), E[S(t+N)|I(t)]\}. \qquad (5.12)\end{aligned}$$

Invoking rational expectations, (5.12) can be rewritten as

$$\mathrm{Cov}[F(t,N), S(t+N)] = \mathrm{Var}\{E[S(t+N)|I(t)]\} + \mathrm{Cov}\{P(t), E[S(t+N)|I(t)]\}. \tag{5.13}$$

The left side of (5.13) is measurable, while the two components of the right side are not. Since the variance of the expected rate of depreciation is nonnegative, the Fama (1984) and Hodrick and Srivastava (1986) findings of a statistically significant negative value for the left side of (5.13) (a negative value of b_1 in (5.7a), for example) implies $\mathrm{Cov}\{P(t), E[S(t+N)|I(t)]\} < 0$ and larger in absolute value than the variance of the expected rate of depreciation. Finally, this last result in conjunction with the variance decomposition of (5.11) implies that the variance of the risk premium exceeds the variance of the expected rate of depreciation.[18]

Cumby (1986) tests and rejects the hypothesis of no ex ante real profits (risk neutrality) from forward speculation. He then examines the hypothesis that the real ex ante returns to forward speculation are consistent with the consumption based model of the risk premium outlined in section 5.1. He finds that these ex ante real returns are qualitatively but not fully explained by the consumption-based models of the foreign exchange risk premium, even when conditional covariances of returns are allowed to vary across time.

How can we reconcile the conclusions drawn by Frankel (1986) with those of Fama (1984), Hodrick and Srivastava (1986), or Cumby (1986)? The answer may lie in the third reaction to the statistical rejection of the UBFR hypothesis: some researchers interpret this rejection as an indictment of the rational expectations hypothesis. In two recent papers Frankel and Froot (1985, 1986a) use survey data collected by the American Express Banking Corporation, the Economist Financial Report, and Money Market Services to test models of investors' expectations formation. In the first paper the authors find that investors' expectations are unconditionally biased forecasts of the actual spot exchange rate process, with the direction of bias strongly dependent on the sample period analyzed. Also, the exchange rate expectations data indicate considerable dispersion in investors' estimates of future spot exchange rates.

In their second paper Frankel and Froot (1986a) use the survey data to interpret the various tests of the UBFR hypothesis and the subsequent attempts to quantify the risk premium (5.1). The authors decompose the coefficient b_1 in equation 5.7a into its value under the null hypothesis (one) minus two additional terms. The first arises from any failure of rational expectations and the second arises from the risk premium. The survey data make both terms observable, and Frankel and Froot (1986a) find that the majority of the deviation from the UBFR hypothesis consists of systematic expectations errors. In all three surveys the expectations errors exhibit bias of an opposite sign to estimates of the risk premium implied by the survey data. Frankel and Froot (1986a) still find that risk premiums are large in absolute value and statistically different from zero. While the authors corroborate the Fama (1984) and Hodrick and Srivastava (1986) conclusion that expected depreciation and the risk premium are negatively correlated, they do not find that the variance of expected depreciation is less than the variance of the risk premium implied by survey data.

We conclude this subsection with a discussion of the last set of reactions to the statistical rejection of the UBFR hypothesis. This statistical rejection in conjunction with the inability of finance-oriented models to fully explain the empirical behavior of risk premiums has led some authors to conclude that exchange markets may be inefficient. The possibility of exchange market bubbles provides yet another possible explanation of the statistical findings; this subject is pursued in the final section and in the discussion of this chapter by Obstfeld (1986).[19] The conclusion of market inefficiency is based on analyses of the profitability of trading rule strategies that have been applied to finely sampled exchange rate data. This line of research has been pursued by Dooley and Shafer (1976, 1983), Logue et al. (1978), Cornell and Dietrich (1978), Bilson (1981), Sweeney and Lee (1985), and Sweeney (1986a, b), among others.

Dooley and Shafer (1976, 1983) were the first to examine the profitability of transaction cost adjusted (and interest rate adjusted) filter rule profits from taking daily open positions in the foreign exchange market.[20] They find evidence of filter rule profits in both the early and more recent years of the modern floating rate period. To assess whether these profits represent abnormal returns requires a model of risk and return. Sweeney's (1986a) paper compares transaction cost-adjusted filter rule profits to a buy and hold strategy, since a single-period CAPM (or a more general asset pricing model) predicts no returns from the active trading rule strategy in excess of buy and hold.[21] His statistical results are inconsistent with market efficiency if the risk premium is constant over time. Sweeney and Lee (1985) use the results of Fama (1984) and Hodrick and Srivastava (1986) to construct a trading strategy based on the negative correlation between the forward premium and subsequent change in the spot rate (a negative b_1 in (5.7a)). Simulations reveal significant profits from this strategy if it is again assumed that the risk premiums are constant over time.

To assess the extent that time-varying risk premiums in forward rates explain the profitability of trading rule strategies, Sweeney (1986b) conducts additional tests that examine whether exchange market risk premiums contain elements of nonsystematic risk in models that allow time variation in β (the $B(t)$ term in equation 5.4), but maintain a constant risk premium on the market or benchmark portfolio in (5.4). Again, his results indicate the possibility of earning positive (ex ante) economic profits from trading rule speculation. The evidence presented in table 5.2 is inconsistent with constant currency β's because both return variances and correlations appear to be time dependent. However, there is also ample evidence of time variation in the risk premium on the market, suggesting the need to estimate consumption based asset pricing models, as in Cumby (1986), that allow both β's and conditional second moments to vary across time.

In a recent paper Bollerslev et al. (1985), also suggest a procedure for estimating CAPMs with time-varying conditional moments.[22] The procedure assumes that the coefficient of relative risk aversion is a constant parameter; conditional covariances and β's are allowed to vary across time, but β's are not directly estimated. In fact, the authors demonstrate that tests of the CAPM using unconditional means and covariances of returns will almost surely fail, because the model will hold for unconditional moments in only very restrictive circumstances. Last, the assumption of a consant utility function parameter makes much more economic sense than the assumption of a constant β. The only drawback to the approach taken by Bollerslev et al. stems from its reliance on a single-period framework.

5.3 Some Conclusions

This chapter provides a cursory review of the theoretical and empirical literature on exchange market risk premiums. While it appears that current econometric techniques are sufficiently powerful to reject the unbiased forward rate (UBFR) hypothesis at very small significance levels, attempts to empirically characterize exchange market risk premiums have met with only limited success. Throughout our review an attempt has been made to highlight the difficulties that confront empirical risk premium research. A partial list of problems includes (1) reliance on the rational expectations hypothesis when survey data suggest the importance of expectations errors when assessing deviations from the UBFR hypothesis; (2) the possibility that a peso problem, process switching,[23] or government intervention subverts the interpretation of the empirical analysis; (3) the need to jointly consider a particular asset pricing paradigm when conducting empirical tests for risk premiums; (4) the absence of small sample distribution theory for many of the sophisticated estimators that are used to study foreign currency risk premiums, (5) the fact that statistical inference is complicated by the particular types of nonstationarities present in both the level (or logarithm) of spot and forward rate data and foreign currency returns; and (6) the possibility that variables omitted from the econometricians' analysis are fundamental determinants of the behavior of foreign currencies. The last point is closely related to the second, and it also includes the recent literature on asset market bubbles.

Our survey attempts to cover foreign currency risk premium empirical work over the past 15 years. The ability of researchers to deal with nonstationarities in both the level (or logarithm) of spot and forward rates and currency returns (point 6) has increased markedly over this period. Econometric models now allow us to account for time variation in conditional second moments of asset returns, and the development of cointegration has provided the profession with a better understanding of the consequences of nonstationarity in the mean of the variables under analysis. GARCH models are natural statistical models to use in the study of asset market data, since it has been clear for some time that exchange markets (as well as domestic stock, commodity, and bond markets) exhibit extended periods of both excessive and diminutive volatility.[24]

Many researchers believe that asset markets exhibit volatility in excess of market fundamentals.[25] Bubbles and irrationality of market participants are two explanations of excess volatility that have received some attention. Bubbles have been defined in the context of forward-looking rational expectations models of asset prices where no natural transversality condition exists (Flood and Garber, 1980). However, the type of trader over reaction documented by French and Roll (1984) in the U.S. stock market (and found by behavioral psychologists in experimental studies[26], is not captured by the explosive dynamics implied by a rational asset market bubble. It is unlikely that this solution indeterminacy bubble will provide much insight into the nature of the important dynamic aspects of any speculative price movements in exchange markets, as convincingly demonstrated by Obstfeld (1986) in his comments on this chapter. Additional avenues for future research might include (1) the investigation of heterogeneous investor expectations (see the evidence offered by Frankel and Froot (1985)), (2) the use of models in which agents behave in a near rational manner,[27] or (3) the construction of exchange rate models where portfolio preference is more directly related to political environments, differential taxation, and country-specific macropolicies.

Notes

1. A partial list of recent surveys includes Adler and Dumas (1983), Branson and Henderson (1985), Isard (1986), Levich (1985), Obstfeld and Stockman (1985), Caramazza et al. (1986), and the staff studies of the Board of Governors of the Federal Reserve System, papers 126–135. The latter papers summarize an extensive research program undertaken by members of the Federal Reserve System to study the effects of exchange market intervention. The *Federal Reserve Bulletin* (November 1983) provides a summary of these staff studies.

2. Private sector bonds net out of the analysis, and government bonds can be considered outside assets to the extent that private agents do not include future tax liabilities generated by the government debt in their portfolio decisions. See Stockman (1979) for a model that utilizes the Ricardian equivalence proposition to demonstrate the ineffectiveness of sterilized intervention even when government bonds are imperfect substitutes.

3. The following notation convention will be followed. A single time index indicates the date that a variable enters agents' information set. Double-time indexes are required to describe variables whose time dimension exceeds the observation interval; the first index indicates the date that a variable enters the information set, while the second indicates time duration. It will be clear from the context whether a variable is forward or backward looking based on the time it enters the information set.

4. See, for example, Krugman (1981) or Frankel (1982, 1983). If investors maximize single-period utility that is a function of mean and variance of end of period wealth, asset demands can be written as linear functions of expected relative rates of return. However, the slope coefficients exhibit nonlinear dependence on the coefficient of relative risk aversion and the covariance matrix of relative rates of return.

5. See also Artus (1976), Kouri and Porter (1977), and Branson (1977, 1979), among others.

6. Contributors to the international asset pricing literature also include Grauer et al. (1976), Kouri (1977), Stockman (1978), Fama and Farber (1979), Frankel (1979a), Roll and Solnik (1979), Dornbusch (1983), Frenkel and Razin (1980), Hodrick (1981), Stulz (1981, 1982), Lucas (1982), Hodrick and Srivastava (1984), and Svensson (1985), among others.

7. See Roper (1975), Stockman (1978), Frankel (1979a), Frenkel and Razin (1980), Adler and Dumas (1983), and Engel (1984), among others.

8. This intuitive discussion parallels an early version of Hodrick and Srivastava (1986). In their published version the intuitive discussion was excised.

9. For an arbitrary time series $x(t)$, the univariate autoregressive (AR) representation $x(t) = C(0) + C(1) * x(t-1) + \ldots + C(k) * x(t-k) + \text{error}(t) = C(L) * x(t) + \text{error}(t)$, where $C(L)$ is a kth-degree polynomial in the lag operator L, is stable if the roots of $C(L)$ lie outside the unit circle. In the case of $k = 1$ this translates into the usual condition $|C(1)| < 1$ for stability. A single unit root in the AR polynomial $C(L)$ means that a stable autoregressive representation exists for the difference of $x(t)$ and $x(t-1)$. The $x(t)$ process is then said to be integrated of order 1.

10. In this case the error term is serially uncorrelated. Allowing for a finer sampling interval than the length of the forward contract (e.g., weekly exchange rate data on one-month foreign exchange contracts) introduces a moving average (MA) component in the error term that will not affect the discussion below. See Hansen and Hodrick (1980) for further discussion, and an econometric procedure that accounts for the MA error component.

11. Two time series are said to be cointegrated of order $f(1)$ and $f(2)$, denoted CI[$f(1), f(2)$], if each time series is integrated of order $f(1)$, and a linear combination of the two time series is integrated of order $f(1) - f(2)$. See Engle and Granger (1987) for precise details.

12. The near equality of sample variances of the logarithms of spot and forward rates also

suggest limitations on the ratio of $v(4, 4)$ to $v(5, 5)$. For our sample of daily observations, the estimate of $v(5, 5)$ is of the same order of magnitude as $v(4, 4)$ when $d=1$.

13. Stock (1987) provides the formal argument. Simulation evidence presented in Mattey and Meese (1986) suggests that a sample of size 100 is sufficient to rely on Stock's (1987) asymptotic results.

14. See also Bilson (1981), Hakkio (1981), Baillie et al. (1983), Hansen and Hodrick (1983), Cumby and Obstfeld (1984), and Hsieh (1984), among others.

15. See Rogoff (1979) or Krasker (1980).

16. Since error terms in regressions of the form (5.6) and (5.7a, b) typically exhibit conditional heteroskedasticity as well as serial correlation (when the length of the forward contract exceeds the sampling interval), procedures for testing the UBFR hypothesis typically employ a sophisticated covariance matrix estimator. The small sample properties of this estimator have not been adequately explored. See MacKinnon and White (1985) or Mattey and Meese (1986) for simulation experiments employing the heteroskedasticity and autocorrelation consistent covariance matrix estimators typically used in tests of the UBFR hypothesis. Cumby and Obstfeld (1984) provide evidence of conditional heteroskedasticity in exchange rate data.

17. The notation ARIMA(0, 1, 1) refers to a time-series model of the form $x(t)-x(t-1)= g(0) + \text{error}\ (t) + g(1) * \text{error}\ (t-1)$, where the g's are parameters and the error term has the usual properties.

18. The finding of a negative correlation between the expected rate of change of the spot exchange rate and the risk premium was originally regarded by Fama (1984) as a puzzle, since it appears reasonable to associate higher required expected nominal return on a dollar investment with a larger expected dollar depreciation. However, this negative correlation is perfectly consistent with the theoretical asset pricing model reviewed in section 5.1, as demonstrated by Hodrick and Srivastava (1986).

19. Papers that investigate the possibility of exchange market bubbles include Evans (1986), Meese (1986), West (1985), and Woo (1984). See Obstfeld and Rogoff (1983, 1986) for a critique of these procedures.

20. Institutional features of foreign exchange markets require that filter rule studies account for interest rates between exchange rate settlement periods. However, it is difficult to find matching, high-quality interest rate data. Sweeney's (1986a) evidence suggests that the filter rule profits depend primarily on exchange rate behavior and not on interest rate differentials.

21. The filter rule used in these studies exploits any positive serial correlation that exists in exchange rate changes. Once the spot exchange rate moves $x\%$ past its last local minimum or maximum, the strategy calls for a position reversal. If the dollar had been appreciating relative to the mark, then once the \$/DM exchange rises $x\%$ past its previous minimum, all funds are transferred from dollar to mark denominated assets.

22. These authors use a multivariate generalized autoregressive conditional heteroskedastic (GARCH) in the mean model. See Engle (1982) for the econometric development of the univariate ARCH model, and Domowitz and Hakkio (1985) for a univariate application of an ARCH model to foreign exchange markets.

23. See Flood and Garber (1983) for further discussion.

24. The GARCH models are also consistent with fat-tailed or leptokurtic distributions of asset returns. See Friedman and Vandersteel (1982) for a documentation of the statistical properties of foreign exchange returns.

25. See, for example, the recent research on stock prices and interest rates by LeRoy and Porter (1981), Shiller (1981a, b), and Singleton (1980). For a critique of these papers see Flavin (1983), Kleidon (1986a, b), and the simulation results of Mattey and Meese (1986). Analogous tests for exchange markets have been proposed and implemented by Meese and Singleton (1983) and Huang (1981), among others.

26. See the paper and literature cited by DeBondt and Thalėr (1985). A typical finding from these experimental studies is that agents tend to overreact to new information when revising forecasts of an ongoing process.

27. For a discussion of near rational models of economic behavior see Akerlof and Yellen (1985).

References

Adler, M. and B. Dumas (1983), "International Portfolio Choice and Corporation Finance: A Survey," *Journal of Finance*, **38**, 925–984.

Akerlof, G. and J. Yellen (1985), "Can Small Deviations from Rationality Make Significant Differences to Economic Equilibria? *American Economic Review*, **75**, 708–720.

Artus, J. (1976), "Exchange Rate Stability and Managed Floating: The Experience of the Federal Republic of Germany, *International Monetary Fund Staff Papers*, **23**, 312–333.

Baillie, R., R. Lippens, and P. McMahon (1983), "Testing Rational Expectations and Efficiency in the Foreign Exchange Market," *Econometrica*, **51**, 553–564.

Bilson, J. (1981), "The Speculative-Efficiency Hypothesis," *Journal of Business*, **55**, 435–451.

Board of Governors of the Federal Reserve System, Staff Studies Nos. 126–135.

Bollerslev, T., R. Engle, and J. Wooldridge (1985), "A Capital Asset Pricing Model with Time Varying Covariances," University of California, San Diego, mimeo.

Branson, W. and D. Henderson (1985), "The Specification and Influence of Asset Markets," in R. Jones and P. Kenen (Eds.), *Handbook of International Economics*, Vol. 2, Elsevier Science, Amsterdam, pp. 749–804.

Branson, W., Halttunen, and P. Masson (1977), "Exchange Rates in the Short Run: The Dollar–Deutschemark Rate," *European Economic Review*, **10**, 303–324.

——— (1979), "Exchange Rates in the Short Run: Some Further Results," *European Economic Review*, **12**, 395–402.

Caramazza, F., K. Clinton, A. Cote, and D. Longworth (1986), "International Capital Mobility and Asset Substitutability: Some Theory and Evidence on Recent Structural Changes," Bank of Canada Technical Reports No. 44.

Cornell, W. and J. Dietrich (1978), "The Efficiency of the Market for Foreign Exchange Under Floating Exchange Rate," *Review of Economics and Statistics*, **60**, 111–120.

Cox, J., J. Ingersol, and S. Ross (1985), "An Intertemporal General Equilibrium Model of Asset Prices," *Econometrica* 53; 363–384.

Cumby, R. (1986), "Is It Risk? Explaining Deviations from Uncovered Interest Parity," New York University mimeo.

Cumby, R. and M. Obstfeld (1984), "International Interest-Rate and Price-Level Linkages under Flexible Exchange Rate: A Review of Recent Evidence," in J. Bilson and R. Marston (Eds.), *Exchange Rates: Theory and Practice*, University of Chicago Press, Chicago.

Danker, D., R. Haas, D. Henderson, S. Symansky, and R. Tryon (1985). "Small Empirical Models of Exchange Market Intervention: Applications to Germany, Japan, and Canada," Board of Governors of the Federal Reserve System Staff Studies No. 135.

DeBondt, W. and R. Thaler (1985), "Does the Stock Market Overreact?" *Journal of Finance*, **40**, 793–805.

Domowitz, I. and C. Hakkio (1985), "Conditional Variance and the Risk Premium in the Foreign Exchange Market," *Journal of International Economics*, **19**, 47–66.

Dooley, M. and P. Isard (1982), "A Portfolio-Balance Rational Expectations Model of the Dollar–Mark Exchange Rate," *Journal of International Economics*, **12**, 257–276.

Dooley, M. and J. Shafer (1976), "Analysis of Short-Run Exchange Rate Behavior, March 1973 to September 1975," Board of Governors of the Federal Reserve International Finance Discussion Paper No. 76.

——— (1983), "Analysis of Short-Run Exchange Rate Behavior, March 1973 to November 1981," in D. Bigman and T. Taya (Eds.), *Exchange Rate and Trade Instability*, Ballinger.

Dornbusch, R. (1983), "Exchange Rate Risk and the Macroeconomics of Exchange Rate Determination," in R. Hawkins, R. Levich, and C. Wihlborg (Eds.), *The Internationalization of Financial Markets and National Economic Policy*, JAI Press.

Engel, C. (1984), "Testing for the Absence of Expected Real Profits from Forward Market Speculation," *Journal of International Economics*, **17**, 299–308.

Engle, R. (1982), "Autoregressive Conditional Heteroskedasticity with Estimates of the Variance of U.K. Inflation." *Econometrica*, **50**, 987–1008.

Engle, R. and C. Granger (1987), "Cointegration and Error Correction: Representation, Estimation and Testing," *Econometrica*, **55**, 251–276.

Evans, G. (1986), "A Test for Speculative Bubbles and the Sterling–Dollar Exchange Rate: 1981–84, "*American Economic Review*, **76**, 621–636.

Fama, E. (1984), "Forward and Spot Exchange Rates," *Journal of Monetary Economics*, **14**, 319–388.

Fama, E. and A. Farber (1979), "Money, Bonds and Foreign Exchange," *The American Economic Review*, **69**, 639–349.

Federal Reserve Bulletin (November 1983).

Flavin, M. (1983), "Excess Volatility in the Financial Markets: A Reassessment of the Empirical Evidence," *Journal of Political Economy*, **91**, 929–956.

Flood, R. and P. Garber (1980), "Market Fundamentals versus Price-Level Bubbles: The First Tests," *Journal of Political Economy*, **88**, 745–770.

——— (1983), "A Model of Stochastic Process Switching," *Econometrica*, **51**, 537–552.

Frankel, J. (1979a), "The Diversifiability of Exchange Risk," *Journal of International Economics*, **9**, 379–393.

——— (1979b), "A Test of the Existence of the Risk Premium in the Foreign Exchange Market versus the Hypothesis of Perfect Substitutability," Board of Governors of the Federal Reserve International Finance Discussion Paper No. 149.

——— (1982), "In Search of the Exchange Risk Premium: A Six-Currency Test Assuming Mean-Variance Optimization," *Journal of International Money and Finance*, **1**, 255–274.

——— (1983), "Estimation of Portfolio-Balance Functions That Are Mean-Variance Optimizing: The Mark and the Dollar," *European Economic Review*, **23**, 315–327.
——— (1986), "The Implications of Mean-Variance Optimization for Four Questions in International Macroeconomics," *Journal of International Money and Finance*, **5**, (Suppl.), s53–s75.
Frankel, J. and K. Froot (1985), "Using Survey Data to Test Standard Propositions Regarding Exchange Rate Expectations," NBER working paper No. 1672.
——— (1986a), "Interpreting Tests of Forward Discount Bias Using Survey Data on Exchange Rate Expectations," University of California, Berkeley, mimeo.
——— (1986b), "The Dollar as a Speculative Bubble: A Tale of Chartists and Fundamentalists," University of California, Berkeley, mimeo.
French, K. and R. Roll (1984), "Stock Return Variances: The Arrival of Information and Reaction of Traders," University of California, Los Angeles, mimeo.
Frenkel, J. and A. Razin (1980), "Stochastic Prices and Tests of Efficiency of Foreign Exchange Markets," *Economic Letters*, **6**, 165–170.
Friedmen, D. and S. Vandersteel (1982), "Short Run Fluctuations in Foreign Exchange Rates: Evidence from the Data, 1973–79," *Journal of International Economics*, **13**, 171–186.
Froot, K. (1986), "Currency Values in a Continuous Time Capital Asset Pricing Model Driven by Asset Supplies," Ph.D. dissertation, University of California, Berkeley.
Geweke, J. and E. Feige (1979), "Some Joint Tests of the Efficiency of the Markets for Forward Foreign Exchange," *Review of Economics and Statistics*, **61**, 334–341.
Giddy, I. and M. Dufey (1975), "The Random Behavior of Flexible Exchange Rates," *Journal of International Business Studies*, **6**, 1–32.
Giovannini, A. and P. Jorion (1986), "Interest Rates and Risk Premia in the Stock Market and in the Foreign Exchange Market," Columbia University mimeo.
Grauer, F., R. Litzenberger, and R. Stehle (1976), "Sharing Rules and Equilibrium in an International Capital Market with Uncertainty," *Journal of Financial Economics*, **3**, 233–256.
Hakkio, G. (1981), "The Term Structure of the Forward Premium," *Journal of Monetary Economics*, **8**, 41–58.
Hansen L. and R. Hodrick (1980), "Forward Exchange Rates as Optimal Predictors of Future Spot Rates: An Econometric Analysis," *Journal of Political Economy*, **88**, 828–853.
——— (1983), "Risk Averse Speculation in the Forward Foreign Exchange Market: An Econometric Analysis of Linear Models," in J. Frenkel (Ed.), *Exchange Rates and International Macroeconomics*, University of Chicago Press, Chicago.
Hodrick, R. (1981), "International Asset Pricing with Time-Varying Risk Premia," *Journal of International Economics*, **11**, 573–577.
——— (1987), *The Empirical Evidence on the Efficiency of Forward and Future Foreign Exchange Markets*, Harwood Academic, Chur, Switzerland.
Hodrick, R. and S. Srivastava (1984), "An Investigation of Risk and Return in Forward Foreign Exchange," *Journal of International Money and Finance*, **3**, 5–29.
——— (1986), "The Covariation of Risk Premiums and Expected Future Spot Exchange Rates," *Journal of International Money and Finance*, **5** (Suppl.) s5–s21.

Hsieh, D. (1984), "Tests of Rational Expectations and No Risk Premium in Forward Exchange Markets," *Journal of International Economics*, **17**, 173–184.

Huang, R. (1981), "The Monetary Approach to Exchange Rates in an Efficient Foreign Exchange Market: Tests Based on Volatility," *Journal of Finance*, **36**, 31–41.

Isard, P. (1986), "The Empirical Modeling of Exchange Rates: An Assessment of Alternative Approaches," International Monetary Fund mimeo.

Kleidon, A. (1986a), "Bias in Small Sample Tests of Stock Price Rationality," *Journal of Business*, forthcoming.

——— (1986b), "Variance Bounds Tests and Stock Price Valuation Models," *Journal of Political Economy*, forthcoming.

Kouri, P. (1977), "International Investment and Interest Rate Linkages under Flexible Exchange Rates," in R. Aliber (Ed.), *The Political Economy of Monetary Reform*, Macmillan, New York.

Kouri, P. and M. Porter (1977), "International Capital Flows and Portfolio Equilibrium," *Journal of Political Economy*, **82**, 443–467.

Krasker, W. (1980), "The 'Peso Problem' in Testing the Efficiency of Forward Exchange Markets," *Journal of Monetary Economics*, **6**, 269–276.

Krugman, P. (1981), "Consumption Preferences, Asset Demands and Distribution Effects in International Financial Markets," NBER working paper No. 651.

LeRoy, S. and R. Porter (1981), "The Present Value Relation and Implied Variance Bounds," *Econometrica*, **49**, 555–574.

Levich, R. (1979), "On the Efficiency of Markets for Foreign Exchange," in R. Dornbusch and J. Frenkel (Eds.), *International Ecomomic Policy: Theory and Evidence*, Johns Hopkins Press, Baltimore.

——— (1985), "Empirical Studies of Exchange Rates: Price Behavior, Rate Determination and Market Efficiency," in R. Jones and P. Kenen (Eds.), *Handbook of International Economics*, Vol. 2, Elsevier Science Amsterdam.

Logue, D., R. Sweeney, and T. Willett (1978), "The Speculative Behavior of Foreign Exchange Rates during the Current Float," *Journal of Business Research*, **6**, 150–174.

Lucas, R. (1976), "Econometric Policy Evaluation: A Critique," in K. Brunner and A. Meltzer (Eds.), *The Philips Curve and Labor Markets, Carnegie-Rochester Conference Series on Public No.* 1, North-Holland, Amsterdam, pp. 19–46.

——— (1982), "Interest Rates and Currency Prices in a Two-Country World," *Journal of Monetary Economics*, **12**, 55–93.

MacKinnon, J. and H. White (1985), "Some Heteroskedasticity Consistent Covariance Matrix Estimators with Improved Finite Sample Properties," Queens University mimeo.

Mattey, J. and R. Meese (1986), "Empirical Assessment of Present Value Relations," *Econometric Reviews*, **5**, 171–234.

Meese, R. (1986), "Testing for Bubbles in Exchange Markets: A Case of Sparkling Rates?" *Journal of Political Economy*, **94**, 345–373.

Meese, R. and K. Rogoff (1983a), "Empirical Exchange Rate Models of the Seventies: Do They Fit Out-of-Sample?" *Journal of International Economics*, **14**, 3–24.

——— (1983b), "The Out-of-Sample Failure of Empirical Exchange Rate Models: Sampling Error or Misspecification?" in J. Frenkel (Ed.), *Exchange Rates and International Macroeconomics*, University of Chicago Press, Chicago.

Meese, R. and K. Singleton (1982), "On Unit Roots and the Empirical Modeling of Exchange Rates," *Journal of Finance*, **37**, 1029–1035.

——— (1983), "Rational Expectations and the Volatility of Floating Exchange Rates," *International Economic Review*, **24**, 721–733.

Mussa, M. (1979), "Empirical Regularities in the Behavior of Exchange Rates and Theories of the Foreign Exchange Market," *Carnegie-Rochester Series on Public Policy*, **11**, 9–57.

——— (1981), "The Role of Official Intervention," Group of Thirty Occasional Papers 6.

Obstfeld, M. (1983), "Exchange Rates, Inflation and the Sterilization Problem: Germany 1975–1981," *European Economic Review*, **21**, 161–189.

Obstfeld, M. and K. Rogoff (1983), "Speculative Hyperinflations in Maximizing Models: Can We Rule Them Out?" *Journal of Political Economy*, **91**, 675–687.

——— (1986), "Ruling Out Divergent Speculative Bubbles," *Journal of Monetary Economics*, 349–362.

Obstfeld, M. and A. Stockman (1985), "Exchange Rate Dynamics," in R. Jones and P. Kenen (Eds.), *Handbook of International Economics*, Vol. 2, Elsevier Science, Amsterdam.

Poole, W. (1967), "Speculative Prices as Random Walks: An Analysis of Ten Time Series of Flexible Exchange Rates," *Southern Economic Journal*, **33**, 468–478.

Richard, S. and M. Sundaresan (1981), "A Continuous Time Equilibrium Model of Forward Prices and Future Prices in a Multigood Economy," *Journal of Financial Economics*, **9**, 347–372.

Rogoff, K. (1979), "Essays on Expectations and Exchange Rate Volatility," Ph.D. dissertation, Massachusettes Institute of Technology, Cambridge.

Roper, D. (1975), "The Role of Expected Value Analysis for Speculative Decisions in the Foreign Currency Market," *Quarterly Journal of Economics*, **89**, 157–169.

Shiller, R. (1981a), "Do Stock Prices Move Too Much to Be Justified by Subsequent Changes in Dividends?" *American Economic Review*, **71**, 421–436.

——— (1981b), "The Use of Volatility Measures in Assessing Market Efficiency," *Journal of Finance*, **36**, 291–311.

Singleton, K. (1980), "Expectations Models of the Term Structure and Implied Variance Bounds," *Journal of Political Economy*, **88**, 1159–1176.

Solnik, B. (1974), "An Equilibrium Model of the International Capital Market," *Journal of Economic Theory*, **8**, 500–524.

Stock, J. (1987), "Asymptotic Properties of Least Squares Estimators of Cointegrated Vectors," *Econometrica*, **55**, 1035–1056.

Stockman, A. (1978), "Risk, Information and Forward Exchange Rates," in J. Frenkel and H. Johnson (Eds.), *The Economics of Exchange Rates*, Addison-Wesley, Reading, MA.

——— (1979), "Monetary Control and Sterilization under Pegged Exchange Rates," University of Rochester mimeo.

Stulz, R. (1981), "A Model of International Asset Pricing," *Journal of Financial Economics*, 383–406.

——— (1982), "The forward Rate and Macroeconomics," *Journal of Monetary Economics*, **12**, 285–299.

Svensson, L. (1985), "Currency Prices, Terms of Trade and Interest Rates: A General Equilibrium Asset-Pricing Cash-in-Advance Approach," *Journal of International Economics*, **15**, 17–41.

Sweeney, R. (1986a), "Beating the Foreign Exchange Market," *Journal of Finance*, **41**, 163–182.

——— (1986b), "Risk Premia in Forward Exchange Rates: Systematic or Non-systematic?" Claremont Graduate School mimeo.

Sweeney, R. and E. Lee (1985), "Trading Strategies in Forward Exchange Markets," Claremont Graduate School mimeo.

Tryon, R. (1979), "Testing for Rational Expectations in Foreign Exchange Markets," Federal Reserve Board International Finance Discussion Paper No. 139.

West, K. (1985), "A Standard Monetary Model and the Variability of the Deutsemark–Dollar Exchange Rate," Princeton University mimeo.

Woo, W. (1984), "Speculative Bubbles in the Foreign Exchange Markets," Brooking Discussion Paper in International Economics.

Commentary by Maurice Obstfeld

One of the most puzzling aspects of the post-1973 floating exchange rate system has been the apparently inefficient predictive performance of forward exchange rates. Richard Meese's survey of research on international asset pricing ably documents both the evidence on forward rate determination and the attempts of researchers to pin down the empirical relationship between forward and spot exchange rates.

Table 5C–1, which reproduces in part results I reported in a 1985 paper, is representative of the empirical record. Shown in the table are regressions linking the one-month percentage change in the spot dollar price of a foreign currency to the corresponding one-month nominal interest rate differential (or forward premium) from the previous month. (The sample period is February 1975–January 1985.) For the four foreign currencies tested, the forward premium tended on average to *mispredict* the direction in which the

I am grateful for discussions with Richard Meese, for helpful comments from the Penn macro lunch group, and for financial support from the National Science Foundation and the Alfred P. Sloan Foundation. I retain full responsibility, however, for any errors and all opinions.

Table 5C–1. One-Month Eurocurrency Interest Rate Differentials and Subsequent Dollar Depreciation, February 1975–January 1985[a]

Depreciation Rate of Dollar Against:	*Constant*	*Lagged Eurocurrency Interest Differential*	*DW*	$\bar{R}^2$
Yen	0.113 (0.056)	−2.188 (0.985)	1.97	0.03
French franc	−0.092 (0.039)	−0.483 (0.773)	2.27	−0.01
Deutschemark	0.040 (0.071)	−1.778 (1.573)	2.23	0.00
Pound sterling	−0.102 (0.037)	−1.477 (0.875)	1.93	0.02

[a] The dependent variable is the percentage change in the dollar price of the foreign currency, expressed on an annualized basis. The independent variables are a constant and the difference between the previous month's one-month Eurodollar deposit rate and one-month foreign Eurocurrency deposit rate. Exchange rate data are end-of-month data from OECD *Main Economic Indicators*. End-of-month interest rates come from Morgan Guaranty Trust Company of New York, *World Financial Markets*. Standard errors are given in parentheses below the coefficient estimates.

dollar exchange rate moved during the subsequent month. Forward premiums have therefore been badly biased predictors of subsequent exchange rate movements. As Meese notes, a further indication of the poor forecasting performance of forward rates is the large body of evidence pointing to the ex ante predictability of forward forecast errors by past information.[1]

Three broad approaches to explaining the preceding facts can be discerned in Meese's review. The first of these approaches holds that the empirical findings may result from distributional peculiarities such as the "peso problem" or from other factors that cause nonstationarities in the data. The second approach posits an important role for speculative bubbles and/or market irrationality in exchange rate determination. The third approach observes that private risk aversion can imply time-varying discrepancies between forward premiums and expected future spot depreciation. Risk aversion thus offers another potential explanation of measured deviations from uncovered interest parity.

Economists have not reached a consensus interpretation of the data. Yet, the answer may have important implications for policymakers. A determination that the foreign exchange market is driven by irrational trading, for example, would stengthen both the case for fixed exchange rates and the case for direct controls on international capital movements.

Below I explore some aspects of each of the three leading explanations of forward rate behavior. Section 5C.1 develops a simple rational–expectations model of the peso problem that generates some key empirical regularities of the foreign exchange market: seemingly predictable and conditionally heteroskedastic forward forecast errors, along with possible directional misprediction by the forward premium. Section 5C.2 discusses the implications of bubbles for tests of forward rate predictive efficiency. Section 5C.3 expands on Meese's discussion of foreign exchange asset pricing under risk aversion. I suggest there that a convincing account of forward rate behavior should also help explain the results found in testing other asset pricing theories, such as the expectations theory of the interest rate term structure.

5C.1 Peso Problems

A peso problem arises when market forecasts reflect the possibility of major events that occur relatively infrequently in the data set available to the econometrician. Even though market expectations may be entirely reasonable ex ante, market forecasts appear biased and forecast errors appear serially correlated in the ex post sample. To the best of my knowledge, the effects of the peso problem on efficiency tests were first noticed by Kenneth Rogoff in connection with the behavior of Mexican peso futures prior to the August 1976 devaluation of that currency. (An elegant formal model of the episode has been developed by José Saúl Lizondo.) Stephen Salant and Dale Henderson presented the first theoretical analysis of a peso-type problem in studying the behavior of gold prices under the threat of official gold market intervention.

The peso problem is essentially one of small-sample inference. An announcement by the United States Treasury Secretary that the dollar is "too strong" may lead the market to repeatedly underestimate the dollar's future strength if macroeconomic policies are not promptly adjusted to push the dollar down. Market expectations will be reassessed if it becomes clear that official pronouncements are not being backed by concrete policy shifts. But an econometrician looking at a limited data set would erroneously interpret hypothesis tests based on asymptotic distribution theory as rejections of market efficiency. Reliable inference would require a data set covering many similar episodes, including some in which official pronouncements did lead to the implied policy actions.

An example of a floating-rate peso problem shows how some aspects of the seemingly anomalous behavior of exchange rates can be modeled without appeal to irrationality or risk aversion. Such a model requires the description of a general equilibrium framework within which exchange rates are determined. To make my main points as simply as possible, I adopt the monetary approach to exchange rate determination, as described by Michael Mussa. Karen Lewis has used this model to construct a complementary example in which a peso problem arises because agents are uncertain about the monetary regime currently in effect.

The monetary approach is based on an exchange rate equation of the form

$$s(t) = \lambda\{E_t[s(t+1) - s(t)]\} + \alpha'\phi(t), \tag{5C.1}$$

where $s(t)$ is the natural logarithm of $S(t)$, the domestic currency price of foreign exchange, λ is a constant that measures the spot rate's response to expected future depreciation, $E_t(\cdot)$ is a rational expectation conditional on time-t information, α is a coefficient vector, and $\phi(t)$ is a vector of exogenous variables. The equation is derived from an uncovered interest rate parity condition together with a theory of nominal interest rates and price levels in which the key variables are $s(t)$ and $\phi(t)$. The vector $\phi(t)$ could, in principle, include an exogenously varying risk premium, but such an exogeneity assumption is implausible. The model embodied in (5C.1) is therefore best viewed as describing a hypothetical world economy with risk-neutral investors.

The "bubble-free" solution to (5C.1) is

$$s(t) = [1/(1+\lambda)] \sum_{i=0}^{\infty} [\lambda/(1+\lambda)]^i E_t[\alpha'\phi(t+i)]. \tag{5C.2}$$

This solution is found by iterating (5C.1) forward and imposing a stationarity condition that is described in detail in the next section. For my example, it is sufficient to assume that $\phi(t)$ consists of a single variable (the log of the money supply) and that $\alpha = 1$.

To model a peso problem, assume that on any date t, the log money supply is the sum of two random variables. The first is a random walk process $m(t)$, the sum of $m(t-1)$, and a completely unpredictable mean-zero disturbance $\omega(t)$. The second random variable contributing to the money supply process is itself the product of two random variables, denoted $d(t)$ and $\mu(t)$. $d(t)$ has the distribution.

$$d(t) = \begin{cases} 1 & \text{(with probability } \pi) \\ 0 & \text{(with probability } 1-\pi) \end{cases} \qquad \text{conditional on } d(t-1) = 0;$$

$$d(t) = 1 \quad \text{(with probability 1)} \qquad \text{conditional on } d(t-1) = 1.$$

Conditional on $d(t-1)=0$, $\mu(t)$ is generated by the first-order autoregressive process $\mu(t)=\rho\mu(t-1)+\varepsilon(t)$, where $0<\rho<1$ and $E_{t-1}[\varepsilon(t)]=0$; but $\mu(t+j)$ $(j>0)$ is constant at $\mu(t)$ conditional on $d(t)=1$. $\phi(t)$ therefore follows the process

$$\phi(t)=m(t)+d(t)\mu(t)=m(t-1)+\omega(t)+d(t)\mu(t). \tag{5C.3}$$

The interpretation of equation 5C.3 is this. One component of the money supply process is a random walk, which in itself would lead to no expected future change in money. It is the second component, the product $d(t)\mu(t)$, which causes a peso problem. In each period, there is a probability π that the money supply will jump permanently by the amount $\mu(t)$, given that no such jump has yet taken place. The expected value of this possible jump is $\rho\mu(t-1)$ in the previous period. The $\mu(t)$ process is assumed to damp out monotonically in mean to capture the intuitive notion that the market expects to put progressively less weight on the significance of a possible policy change the longer the interval over which the change has not occurred.[2]

The simple exchange rate model set out above can now be used to analyze the difficulties associated with peso problems. For this purpose, it is assumed that $d(t)=0$ for all observations t available to the econometrician. In other words, even though the market viewed a major policy switch as a possibility, the available data are conditioned on the nonoccurrence of that event. The peso problem modeled here has three major implications:

1. *Apparent conditional bias in market exchange rate forecasts.* Assume for simplicity that the econometrician can directly observe the market's expectation $E_t s(t+1)$ of next period's exchange rate, but not the true, ex ante money supply process itself. In forecasting the exchange rate, the market took into account the possibility that d might equal 1 on some future date, even though the event $d=1$ turned out not to occur ex post. The possibility that d might equal 1 is reflected in the sequence of expected future money supplies $E_t\phi(t+i)$, $i>0$.

That sequence is computed as follows. If $d(t)=0$, the event $d=1$ will have occurred by date $t+i$ with probability $1-(1-\pi)^i=\pi+\pi(1-\pi)+\pi(1-\pi)^2+\cdots+\pi(1-\pi)^{i-1}$. On date t, the expected value of $\phi(t+i)$ is therefore the sum of $m(t)$ and $\{\pi+\pi(1-\pi)\rho+\pi[(1-\pi)\rho]^2+\cdots+\pi[(1-\pi)\rho]^{i-1}\}\rho\mu(t)$, where the latter term is just the expected date-$(t+i)$ value of the second component of the money supply process. Thus, conditional on $d(t)=0$,

$$E_t\phi(t+i)=m(t)+\frac{1-[(1-\pi)\rho]^i}{1-(1-\pi)\rho}\pi\rho\mu(t) \tag{5C.4}$$

for all $i>0$.

Combined with equation 5C.2 (for the case $\alpha = 1$), the above formula implies

$$s(t) = m(t) + \frac{\pi\lambda\rho}{1 + \lambda - (1 - \pi)\lambda\rho}\mu(t). \tag{5C.5}$$

A similar calculation shows that the rational one-period-ahead exchange rate forecast is

$$E_t[s(t + 1)] = m(t) + \frac{\pi(1 + \lambda)\rho}{1 + \lambda - (1 - \pi)\lambda\rho}\mu(t). \tag{5C.6}$$

Together, (5C.5) and (5C.6) yield a date $(t + 1)$ forecast error of

$$s(t + 1) - E_t[s(t + 1)] = \omega(t + 1) + \frac{\pi\lambda\rho\varepsilon(t + 1) - [\rho + (1 - \rho)\lambda\rho]\pi\mu(t)}{1 + \lambda - (1 - \pi)\lambda\rho}, \tag{5C.7}$$

given that $d(t + 1) = 0$.

Note that the forecast error conditional on $d(t + 1) = 0$ depends on the lagged variable $\mu(t)$. If $\mu(t) > 0$ over some interval, for example, the market appears systematically to overestimate the home currency's future depreciation. This pattern of ex post forecast errors does not imply a conditionally biased forecast: the market also took into account the likelihood of the event $d(t + 1) = 1$, which would have occasioned a sharp increase in the money supply.

More formally, if $d(t + 1) = 1$ had occurred, the equilibrium exchange rate $s(t + 1) = m(t + 1) + \mu(t + 1)$ would have resulted in a forecast error of

$$s(t + 1) - E_t[s(t + 1)] = \omega(t + 1) + \varepsilon(t + 1) + \frac{[\rho + (1 - \rho)\lambda\rho](1 - \pi)\mu(t)}{1 + \lambda - (1 - \pi)\lambda\rho}. \tag{5C.8}$$

The conditional expectation of the forecast error with respect to time t information only is

$$\pi E_t[\text{error}(t + 1)|d(t + 1) = 1] + (1 - \pi)E_t[\text{error}(t + 1)|d(t + 1) = 0]$$
$$= E_t\left(\omega(t + 1) + \frac{\pi(1 + \lambda)\varepsilon(t + 1)}{1 + \lambda - (1 - \pi)\lambda\rho}\right) = 0.$$

Expectations are therefore conditionally unbiased.

An econometrician viewing a sample conditioned on $d(t) = 0$ would fail to reach this last conclusion using standard methods of inference. If the forecast error (5C.7) is regressed on the lagged depreciation forecast, for example, a negative regression coefficient will be found with high probability (as implied by results in the next paragraph). But such a finding is not evidence of an inefficient market in the present context. The resulting regression equation provides an estimate of $E_t[\text{error}(t+1)|d(t+1)=0]$, which is generally nonzero. Since $E_t[\text{error}(t+1)]=0$, however, forecast errors are indeed uncorrelated with past information given the true distribution of the money supply (and hence of forecast errors).

2. *Exchange rate misprediction.* This particular model also implies that rational market forecasts will on average mispredict the exchange rate's direction of change as long as $d=1$ does not occur. By (5C.5) and (5C.6), the market forecast of currency depreciation, given that $d(t)=0$, is

$$E_t[s(t+1)]-s(t)=\frac{\pi\rho}{1+\lambda-(1-\pi)\lambda\rho}\mu(t).$$

If $\mu(t)>0$, for example, the market expects the currency to depreciate, and the home interest rate consequently exceeds the foreign rate under uncovered interest parity. The actual change in the exchange rate, however, is

$$s(t+1)-s(t)=\omega(t+1)+\frac{\pi\lambda\rho\varepsilon(t+1)-(1-\rho)\pi\lambda\rho\mu(t)}{1+\lambda-(1-\pi)\lambda\rho}.$$

If $\omega(t+1)=\varepsilon(t+1)=0$, the currency *appreciates* (still assuming $\mu(t)>0$) as the market revises downward by the factor $1-\rho$ the expected future path of the money supply's second component. In a sample where $d(t)=0$ for all t, realized and expected depreciation will therefore be negatively correlated, even though interest parity holds and expectations are rational. (Table 5C–1 showed that recent data are characterized by a negative correlation between forward premiums and subsequent depreciation rates.)

3. *Conditional heteroskedasticity of forecast errors.* Peso problems can result in time dependence in the conditional covariances of forecast errors. Robert Cumby and I first presented evidence of such conditional heteroskedasticity in forward rate forecast errors, and our finding has been confirmed by Robert Hodrick and Sanjay Srivastava, Alberto Giovannini and Philippe Jorion, and many others. As Meese notes, conditional heteroskedasticity may pose problems for statistical inference. In a world of risk-averse investors, the phenomenon also has a crucial implications about the nature of foreign exchange risk premiums, as detailed in section 5C.3.

Assume that the random variables $\omega(t)$ and $\varepsilon(t)$ themselves have constant conditional variances, so that $E_t[\omega(t+1)^2]=\sigma_\omega^2$ and $E_t[\varepsilon(t+1)^2]=\sigma_\varepsilon^2$. In spite of these assumptions, the conditional variance of the exchange rate forecast error depends on lagged information in the preceding model. If $d=1$ has occurred, then the exchange rate forecast error is just $\omega(t)$. Thus, $E_t[\text{error}(t+1)^2]=\sigma_\omega^2$, where the conditioning set contains $d(t)$. If $d=1$ has not occurred, however, the conditional variance of the forecast error, is different. For simplicity, assume $\rho = 0$. Under that assumption, the population conditional variance of the forecast error, $E_t[\text{error}(t+1)^2]$, is $\pi(\sigma_\omega^2 + 2\sigma_{\omega\varepsilon} + \sigma_\varepsilon^2) + (1-\pi)(\sigma_\omega^2) = \sigma_\omega^2 + \pi(2\sigma_{\omega\varepsilon} + \sigma_\varepsilon^2)$, where the conditioning set again contains $d(t)$.

An econometrician may well find evidence of conditional heteroskedasticity in a sample conditioned on $d(t) = 0$. For example, regressions of the squared forecast error (5C.7) on variables including the squared forward premium, $\pi^2\rho^2\mu(t)^2/[1 + \lambda - (1-\pi)\lambda\rho]^2$, are likely to be significant. Cumby and I used this type of regression specification to test for conditional heteroskedasticity.

5C.2 Speculative Bubbles

Speculative bubbles can be modeled within the monetary model of the previous section. Equation 5C.2, which gives the equilibrium exchange rate just analyzed, is only one possible solution to the stochastic difference equation 5C.1. A general solution takes the form

$$s(t) = [1/(1+\lambda)] \sum_{i=0}^{\infty} [\lambda/(1+\lambda)]^i E_t[\alpha'\phi(t+i)] + x(t)[(1+\lambda)/\lambda]^t, \quad (5C.9)$$

where $\{x(t)\}$ is any stochastic process with the martingale property,

$$E_t[x(t+1)] = x(t).$$

Solution (5C.2) corresponds to the choice $x(t) = 0$, for all t, but because $x(t)$ is multiplied in (5C.9) by the exploding term $[(1+\lambda)/\lambda]^t$, choice of a nonzero x process will impart explosive behavior to the exchange rate. Such explosive paths capture the idea of speculative bubbles driven by self-fulfilling anticipations.

It is sometimes asserted that bubbles give rise to serially correlated market forecast errors or to biased forecasts, but this is not the case when the bubble's path is described by an equation like (5C.9). Define $v^{t+i}(t+1) = E_{t+1}[\alpha'\phi(t+i)] - E_t[\alpha'\phi(t+i)]$ and $\eta(t+1) = x(t+1) - E_t[x(t+1)] = \Delta x(t+1)$. When expectations are rational and the model (5C.9) is used to forecast future exchange rates, the one-step ahead forecast error is

$$s(t+1) - E_t[s(t+1)] = [1/(1+\lambda)] \sum_{i=0}^{\infty} [\lambda/(1+\lambda)]^i v^{t+i+1}(t+1)$$
$$+ \eta(t+1)\{(1+\lambda)/\lambda]^{t+1}.$$

This error, however, is uncorrelated with time-t information (including lagged forecast errors), and the market forecast is therefore conditionally unbiased.

While market forecasts remain efficient, the presence of bubbles will generally invalidate the usual efficiency tests. Consider, for example, a test for bias in exchange rate forecasts. Assume, for simplicity, that $\alpha'\phi(t)$ itself follows a martingale process, so that its conditional expectation equals its own lagged value. Then

$$s(t+1) - E_t[s(t+1)] = v^{t+1}(t+1) + \eta(t+1)[(1+\lambda)/\lambda]^{t+1}. \quad \text{(5C.10)}$$

A significance test for the sample mean

$$M(T) = (1/T)\sum_{t=1}^{T} \{s(t+1) - E_t[s(t+1)]\}$$

is a test for unconditional bias in exchange rate forecasts. But the variance of $M(T)$ can be calculated as

$$\text{Var}[M(T)] = (1/T^2)\sum_{t=1}^{T} \{\sigma_v^2 + \sigma_\eta^2[(1+\lambda)/\lambda]^{2(t+1)}\}$$

when v and η are stationary and uncorrelated. This variance does not go to zero as $T \rightarrow \infty$. It follows that the statistic $M(T)$ will not necessarily give a consistent estimate of the mean forecast error in the presence of a bubble. Even though agents are making optimal forecasts, the usual tests might give strong indications of inefficiency.

As Meese notes, however, bubbles are an unlikely explanation of the puzzle of forward exchange rate behavior. Under the type of bubble described by (5C.9), the variance of one-step-ahead forecast errors explodes over time at rate $[(1+\lambda)/\lambda]^2$, as (5C.10) shows. Taking the logarithm of the forward rate as an approximation to the expected logarithm of the future spot rate gives a rough empirical measure of this forecast error under risk neutrality. The stylized facts recounted by Meese imply that the variance of forward forecast errors does not explode over time. Nor is such behavior observed over subperiods. In particular, a bubble as in (5C.9) would be inconsistent with the approximate random walk followed by spot and forward rates.[3]

There are two other reasons for dismissing divergent speculative bubbles as a characterization of exchange rate behavior. First, there is a strong theoretical case for ruling them out (as discussed in my paper with Rogoff). Second, as first pointed out by Robert Flood and Peter Garber, bubbles are observationally equivalent to possible changes in the $\phi(t)$ process that the public may expect with good reason.

The observational equivalence of bubbles and anticipated future changes is illustrated by an example related to the one analyzed in the previous section.[4]

Suppose again that α is a scalar equal to 1 and that $\phi(t)$ is the money supply. Until a known date T in the future, $\phi(t)$ is expected to equal the random variable $m(t)$ with probability 1, where $m(t) = m(t-1) + \omega(t)$, as before. There is a possibility, however, that the $\phi(t)$ process will change permanently on date T. Specifically, the public knows that the money supply for $t' \geqslant T$ will be given by the random variable $\phi(t') = m(t') + \mu(T)$, where $\mu(t) = [1 - d(t)] \times [\mu(t-1) + \varepsilon(t)]$ (for $t \leqslant T$) and $d(t)$ and $\varepsilon(t)$ are as defined earlier. In words, the public expects a sharp jump in the money supply at time T if the event $d(t) = 1$ does not occur in the interim. The expected size of the possible jump $\mu(t)$ evolves as a random walk.

Consider next the "bubble-free" exchange rate solution (5C.2), which is now equal to

$$s(t) = m(t) + (1-\pi)^{T-t}[1/(1+\lambda)] \sum_{i=T-t}^{\infty} [\lambda/(1+\lambda)]^i \mu(t).$$

Rewrite this equation as

$$s(t) = m(t) + K[\mu(t)/(1-\pi)^t][(1+\lambda)/\lambda]^t$$

where $K = [(1-\pi)\lambda/(1+\lambda)]^T$; since $E_t[\mu(t+1)/(1-\pi)^{t+1}] = (1-\pi)\mu(t)/(1-\pi)^{t+1} = \mu(t)/(1-\pi)^t$ (conditional on $d(t) = 0$), the result is a special case of (5C.9), corresponding to $E_t[\alpha'\phi(t+i)] = m(t)$ for all i. The equation therefore shows that an econometrician who is unaware that the public expected a possible change in the money supply process will be unable to distinguish the exchange rate's bubble-free path from that of a "crashing" bubble such as the one analyzed by Olivier Blanchard. The strong theoretical case against divergent bubbles suggests that econometric results purporting to show their existence are more likely to be the result of misspecifying agents' information sets.

It is noteworthy that the example just given and (by implication) some bubbles may lead to peso problems. This coincidence does not imply that peso problems and bubbles are the same. The model of the last section, for example, shows that peso problems need not give rise to explosive exchange rate behavior.

The bubble model embodied in equation 5C.9 assumes rational one-step-ahead forecasting by market participants, but it imposes no terminal convergence condition to tie the exchange rate to economic fundamentals. As Meese notes, some researchers have suggested that market forecasts are *not* rational, and that exchange rates may be prone to "overreaction" or "excessive" volatility. Under risk neutrality, the recently developed volatility tests applied to stock and bond markets offer a "portmanteau" methodology that potentially detects bubbles as well as other deviations from efficient asset pricing based on fundamentals. How one should interpret these tests in practice is currently a matter of some controversy. (Joe Mattey and Meese provide a survey of the econometric issues in the debate, together with the results of Monte Carlo experiments.) In particular, volatility tests, like tests for bubbles, require strong identifying assumptions about market expectations.

Even if one accepts the methodology of volatility testing in principle, it is not clear how it can be applied to the foreign exchange market. Economists have developed widely accepted theories of both stock pricing and the term structure of interest rates under risk neutrality and rational expectations; it is these theories upon which the volatility tests build. No correspondingly clear-cut theory of risk-neutral nominal or real exchange rate determination exists. A consensus theory of exchange rates would require agreement on the determinants of relative demands for fiat monies, as well as on the dividing line between money and near-money. Such a theory would also require a consensus model of demand and supply in national output markets.

5C.3 Risk

Risk aversion on the part of market participants provides a third potential explanation of apparent deviations from uncovered interest parity. Although much of the empirical literature on the risk premium reports negative results, more recent research lends limited support to the empirical relevance of risk-averse asset pricing.

To see how risk aversion gives rise to departures from interest parity, consider the relation between the nominal interest rates on one-period bonds denominated in home and foreign currency. An international investor following an optimal consumption/investment plan must be indifferent among the three alternatives of using an additional domestic currency unit to augment his domestic currency assets, allocating the money to foreign currency assets, or spending the money on consumption goods today. Indifference occurs when each course of action yields the same expected marginal return. Let the investor's period utility function be $u[C(t)]$, let $\beta < 1$ denote the subjective time-preference factor, let $R(R^*)$ denote the domestic (foreign) one-period nominal interest rate, and let $P(P^*)$ be the local money price of the typical home (foreign) consumption bundle. For a domestic investor, the optimality condition described above is

$$\frac{u'[C(t)]}{P(t)} = \beta[1 + R(t)]E_t\frac{u'[C(t+1)]}{P(t+1)} = \beta[1 + R^*(t)]E_t\frac{u'[C(t+1)]S(t+1)}{P(t+1)S(t)},$$

where $S(t)$, as before, is the level (rather than the log) of the exchange rate. Define $Q(t+1)$ to be the ex post marginal rate of substitution between domestic currency units available on dates t and $t+1$; thus, $Q(t+1) = \{\beta u'[C(t+1)]/P(t+1)\} \div \{u'[C(t)/P(t)]\}$. The equation above can be rewritten in terms of this definition as

$$1 = [1 + R(t)]E_t[Q(t+1)] = [1 + R^*(t)]E_t[Q(t+1)S(t+1)/S(t)], \qquad (5C.11)$$

which implies

$$[1 + R(t)]/[1 + R^*(t)] = E_t[Q(t+1)S(t+1)/S(t)]/E_t[Q(t+1)]. \qquad (5C.12)$$

Because the one-period forward exchange rate $F(t)$ is equated by covered interest parity to $S(t)[1 + R(t)]/[1 + R^*(t)]$, equations 5C.11 and 5C.12 above lead to Meese's equation 5.2 for the forward rate.

While (5C.11) and (5C.12) were derived by considering the alternatives available to a typical domestic investor, consideration of a foreign investor would lead to the same expressions. As noted earlier, $E_t[Q(t+1)]$ is an expected marginal rate of substitution between present and future home currency units. $E_t[Q(t+1)S(t+1)/S(t)]$ can likewise be interpreted as an expected marginal rate of substitution between present and future units of the *foreign* currency. In the equilibrium of an internationally integrated asset market, all investors should have the same expected intertemporal substitution rate for each currency they trade. Both the numerator and the denominator on the right side of (5C.12) are therefore independent, in equilibrium, of the particular investor considered, provided all investors have access to the same bond markets.[5]

The implications of (5C.12) for uncovered interest parity are understood most easily if that equation is written in the form

$$\frac{1 + R(t)}{1 + R^*(t)} - E_t\frac{S(t+1)}{S(t)} = \frac{\mathrm{Cov}_t[Q(t+1), S(t+1)/S(t)]}{E_t[Q(t+1)]}. \qquad (5C.13)$$

Equation 5C.13 shows the deviation from uncovered interest parity that arises in the present model; the right side of the equation is usually referred to as the (one-period) foreign exchange risk premium on domestic currency. The risk premium is positive if the home currency's depreciation against foreign currency is unexpectedly high at times when the increase in the marginal utility from spending a domestic currency unit is also unexpectedly high. In other words, the home currency is riskier if it tends to lose foreign exchange value in states of the world where it is most needed. A positive risk premium implies that the domestic–foreign interest ratio exceeds the expected depreciation of home currency, while a negative risk premium implies the opposite.

The right side of equation 5C.13 equals the one-period forward premium $F(t)/S(t)$ less expected depreciation. Thus, the equation also reveals that the forward premium forecast error $[S(t+1)-F(t)]/S(t)$ consists of a true, random forecast error less a risk premium that generally varies over time. Since the risk premium is a function of time-t information, forward premium forecast errors are also predictable on the basis of that information. Many researchers therefore ascribe the apparent partial predictability of forward premium errors to time-varying risk premiums. This explanation is sensible only if risk premiums are sufficiently variable that their influence is not dominated by that of the pure expectational errors.

If the relevant economic variables are jointly log-normally distributed (because their logs are generated by a linear Gaussian process), then (5C.12) becomes

$$r(t)-r^*(t)-E_t[\Delta s(t+1)] = \mathrm{Var}_t[\Delta s(t+1)]/2+\mathrm{Cov}_t[q(t+1), \Delta s(t+1)], \tag{5C.14}$$

where $r(t)=\log[1+R(t)]$, $r^*(t)=\log[1+R^*(t)]$, and $q(t)=\log[Q(t)]$. Lars Peter Hansen and Hodrick (1983) first derived this widely tested logarithmic model within a utility-maximizing framework. A major implication of this model is that the conditional variance and covariance on the right side of (5C.14) are both constant (given stationarity), implying a constant risk premium. Constancy follows from the fact that the innovations in $q(t+1)$ and $\Delta s(t+1)$, being normal, are independent of time-t variables, not just uncorrelated with them. Since the risk premium must vary over time to explain the predictability of forward forecast errors by past information, the logarithmic model is clearly inconsistent with the data. Another of the model's implications, the conditional homoskedasticity of forward rate forecast errors, also contradicts the facts. Conditional heteroskedasticity may be caused by peso problems, as noted above, but there are obviously other possible causes.

As Meese documents, alternative models of the risk premium also seem to do poorly when confronted with the data. But I think it is too early to conclude, as does Jeffrey Frankel, that risk-averse behavior can explain only a negligible fraction of the observed serial correlation in forward forecast errors. In recent work, Cumby (1986a) presents direct estimates of foreign exchange risk premiums that provide some support for the risk-averse asset-pricing model described by equation 5C.13.[6] My own preliminary estimates (1988) of a logarithmic, consumption-based model of real interest rate differentials are also encouraging. The problems discussed in section 5C.1 are almost certainly important, however, and one goal of research should be to take these data problems explicitly into account. The role of risk aversion cannot be assessed adequately until more refined procedures for purging the data have been developed.

Another promising direction for future research is to integrate studies of foreign exchange pricing with studies of price determination in other asset markets. The (rational) expectations model of the term structure, like uncovered interest rate parity, has been widely tested and rejected. As documented by Robert Shiller, John Campbell, and Kermit Schoenholtz, the interest rate forecasts implicit in the term structure, like forward foreign exchange premiums, often mispredict the direction of future rate movements in post-1959 data. It is more than an appeal to Occam's razor to suggest that a single theory should explain these similar phenomena. In view of the increasingly tight links between onshore and offshore asset markets, it is difficult to conceive of a convincing account of the foreign exchange risk premium that does not simultaneously throw light on the characteristics of term premiums and stock market risk premiums.

Consider, for example, the tight connection between term premiums and foreign exchange premiums implied by covered interest parity. Let $F^{(i)}$ denote the i-period forward exchange rate and $R^{(i)}$ $(R^{*(i)})$ the i-period interest rate on a domestic (foreign) bond. Covered interest parity ensures that for any i,

$$F^{(i)}(t)/S(t) = [1 + R^{(i)}(t)]^i/[1 + R^{*(i)}(t)]^i.$$

To be concrete, apply the above expression to compute the ratio of the two-period forward premium to the one-period forward premium. The result is

$$\frac{F^{(2)}(t)/S(t)}{F^{(1)}(t)/S(t)} = \frac{[1 + R^{(2)}(t)]^2/[1 + R^{(1)}(t)]}{[1 + R^{*(2)}(t)]^2/[1 + R^{*(1)}(t)]}. \tag{5C.15}$$

Let $\tau(\tau^*)$ denote the domestic (foreign) one-period term premium and let $\theta^{(i)}$ $(i = 1, 2)$ denote the i-period foreign exchange risk premium. Reasoning similar to that followed above shows that

$$\tau(t) = \mathrm{Cov}_t\{Q(t+1)Q(t+2), [1 + R^{(1)}(t+1)]\}/E_t[Q(t+1)Q(t+2)].$$

The foreign term premium $\tau^*(t)$ depends in the same way on the covariance between the foreign one-period interest rate and the ex post marginal rate of substitution between foreign currency units delivered on dates t and $t+2$. Equation 5C.15, expressed in terms of these risk premiums, can be shown to be

$$\frac{E_t[S(t+2)/S(t)] + \theta^{(2)}(t)}{E_t[S(t+1)/S(t)] + \theta^{(1)}(t)} = \frac{E_t[1 + R^{(1)}(t+1)] + \tau(t)}{E_t[1 + R^{*(1)}(t+1)] + \tau^*(t)}.$$

Expressions such as this one imply restrictions on the joint behavior of foreign exchange risk premiums and bond market term premiums.

Intriguing results have come out of research that examines several asset markets at the same time, Richard Clarida and John Campbell, for example, find that variables with explanatory power for term premiums also help predict returns to forward foreign exchange speculation. Giovannini and Jorion report similarities in the conditional distributions of foreign exchange and U.S. stock market risk premiums. In time, further investigation into findings such as these may help explain the puzzling behavior of forward exchange rates.

Notes

1. The table also shows that forward premiums have virtually no predictive value with respect to future depreciation. This fact is not necessarily evidence of some market failure; it is consistent with a world in which exchange rate movements are dominated by rational market reactions to unpredictable events. It is noteworthy that the early regressions of spot exchange rate *levels* on lagged forward rate levels seemed to indicate a greater predictive value of the forward rate than is evident in table 5C–1. Meese's argument that the forward and spot rate processes are cointegrated suggests that the latter findings are the spurious result of a common stochastic trend.
2. Alternatively, one could assume a time-varying π to capture this type of effect.
3. There are some models in which the bubble term involves the power of a root that is smaller than unity in absolute value. These convergent bubbles are difficult to rule out by inspecting the data, but, on the other hand, they do not necessarily destroy the validity of the standard efficiency tests. It is therefore unlikely that convergent bubbles are responsible for the apparent failure of risk-neutral foreign exchange pricing.
4. A similar example illustrating this equivalence is given by James Hamilton.
5. In my 1988 paper I test the international equality of intertemporal marginal substitution rates between the United States and Germany and between the United States and Japan. For post-1972 data, the tests I conduct fail to reject those equalities.
6. Cumby's (1986b) results on stock market prices in Germany, Japan, the United Kingdom, and the United States appear less supportive of the model

References

Blanchard, O. J. (1979), "Speculative Bubbles, Crashes, and Rational Expectations," *Economics Letters*, **3**, 387–389.

Campbell, J. Y., and R. H. Clarida (1987) "The Term Structure of Euro-market Interest Rates: An Empirical Investigation," *Journal of Monetary Economics*, **19**, 25–44.

Cumby, R. E. (1986a) "Is it Risk? Interpreting Deviations from Interest Parity," Working Paper, Graduate School of Business Administration, New York University.

——— (1986b) "Consumption Risk and International Asset Returns: Some Empirical Evidence," Working Paper, Graduate School of Business Administration, New York University.

Cumby, R. E. and M. Obstfeld (1984), "International Interest Rate and Price Level Linkages under Flexible Exchange Rates: A Review of Recent Evidence," in J. F. O.

Bilson and R. C. Marston (Eds.), *Exchange Rate Theory and Practice*, University of Chicago Press, Chicago.

Flood, R. P. and P. M. Garber (1980), "Market Fundamentals versus Price-Level Bubbles: The First Tests," *Journal of Political Economy*, **88**, 745–770.

Frankel, J. A. (1986) "The Implications of Mean-Variance Optimization for Four Questions in International Macroeconomics," *Journal of International Money and Finance* **5**, S53–S75.

Giovannini, A. and P. Jorion (1987), "Interest Rates and Risk Premia in the Stock Market and in the Foreign Exchange Market," *Journal of International Money and Finance*, **6**, 107–123.

Hamilton, J. D. (1986) "On Testing for Self-fulfilling Speculative Price Bubbles," *International Economic Review*, **27**, 545–552.

Hansen, L. P. and R. J. Hodrick (1983). "Risk Averse Speculation in the Forward Foreign Exchange Market: An Econometric Analysis of Linear Models," in J. A. Frenkel (Ed.), *Exchange Rates and International Macroeconomics*, University of Chicago Press, Chicago.

Hodrick, R. J. and S. Srivastava, (1984), "An Investigation of Risk and Return in Forward Foreign Exchange," *Journal of International Money and Finance*, **3**, 5–29.

Lewis, K. K. (1986), "The Persistence of the 'Peso Problem' When Policy Is Noisy," Working Paper, Graduate School of Business Administration, New York University.

Lizondo, J. S. (1983), "Foreign Exchange Futures Prices under Fixed Exchange Rates," *Journal of International Economics*, **14**, 69–84.

Mattey, J. and R. Meese (1987), "Empirical Assessment of Present Value Relations," *Econometric Reviews*, forthcoming.

Meese, R. (1988), "Empirical Assessment of Foreign Currency Risk Premiums," in C. C. Stone (Ed.), *Financial Risk: Theory, Evidence, and Implications*, Kluwer Academic, Boston.

Mussa, M. (1986), "The Exchange Rate, the Balance of Payments, and Monetary and Fiscal Policy under a Regime of Controlled Floating," *Scandinavian Journal of Economics*, **78**, 229–248.

Obstfeld, M. (1985), "Floating Exchange Rates: Experience and Prospects," *Brookings Papers on Economic Activity*, **15**, 369–450.

——— (1988), "How Integrated are World Capital Markets? Some New Tests," in G. A. Calvo et al. (Eds.), *Debt, Stabilization and Development: Essays in Memory of Carlos Diaz Alejandro*, Basil Blackwell, London.

Obstfeld, M. and K. Rogoff (1986), "Ruling Out Divergent Speculative Bubbles," *Journal of Monetary Economics*, **17**, 349–362.

Rogoff, K. (1979), "Essays on Expectations and Exchange Rate Volatility," doctoral dissertation, Massachusetts Institute of Technology, Cambridge.

Salant, S. W. and D. W. Henderson (1978) "Market Anticipations of Government Policies and the Price of Gold," *Journal of Political Economy*, **86**, 627–648.

Shiller, R. J., J. Y. Campbell, and K. L. Schoenholtz (1983), "Forward Rates and Future Policy: Interpreting the Term Structure of Interest Rates," *Brookings Papers on Economic Activity*, **13**, 173–217.

6 COUNTRY RISK AND THE STRUCTURE OF INTERNATIONAL FINANCIAL INTERMEDIATION

Donald R. Lessard

Country risk stands out in today's global financial system for several reasons. It is perceived to be a major threat to the system's stability, more so than virtually any other single category of risk. It also is perceived to follow different rules than most other types of risks, and hence to require different institutional approaches. This is reflected in the specialization of particular institutions in bearing country risk, the important risk mitigating role of multilateral institutions or arrangements, including the International Monetary Fund, the World Bank, and the Paris Club, and the lack of specialized markets for laying off this risk.

A major distinction between finance in a single-country and in an international context is that various assets are denominated or determined in different currencies and hence are subject to differing currency risks. An even

---

This chapter draws substantially on an earlier, unpublished paper prepared for the Canadian Department of Finance (Lessard et al., 1983). I gratefully acknowledge my colleagues' collaboration and the support of Canada Finance, but take full responsibility for my interpretations and conclusions. I also have benefited substantially from joint work with John Williamson (Lessard and Williamson, 1985) and the comments of Thierry Bollier and Tom Willett.

more important distinction, though, is that the cash flows associated with various assets are generated in different countries. As a result, assets are subject to different tax regimes, to different political and regulatory risks, and to different actual or potential restrictions regarding their convertability and remittability. In general, these *jurisdiction specific* factors have two effects:

1. They *alter the expected net of tax cash flows* that any investor can appropriate.

2. They *cause divergences in appropriable returns* among investors located in different jurisdictions and, as a result, lead them to skew their portfolios away from the "world market portfolio" toward assets for which they have resulting comparative advantage. This, in turn, alters the *risk premium demanded* on various assets in equilibrium and *reduces the efficiency of resource allocation.*

This chapter raises several issues regarding country risk and offers some views on how these issues might be incorporated in a more comprehensive perspective. The issues raised include:

- What is country risk?
- How do its effects differ across assets or investors?
- Who has comparative advantage in bearing it?
- How does it change the pattern of financial intermediation?
- How does it affect the efficiency of resource allocation?
- What can be done about it?

Clearly, this is far too large a range of issues on which to provide definitive explanations, models, or prescriptions. Instead, an attempt will be made to link various aspects of the phenomena that have been discussed in the literature. In examining the impact of country risk on the structure and efficiency of international financial intermediation, I focus on two salient features of the current structure: (1) the home bias in risky asset holdings among financially developed countries and (2) the apparent crowding out of domestic claims and cross-border risk-bearing claims by sovereign borrowing in the the case of less-developed countries.

This chapter is organized in four sections. Section 6.1 focuses on the definition of country risk with particular attention to its sources and incidence across classes of assets and investors. Section 6.2 develops the concept of comparative advantage in bearing country risk. Section 6.3 examines the impact of country risk on the valuation of assets and capital market equilibrium and its consequent implications for the efficiency of international financial intermediation. Section 6.4 concludes with an exploratory discussion of policy measures that might address some of the most critical undesired effects of country risk.

6.1 What Is Country Risk?

Country risk, broadly defined, comprises those risks associated with claims against (economic agents in) a particular country, including but not limited to claims on the government of that country. In the financial press and academic journals, it typically is associated with the risks of loans by commercial banks to less-developed countries (LDCs). However, it encompasses a much wider range of uncertainties in returns on various types of claims held against a country or economic agents within a country either by foreign or domestic claimants. In the cases of loans to sovereign borrowers, for example, it refers to the possibility of nonperformance in the form of default or delayed repayment. In contrast, in the case of direct foreign investment claims, for example, country risk includes not only the risks associated with aggregate payments crises—typically termed transfer risks—but also may include a variety of other fiscal and policy risks as well as risks of outright expropriation typically included under the heading of political risk.

An understanding of the issues associated with country risk is complicated by differences in the definitions employed in the existing literature. In the literature on international lending, the terms *country* or *sovereign risk* typically refers to the risk of rescheduling or outright default resulting from external payments crises.[1] These crises are viewed as stemming from either bad luck, bad faith, mismanagement, or, more typically, an indistinguishable mix of the three. *Transfer risk* applies to the exposure of claims against domestic corporations or projects to various policy responses to aggregate exchange crises. In contrast, in the literature on direct foreign investment, *political risk* typically is viewed as the risk of political discontinuities resulting in losses through expropriation or major policy shifts.[2] In the case of portfolio equity investment, in turn, *country risk* is defined as the common variability in returns of shares of firms based in or operating in a given country.[3] Finally, with references to the international integration of money markets, *political risk* is typically viewed as the risk of imposition of exchange controls.[4]

These risks have several traits in common. First, they all apply to claims on governments of or activities within particular jurisdictions. Second, most of them involve elements of policy choice as well as chance. Third, many of them have different impacts across classes of claims or claimants.

Before trying to provide a more general definition, I illustrate risks that might be considered country risks in order to explore the extent that these risks are the result of chance, choice, or some interaction of the two as well as the extent to which the impacts of the risks are general or are specific to particular classes of claims or claimants. Since country risk is a factor that changes the probability of a particular set of actions with particular impacts on the distribution of payoffs to various classes of assets and/or investors.[5]

6.1.1 Sources of Country Risk

Country risks can result from exogenous shocks (chance), endogenous behavior (choice), or the interaction of the two. Extreme exogenous economic events, such as the collapse of external markets for a country's key exports, clearly can lead to nonperformance on most of its obligations. Similarly, extreme political events, such as wars or coups, may result in the repudiation of all claims. In most cases, though, country risks will be the result of sequences of events and policy responses that may be initiated either by shifts in political values or changes in economic circumstances.

Economic circumstances are strongly influenced by world economic circumstances, but also reflect the success of existing domestic policies. Political values can shift due to discontinuities in power relationships such as coups or revolutions, but also from "normal" political processes, including elections or evolving values within the ruling groups. These sources of country risk, ranging from microeconomic and micropolitical to macrointeractive, are depicted in table 6–1.

In the case of countries with relatively stable political regimes, most country risks will result from the interaction of policy responses and exogenous events. At a macroeconomic level, external shocks and internal power realignments can lead to overall distress. At a microeconomic level, changes in circumstances may facilitate changes in underlying political forces, but policies may also respond directly to circumstances with no change in the underlying policy frames, especially in seeking to capture windfalls earned by particular sectors, firms, or investors, and in preserving firms or activities that themselves are in distress because of changing circumstances. LDCs, given their typical relatively undiversified economic structures, dependence on external finance, and internal rigidities, are particularly vulnerable to external shocks, such as swings in world economic activity or variations in world interest rates. In addition, they typically display less political stability than industrialized countries, at least in part because of their external economic vulnerability.

Table 6–1. Sources and Dimensions of Country Risks

Nature of Exogenous Risk Factors[b]	*Nature of Endogenous Risk Factors*[a]		
	Not Significant	*Specific*	*General*
		Micropolitical	*Macropolitical*
Not significant	No risk	Targeted expropriation, shift in regulation	Blanket expropriation, breakdown in public order
	Microeconomic	*Microinteractive*	
Affecting particular sectors	Firm-specific commercial losses	Windfall taxes	More of same
	Macroeconomic	*Macrointeractive*	
Affecting general economy	Commercial losses	Commercial losses, transfer losses	Total loss

[a] For example: *Public order*—wars, coups, violence; *Policy shifts*—change of party, change of government, change of minister, change of priorities; *macroeconomic policy*—level of public expenditure, real exchange rates, exchange controls, credit conditions, commercial policy, labor market policy, etc.; *management*—efficiency, honesty.

[b] For example: *trade*—protectionism, reduced global demand, shifting, terms of trade; *financial*—increased interest rates, loss of acess to markets or institutions.

The distinction between exogenous and endogenous risks closely parallels the distinction drawn in the literature on sovereign debt between a country's ability and its willingness to pay. Since the ability to pay at any point in time reflects previous strategic choices as well as choices about the future, it often is difficult or impossible after the fact to distinguish chance outcomes and policy choices. The same difficulty applies to contracts at the project or enterprise level and acts as a major barrier to writing enforceable contracts across borders. This mixture of choice and chance has major implications for the structure of international financial intermediation, which is discussed in later sections. In particular, it gives rise to comparative advantage in managing international risks, the subject of section 6.2, since risk mitigation, in this case the ability to deter opportunistic behavior at the country or firm level, takes on paramount importance. And it contributes to the skewing of the structure of external financing for LDCs, which is discussed in section 6.3.

Factors Influencing Policy Choices. A country's choice of strategic actions will depend on its economic circumstances, its political values, and the internal and external consequences of various actions. The domestic consequences include the impact on future savings as the result of actions that jeopardize particular classes of claims and the distributional effect of these actions. The external consequences of a given action involve both the avoidance of the current onerous obligations and the loss of the future benefits associated with continued compliance. In the case of outright default on foreign obligations, for example, the current gain — the obligations that are avoided — must be traded off against the sanctions, including reduced access to future trade and finance, that will be imposed by the lender and other countries that recognize the validity of its claims.

In the absence of an effective supranational legal framework for enforcing cross-border claims, a contract's self-enforceability, that is, the extent to which the benefits of continued compliance outweigh those of default, becomes a critical consideration in this regard. Both internal and external considerations contribute to self-enforceability. Further, self-enforceability increasingly is buttressed by legal sanctions that apply to transactions of a commercial nature even if one party is a sovereign and by institutional enforcement provided by collective entities including the International Monetary Fund (IMF) and the World Bank.

In the case of an industrialized country with a democratic government, domestic considerations are likely to play a major role in the enforcement of any particular class of claims. Foreign investors, especially if they cannot be effectively singled out, become free riders on these domestic forces. Thus, the risk of strategic actions is likely to be a function of the magnitude of claims held by foreign investors relative to those held by their domestic bedfellows. Further, the complex and pervasive commercial interactions of local firms and foreign-owned multinational firms, as well as of the government with foreign-owned multinationals and financial institutions, imply that substantial legal sanctions would apply in the case of any across-the-board action resulting in nonperformance on specific claims. These legal sanctions, coupled with the existence of politically influential local bedfellows, can be expected to make external financial nonperformance more costly and hence less likely. Nevertheless, cross-border claims are still likely to differ from claims issued within the home jurisdiction, especially when the concept of country risk is extended to include a lesser likelihood of government interventions on behalf of foreign investors relative to domestic investors as well as to a greater likelihood of prejudicial government actions against foreigners.

In the case of less-developed countries, with shallow domestic financial markets, the bedfellow effect is much less important. External sanctions play a greater role, with the usual conclusion being that the "best credit risks" are those countries that would suffer most if they were forced to become commercially or financially autarkic.

Relative Importance of Chance and Policy Choice. Generalized macroeconomic or macropolitical risk factors are common to most claims against a given country. Some are the result of exogenous shocks to the national economy, others of the country's policy choices, which may or may not represent a response to exogenous events. For a country such as Canada, for example, with close trade and investment links with the United States and other OECD countries and significant concentration of activity in the natural resource sector, major exogenous forces will be variations in world economic activity, interest rates and commodity prices. Policy risk variables involve the array of monetary, fiscal, and regulatory choices available to Canada for influencing overall economic activity and for shifting economic benefits among various groups. An LDC such as Mexico faces a similar set of exogenous forces, albeit with a far greater negative exposure to fluctuations in world interest rates. Further, its range of possible policy responses is quite different, especially if one includes the possibility of a major change in political regimes as well as the substantial variations that can occur within the "institutional revolution."

If all claims on Canada or Mexico were shares in Canada or Mexico, Inc., respectively, and if government policies did not result in any transfers among claimants, then the country risk in each case would be the risk of variations in the value (permanent income) of national assets, However, given the complexity of the claims structure, as well as the array of mechanisms available to either sovereign to affect transfer between labor and capital, various regions of the country, the employed and unemployed, and so forth, the country risk of any particular claim will depend to a considerable extent on policy choices as well as potential exogenous shifts in national wealth. This is likely to be even more marked in the case of Mexico, given the greater potential for conflict between external and internal claimants.

6.1.2 Incidence of Country Risk

The possibility of extreme shifts in a country's economic or political circumstances gives rise to generalized country risks that have the same effect on all classes of claims and claimants. Such "all or nothing" risks, which include extreme cases of sovereign risk—the risk of nonperformance on sovereign claims—and transfer risk—the risk of nonavailability of foreign exchange to cover private foreign obligations—are, for most countries, much less likely than asset or investor-specific risks—risks whose incidence differs across classes of claims and, perhaps, claimants.

Consider the case of an LDC experiencing a balance of payments crisis. The usual prescription applied by the IMF is a reduction in the deficit and devaluation of the currency. Government deficit reduction may be achieved by tax increases or expenditure reduction. This typically is accompanied by limits on the expansion of the money supply or on bank credit. The object is to squeeze the domestic economy enough to reestablish foreign balance by reducing import demand. Other instruments used to ameliorate payments crises include export subsidies, special import levies, interest rate policies, additional government borrowing, or, alternatively, foreign exchange controls. While many of these steps are associated with LDCs, steps taken by the recent socialist government of France serve as a reminder that most industrialized countries have at one time or another resorted to such measures.

The exposure of particular types of claims to various policy responses to a payments crisis is illustrated in table 6–2. The risk of repudiation of foreign claims applies directly only to sovereign claims, but in practice it is likely to coincide with the imposition of exchange controls or other measures that affect other classes of claims. A moratorium on all external payments will affect all obligations, but in most cases, will result in a larger loss on fixed-income claims than on equity claims where the value of income not remitted can be protected more easily. A devaluation, in contrast, will have no direct negative effects on foreign currency-denominated claims, but it will result in a loss on domestic currency-denominated claims. Indirectly, it may enhance the value of foreign currency-denominated claims by reducing the value of other competing claims. However, it may also lead to losses on foreign currency-denominated debt if it results in a worsened financial situation of borrowing firms. Its effects on portfolio or direct equity investment will be only indirect, and will depend on the operating and financial exposure of the firms in question and may be positive, negative, or neutral. The choice of measures and, consequently, the degree of loss to various classes of claims and claimants, will depend on many factors including the relative bargaining power of the various parties as well as the degree of self-enforceability of each financial arrangement.

In general, asset-specific and investor-specific risks can result from the differing incidence of general policy measures, from selective responses to

Table 6–2. Incidence of Country Risk by Type of Claim

	Type of External Claim					
Type of Risk	*Foreign Currency Government Debt*	*Home Currency Government Debt*	*Foreign Currency Debt of Private Firms*	*Home Currency Debt of Private Firms*	*Portfolio Equity in Local Private Firm*	*Direct Equity in Foreign-Controlled Local Firm*
Government default on external claims	X	X	X	X	X	X
Exchange controls		X	X	X	X	X
Inflation/devaluation		X	X[a]	X[b]	X[a]	X[a]
Adverse changes in fiscal policy		X	X[a]	X[a]	X[b]	X[b]
Credit controls				X[a]	X[a]	X[a]
Changes in limits on foreign ownership					?	X
Limits on behavior of foreign-controlled firms						X

Source: Lessard et al. (1983).

[a] Indirect effect via impact on borrowing firm's cash flows.

[b] Direct and indirect effect.

changes in general economic or political circumstances, from selective policies oriented toward goals such as limiting foreign ownership, and from policies triggered by either windfall profits or financial distress of specific firms. Example of some of the possibilities are presented below.

General Policy Measures with Differing Incidence. Not only will different events give rise to different actions, but the incidence of various event–action–effect chains will differ across classes of claims and, perhaps, classes of claimants holding particular types of claims. Only an extreme loss of wealth due to external changes or a radical political shift resulting in a severing of all existing external trade and financial linkages is likely to result in a total loss on all foreign claims. Such a zero–one view of country risk is not valid even for the foreign currency-denominated sovereign debt of most LDCs, and certaintly not for the wider range of claims held against more advanced countries by local and foreign investors. Because of their differing political values as well as the internal and external constraints they face, different nations are likely to respond to macroeconomic distress leading to problems with foreign obligations through different mixes of general fiscal, monetary, and regulatory measures rather than through explicit nonperformance on any particular class of claim, although the use of foreign exchange restrictions has been quite common. Macroeconomic crises typically are the result of both exogenous economic circumstances and endogenous policy choices. Further, given a state of crisis, a country's response, and its implications for various classes of claims and claimants, is to a large extent a strategic choice and not merely a mechanical passing through of the existing state of affairs to external claimants.

Selective Response to General Circumstances. In addition to general measures with differing incidence, a government can respond to changes in political or economic circumstances through selective measures. Examples include price controls, performance requirements, or taxes imposed on specific sectors of the economy. Such selective measures are particularly likely in response to macropolitical shifts that change the values and/or constraints faced by the state. Examples of selective measures in response to a general economic crisis coupled with political shifts include the imposition of limits on foreign travel for local residents by France and the adoption of dual exchange rates by Mexico.

Selective Measures in Response to Specific Policy Objectives. Asset-specific and investor-specific risks often result from the possibility of selective measures oriented toward specific policy goals. A common case is the attempt by government to maintain or increase indigenous control of economic institutions. In the mid 1970s, for example, Canada enacted the National Energy Policy (NEP) and the Foreign Investment Review Act (FIRA), both of which discriminated directly or indirectly against foreign investors, and it enacted programs in the high-technology sector to benefit Canadian-owned firms. Germany integrated its personal and corporate income taxes in a way that imposes a substantially higher tax on foreign shareholders than on domestic ones, and many countries, including Japan and Switzerland, maintain restrictions on foreign owership of shares.

In addition to these direct, specific policies, policies with similar indirect effects are common. A case in point is Canada's preferential tax treatment of the manufacturing sector. Because of the interactions with the U.S. tax system, this measure results in higher effective tax rates on U.S.-owned than on Canadian-owned manufacturing facilities. Measures to integrate corporate and investor taxation often have similar effects.

Selective Measures Triggered by Circumstances of Specific Firms or Sectors. A final category of policies that give rise to asset-specific and investor-specific risks are interventions to limit or tax windfall profits or to support firms or sectors encountering financial distress.

Virtually all governments of industrialized natural resource-producing countries imposed some form of price regulation or windfall profit tax to recover a share of the rents accruing oil production resulting from the first and second oil shocks. Clearly, this is an asset-specific risk. However, it also is an investor-specific risk to the extent that the likelihood or severity of the tax depends on the nationality of the owners. Canada, through its NEP, attempted to ameliorate the impact of provincial and federal taxes and price controls on Canadian firms, thus signaling that there was a risk of differential treatment in the energy sector.

Another asset-specific risk that is likely to be investor-specific to the prejudice of foreigners is the uncertainty regarding the extent to which the local government will intervene on behalf of financially distressed firms or act as lender of last resort to local financial institutions. Most governments, regardless of their professed belief in markets, from time to time intervene to rescue distressed firms. While such interventions typically are motivated by the desire to maintain employment or a significant technological capacity, they often benefit lenders or bondholders, and in some cases even shareholders. If these interventions are less likely when the owners or lenders are foreign, they are a source of cross-border investment risk. Such was the case with the refusal of the Italian authorities to take responsibility for the liabilities of Banco Ambrosiano's foreign subsidiaries. Of course, the opposite may occur at times because of the greater leverage of foreign lenders. Chile, for example, was forced to assume the external obligations of its private banks.

6.1.3 *Toward a General Definition*

While the various types of risks described vary greatly in their sources and incidence, a common feature of virtually all of them is that they involve some element of policy choice on the part of a sovereign. Therefore, country risk can be defined as the risk of changes in an asset's value due to sovereign policy responses that involve general or selective default on, confiscation of, or taxation of claims in response to circumstances under which either or both the ability and willingness of the sovereign to meet all the claims placed on it is impaired. Clearly, these risks can apply to assets within a single jursidiction as well as to claims across jurisdictional boundaries. Therefore, the more restrictive term *cross-border risk* should be applied to those risks affecting only cross-border claims.

6.2 Who Has Comparative Advantage in Bearing Country Risk?

Comparative advantage in bearing or managing risk can arise in any stage of the risk management process including identification, analysis of consequences, mitigation, and allocation and diversification. Some parties will be better than others at identifying risks and assessing their impacts on particular contracts or undertakings. This depends in large part on a party's prior experience and scope of activities. To the extent that the risks in question entail an element of choice, comparative advantage in mitigation will reflect various parties' leverage or bargaining power, which in turn reflects the direct or indirect sanctions it can bring to bear on the nonperforming party. Comparative advantage in risk allocation, in contrast, will reflect the parties' appetite for risk and, more importantly, the diversity of its exposures and hence its ability to ameliorate risk through diversification. These sources of comparative advantage are summarized in table 6–3.

In some cases, these functions are separable, and optimal risk management will involve specialization by function as well as by type of risk. In other cases, one function may not be separable from another and comparative advantage will reflect some averaging of the various functions. Consider the case of commercial banks lending to LDCs. They have an advantage in risk

Table 6–3. Sources of Comparative Advantage in International Risk Management

Identification	Superior information: experience, scope, access
Analysis of incidence	Superior information: experience scope, access
Mitigation	Leverage: ability to monitor behavior and to impose sanctions, seniority, perception of legitimacy on part of debtor and other creditors
Allocation/ Diversification	Diversification: degree of exposure to same or related risks

mitigation relative to most other potential lenders because of their relatively high degree of bargaining power vis-à-vis LDCs, but a disadvantage in risk allocation, given their relative overexposure to LDC credits.

6.2.1 Application to Country Risks

The concept of comparative advantage in risk management is a general one. However, the strength of this comparative advantage in terms of each of the risk management functions and the relative importance of the functions will depend on the type of risk being addressed.

The dimensions of risk affecting international contracts can now be related to the sources of comparative advantage in different risk management functions in order to judge the comparative advantage of different classes of institutions in managing particular aspects of country risk. Table 6–4 focuses on three functions: a combination of risk identification and analysis of incidence, risk mitigation, and risk allocation. While admittedly subjective, this table suggests that exploiting comparative advantage requires an unbundling of macro and micro risks as well as some specialization by institution in terms of the functions they perform.

Official lenders, such as the World Bank, have an advantage in the assessment and mitigation of endogenous macro level risks, given their access to policymakers, the sanctions they can exert if their suggestions are not followed, and the seniority of their claims in case of rescheduling. However, their capacity and willingness to take on various exogenous risks inherent in specific LDC economic undertakings are quite limited. Typically, they lend

Table 6–4. Comparative Advantage in International Risk Management

	Institution				
Risk Management Function 2	*Official Lenders*	*Commercial Banks*	*Institutional Investors*	*Direct Investors*	*Local Investors*
Macro risks					
Assessment	++	++	0	0	+
Mitigation	++	++	0	–	–
Diversification	0	–	+	0	–
Micro risks					
Assessment	+	0 to +[a]	–	++	++
Mitigation	+ to –[b]	+	–	++	++
Diversification	+	0	+	0[c]	–

[a] ++ if allowed to have significant local operations.

[b] Multilateral financial institutions appear to have an advantage in influencing micro level policy choices such as output pricing as limiting diversion of funds in capital goods purchasing. However, they appear to be at a disadvantage in monitoring management performance and limiting the diversion of proceeds in commercial ventures. The International Finance Corporation, for example, a significant lender and investor in third world enterprises, finds that it shares joint ownership of many "poor projects" with local owners who are doing extremely well.

[c] Depends on whether micro risk is country-specific or project-specific or if it is specific to the industry on a worldwide basis.

only on a general obligation basis and thus do not bear specific risks such as shifts in commodity prices or the commercial failures of sectoral programs or specific projects. Further, because of their senior creditor status, they are able to shift many of the remaining risks to less senior claimants.[6] At the micro level, they have substantial advantages in mitigating risks associated with the selection and execution of standard types of projects. However, they lack the commercial knowledge and profit incentives necessary to monitor more entreprenurial activities.

Commercial banks, because of their demonstrated ability to act collectively, also have strong leverage at the macro level. However, the current spotlight on their precarious capital positions makes it painfully clear that they are overexposed to such risks. At the micro level, they may be advantaged or disadvantaged depending on whether they operate extensively within the local economy and are allowed to bring full sanctions to bear on local borrowers in the case of nonperformance.

Institutional investors, including insurance companies and pension funds, have little or no leverage over macro or micro risks, but could diversify various LDC risks to a much greater extent than the much more highly exposed banks and credit agencies. Direct investors clearly have greater expertise in managing micro-level risks, but typically are at a disadvantage in terms of mitigating macro-level risks.

Local investors presumably have information advantages at the micro-level, but they may or may not have advantages in terms of mitigating particular risks or the incidence of those risks. With regard to risk of loss resulting from changes in government policy, locals could conceivably have more or less leverage than foreign governments, banks, or firms. In those cases where foreign borrowing is accompanied by capital flight, though, it would appear that foreign entities have the upper hand. Local investors may also differ in the impact of particular measures, particularly those associate with foreign exchange transfer. Since they value local expenditures more highly than do foreign investors, they have an option to switch their expenditures to the local goods that foreigners do not.[7]

6.3 Country Risk and the Structure and Efficiency of International Financial Intermediation

A complete model of the effects of country risk on the structure of international financial intermediation lies beyond the current frontier of financial economics, and certainly beyond the scope of this review. Substantial insights regarding the nature and impact of country risk, however, can be gained by observing, *grosso modo*, departures of asset holdings from idealized patterns and assessing the extent to which these departures might be attributable to various aspects of country risk.

In an idealized world capital market as characterized by the capital asset pricing model (CAPM), the introduction of generalized country risk — where all claims on a given country regardless of who holds them are subject to the same risk — would have little or no effect on the optimal pattern of asset holdings by different investor groups.[8] In such a market, with no barriers to cross-border investment, no differences in consumption preferences, and no asset-specific or investor-specific country risks, optimal asset holdings for all investors would consist of a universal portfolio of risky assets combined with varying proportions of a minimum risk portfolio depending on the investor's risk aversion.[9]

The structure of international financial intermediation that we observe differs substantially from this idealization. Among industrialized countries, the pattern of financial intermediation differs considerably from that within single, representative jurisdictions. Both gross and net cross-border claims represent a small fraction of domestic financial claims either on a gross or net basis. Further, the pattern of cross-border claims is quite skewed, with relatively larger proportions of cross-border holdings taking the form of sovereign claims (treasury bills, bonds, etc.), private debt, and direct investment than portfolio investment in risky, equity claims than the fractions of total financial claims represented by each class of claim. This is ironic, since risky claims provide the prime benefits of international diversification, while investors could be expected to hold relatively home-biased portfolios of less risky claims such as bonds in order to match their differing consumption patterns. As a result, cross-border risks with relatively small associated costs would eliminate international holdings of (nearly) riskless claims, but the costs required to justify holding a only domestic risk assets would be much larger. Cooper and Kaplanis (1986b), for example, using historical return covariances and market risk premia, estimate that the cross border "penalty" required to explain the difference between the observed holdings of a U.S. investor and the fully diversified world portfolio is less than 3% per annum, the same order of magnitude as real interest rates and risk premia; but this required penalty would have to be considerably higher to explain investor behavior in some other countries, ranging up to 40% for Italy!

In the case of LDCs, especially those in external financial difficulty, the pattern is even more extreme. Virtually all external claims against the major borrowers are in the form of sovereign borrowings, or private borrowings that are implicitly or explicitly guaranteed by the sovereign, and a majority of them are in the form of floating rate loans from commercial banks. Further, in some cases these external claims exceed total internal claims.[10]

The features of country risk that may account for these divergences in patterns of international intermediation from CAPM idealizations include its asset and investor specificity, its element of moral hazard, and the resulting information assymetry between various agents. I begin with a general discussion of the impact of country risk on asset holdings and prices. I then explore the extent to which it may account for (1) the home bias in risky asset holdings among financially developed countries and (2) the apparent crowding out of domestic claims and cross-border risk-bearing claims by sovereign borrowing in the case of LDCs.

6.3.1 Country Risk and Asset Evaluation

If country risks were simply the passing through of exogenous risks faced by countries, they would have no unique effects on the structure of asset holdings and prices. Of course, they would be reflected in asset values both through their impact on expected cash returns (cash flow effects) and on the (co)variability of future returns (risk premium effects), but these effects would be no different than those of the exogenous risks. It is the discretionary policy choice element of country risk and the ensuing information and enforcement issues that give rise to its stylized special effects: an uneven impact across assets and investors, with a virtual elimination of particular types of financial contracting and non-price clearing for others.

Consider the simplest case, sovereign borrowings in foreign currencies. A risk that the sovereign will be unable to pay due to external circumstances, if recognized by both borrower and lender, will result in an adjusted promised rate that maintains the expected rate of return at the riskless level as long as the risk of default is uncorrelated with undiversifiable external factors.[11] If the risk of nonperformance is systematic in the sense that it is related to, say, the world business cycle, the equilibrium expected return will include a risk premium reflecting the contribution of this asset to the variance of investors' portfolios. In either case, the borrower, if small, will face an elastic supply of credit at the risk-adjusted promised rate.[12]

If the risk of nonperformance includes an element of policy choice, the claim becomes unenforceable when the cost in terms of borrower utility of meeting its obligations exceeds penalties associated with nonperformance, also measured in terms of the borrowers' utility. Therefore, the total amount of credit must be limited and, in general, some structure of penalties must be imposed to provide the borrower with the incentive to honor its obligation. Many variations on this theme have been developed, with most attention being focused on optimal default strategies and their effect on the price of debt and on borrowers' growth while the nature of the penalties of default and the mechanisms by which lenders can credibly impose these penalties have been simply assumed.[13]

When the analysis is extended to other types of claims, the range of situations that can be termed nonperformance becomes much broader, the potential cash flow and risk premium effects become more complex, and the problems of enforcement/incentives for performance become more problematic. In the case of obligations denominated in the national currency, nonperformance encompasses not only explicit default, but implicit default in the form of opportunistic inflation and, if the claims are held by foreigners, the imposition of exchange controls and other measures that may partially or totally preclude the foreigner from realizing the value of the claim. In the case of credit or equity claims against private entities within the country, nonperformance is further extended to include a whole host of policies, including tax policies, price control policies, competitive policies, and labor market policies, that may affect the ability of a firm to meet its obligations and the ability of the lender or investor to appropriate its claim, as well as the ability of the sovereign to alter the internal or external purchasing power represented by the claim.

The *cash flow effects* of the various nonperformance risks, can be traced for any specific claim, although in most cases the possibility of nonperformance will transform the payoff into a nonlinear function of the underlying risk factors, thus requiring a more complex contingent claims analysis. The *risk premium effects* will depend primarily on whether the risks of nonperformance enhance or mitigate the systematic risk of the underlying claim.

The enforcement/incentive aspects of country risk associated with these more penetrating claims are particularly problematic. Since most nonperformance here involves violation of implicit claims with widely varying incidence across asset and investor groups, the concerted imposition of external sanctions is less likely than in the case of nonperformance on explicit, external contracts and the strength of domestic claimants will depend on the voice in the political system and the credibility of their threat to shift assets elsewhere, transforming themselves into external claimants.

6.3.2 Country Risk and Cross-Border Asset Holdings

Since country risk differs in incidence both across assets and investors, it can be expected to alter the structure of asset holdings in equilibrium. The possible role of country risk in explaining two observed departures from world-wide diversification—the home bias of investors' risky asset holdings in industrialized countries and the virtual absence of explicitly risk shifting cross-border claims on LDC—is examined below.

Country Risk as a Barrier to Cross-Border Investment in Risky Assets. It is plausible that the risk of violations of the various implicit contracts that give value to equity claims would increase with the degree of foreign ownership of equity claims. At significant levels of foreign ownership, the ever-present conflict between the interests of capital, labor, and other stakeholders would be transformed into a conflict among domestic and foreign interests and the behavior of the state in mediating these claims would be fundamentally altered. Foreign investors would no longer be able to rely on domestic bedfellows for political representation, and unless they could exercise similar power directly, they would be forced to rely on other enforcement mechanisms that typically would require absolute control of local firms and would involve substantial costs. If capital markets were globally integrated and all investors held similar portfolios of risky assets, as the CAPM implies they should, the degree of foreign ownership of equities in most countries would be overwhelming: foreign investors would hold 95% of

Swiss assets, 90% of U.K. assets, 80% of Japanese assets, 50% of U.S. assets, and so on.

The problem with this story is that there is no plausible mechanism by which individual foreign investors would jointly agree to limit their holdings of equities in a particular country to the optimal level given country risk. Individual investors could improve their risk/return frontiers by increasing local holdings, thus imposing a cost on other holders of such claims. Many countries, though, have regulations in place that serve the same purpose. Whether this is a politically rational response to the risk diversification–enforceability dilemma or an effort to preempt actions by foreigners with significant stake in that country, though, is an open question. Foreign ownership of shares either is restricted to an acceptable proportion of shares (e.g., Japan), limited to nonvoting shares (e.g., Switzerland), or discouraged through discriminatory taxation (e.g., Germany).

Country Risk and Sovereign Subordination. While country risk appears to be a factor in the home biasedness of investor portfolios in industrialized countries, especially in the case of risky holdings where the greatest gross cross-border holdings should occur, it appears to have a radically different effect on LDCs in extreme financial difficulty. In these countries, country risk in the form of a significant probability of a government credit crisis appears to drive out not only cross-border risky flows, but also domestic financial intermediation. The result is the substitution of cross-border sovereign claims that represent explicit, general obligations of the state for its implicit, domestic claims as well as for "more penetrating" claims whose value depends on outcomes of specific projects or enterprises, but also on implicit claims on the sovereign.[14]

The mechanism for this crowding out of private foreign claims and virtually all domestic claims by external sovereign claims is the effective subordination of these other claims to sovereign obligations.[15] Recall that the enforceability of any particular claim depends on the trade-off between the benefits of default and the sanctions that will apply in such a case. A default on foreign obligations is likely to trigger collective action imposing partial or total real and financial autarky, while a default on implicit domestic obligations, depending on its impact on expectations of future behavior, will result in further capital flight and a consequent reduction in domestic capital formation.

With hindsight, severe debt problems in LDCs have involved a slippery slope whereby:

1. To increase or maintain domestic absorption in the face of external shocks and/or increase the power of the state in allocating resources, the

sovereign has borrowed abroad, increasing its future fiscal and foreign exchange requirements.

2. In reaction to some internal or external shock, the state absorbs a significant proportion of the external obligations of the private sector to prevent failures that would reduce domestic confidence and/or violate its implicit or explicit guarantees to foreign lenders, thus increasing is fiscal and foreign exchange burdens.[16]

3. Private claimants, recognizing their subordination to increased foreign claims on the sovereign, often as the result of the violation of some implicit contract by the increasingly pressed sovereign, seek to transfer assets to other jursidictions.

4. In the absence of a securities market where such attempted transfers depress asset prices and, hence, face an implicit penalty, these attempted transfers create a run on foreign exchange reserves, forcing either further foreign borrowing (and subordination of private claims) or some form of default on existing claims.

Variations on this theme have occurred in most Latin American countries.

6.3.3 Country Risk and the Efficiency of International Resource Allocation

Country risk affects the efficiency of resource allocation through international capital markets in several ways. First, it reduces the completeness of financial markets both within and across jurisdictions, reducing the potential for bridging differences in time and risk preferences among different agents and reducing the impact of risk through diversification or pooling, which, in turn, alters required returns for various activities and shifts patterns of real investment. Second, it creates divergences between public and private returns or costs, reducing the social efficiency of private choices. Investment in exposed assets, for example, is reduced to a socially suboptimal level.[17] Third, by altering the structure of financial claims, it also alters incentives. In particular, it reduces the role of private agents in allocating funds within countries with the consequent loss of efficiency if such involvement provides important roles in project selection and management. Each of these is discussed briefly.

Changes in Required Private Returns. To the extent that country risks increase contracting costs and/or that their incidence differs between groups of investors, they will change the extent to which claims are exchanged among agents and, hence, the extent to which differences in time and risk preferences are bridged and various risks are diversified. In the case of cross-border risks, for example, real interest rates in net borrower countries will remain above the general world level while those in net lender countries will be below that level. Further, to the extent that cross-border exchanges of risky assets are limited, domestic investors will choose to bear some potentially diversifiable exogenous risks. The cost of this incomplete diversification will be reflected in derived risk premia (described below), which may be substantial in the case of risky claims (equity, risky debt, etc.) with little systematic risk within a fully diversified world portfolio, but substantial systematic risk within the resulting local portfolio.

Costly Contracting. Risks with a strategic element are likely to result in deadweight costs, that is, costs to one party in the form of a loss in efficiency or a "leakage" to third parties rather than a transfer between the parties to the contract. If borrowers are price takers, these deadweight costs increase their cost of funds. Several alternative reasons for such divergences between the expected cost of funds to the borrower and the required expected return to investors have been identified, including uninformed equilibria, nonprice market clearing, enforcement costs, efficiency costs of self-enforcing contracts, and costs of financial distress.

Uninformed market equilibria refers to conditions under which a borrower pays a higher rate than it should given the objective probability of nonperformance because of some type of information market failure. Several alternative versions involving sovereign borrowing have been articulated in the literature. Harberger (1976) argues that foreigners will persistently overestimate the risks of nonperformance by a particular nation and, hence, demand too high a promised rate of interest. While possible, this version is implausible since it relies on persistent information asymmetries, but does not explicitly incorporate the moral hazard aspects of strategic country risks. Buiter (1983), in contrast, drawing on Ackerlof's "lemons" analogy, suggests that lenders may not be able to distinguish good from bad borrowers ex ante and, therefore, set a promised rate that incorporates the average risk of nonperformance. Aizenman (1985) relies on the uncertainty regarding the penalties of default to reach a similar result.

Monitoring and enforcement costs refer to costs borne by lenders or investors to monitor performance and penalize nonperformance without necessarily obtaining the desired performance. Such costs include the costs of gathering information on borrowers' performance, losses of gains from trade if trade is cut off as the result of a breach if a particular contract, or legal fees incurred by private or public claimants.

Derived Risk Premia. Various authors, including Black (1972), Stulz (1983), Errunza and Losq (1985) and Cooper and Kaplanis (1986a), have modeled the effect of various types of risks or constraints to cross-border investment as "taxes" on cross-border investment.[18] While the specifics of each model differ, the main conclusions, not surprisingly, are that in each country all investors hold the same portfolio of risky assets, but the world portfolio is inefficient; that is, nobody would hold the world portfolio as his sole risky investment. In consequence, the traditional relation between systematic risk (β) with respect to the world market portfolio and expected return does not hold.

Consider the case of a small country government that imposes a linear tax θ on foreign holdings of asset i. If the asset should be held by both foreign and domestic investors, its gross of tax return R_i must lie on the domestic security market line (SML), and its net of tax return $R_i - \theta$ must lie on the foreign security market line. The tax on foreign holdings induces two effects:

1. Because domestic and foreign investors now face different opportunity sets, the security market lines will not be identical and, given the assumption that the tax applies only to foreign investors, the domestic price of risk will be higher.

2. By shifting away from asset i, foreign investors reduce its systematic risk (covariance with their portfolio), while by shifting into this asset domestic investors increase its systematic risk from their perspective, thus further increasing the required return on this activity.

Figure 6–1 shows the "knife-edge" case where the difference in systematic risk from the perspective of the two classes of investors just offsets the difference in return (θ) between the two groups. In many cases, though, it is unlikely to fall exactly on both security market lines. If the aggregate value of the "taxed" asset is large and it has substantial covariance with other assets, for example, the result of the tax would be a relatively small movement along the domestic SML, with the resulting change in expected returns being too small to induce foreigners to hold that asset as shown in figure 6–2.[19]

Divergences Between Private and Social Returns or Costs. Many aspects of country risk are similar to taxes in that they involve a taking by the state. In such cases, of course, the social returns of a given activity will exceed its private returns and the efficiency of private choices will be reduced.

Country risk will result in a further wedge between private and social returns to the extent that it results in a supply curve of external finance to a country will be upward sloping (in terms of expected and not just promised

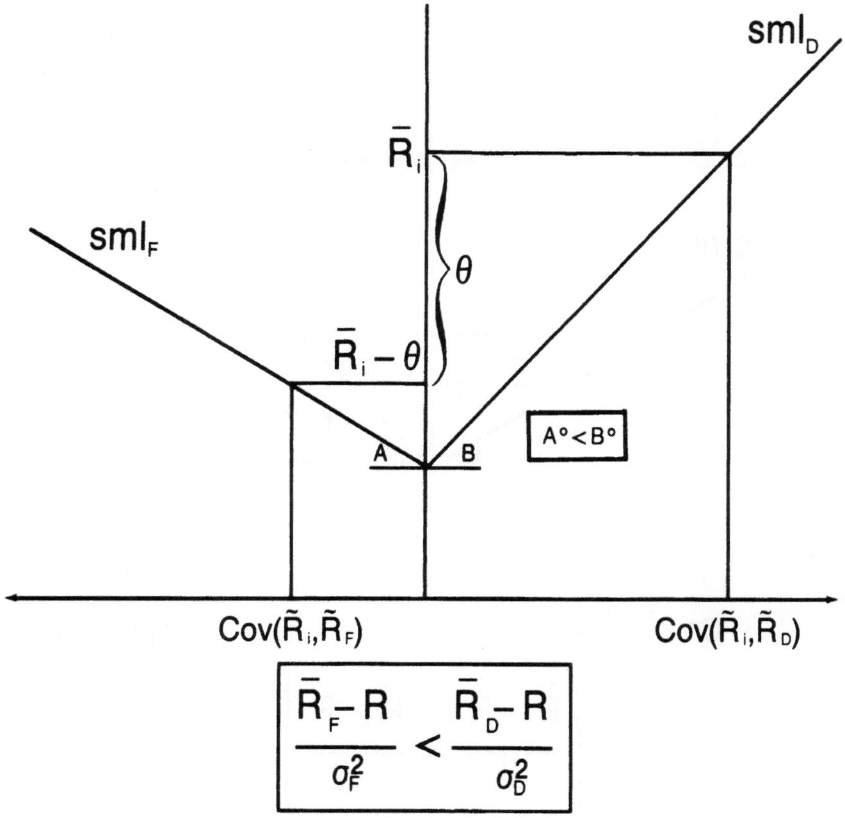

Figure 6–1. Impact of country risk on risk premium: Asset traded domestically and internationally.

rates) and, eventually, vertical as credit is rationed. Buiter, for example, argues that in order not to reveal their hand, "dishonest" borrowers will restrict their borrowing and "honest" borrowers will limit their borrowing both because of the deadweight cost they bear and because to seek increased loans would signal "dishonesty" and thus preclude them from the market. Various authors, including Sachs (1984) and Aizenman (1985), in contrast, show that credit rationing will result from creditors seeking to limit total leanding to a level that will not induce nonperformance on the part of the borrower. Bollier (1986) shows that in an uncertain environment a sovereign agent would also face an upward sloping supply of debt and that at optimal levels of borrowing this debt would be both risky and priced accordingly.

With an upwardly sloping supply curve and/or credit rationing of course, the social cost of borrowing will exceed the private cost by its contribution to

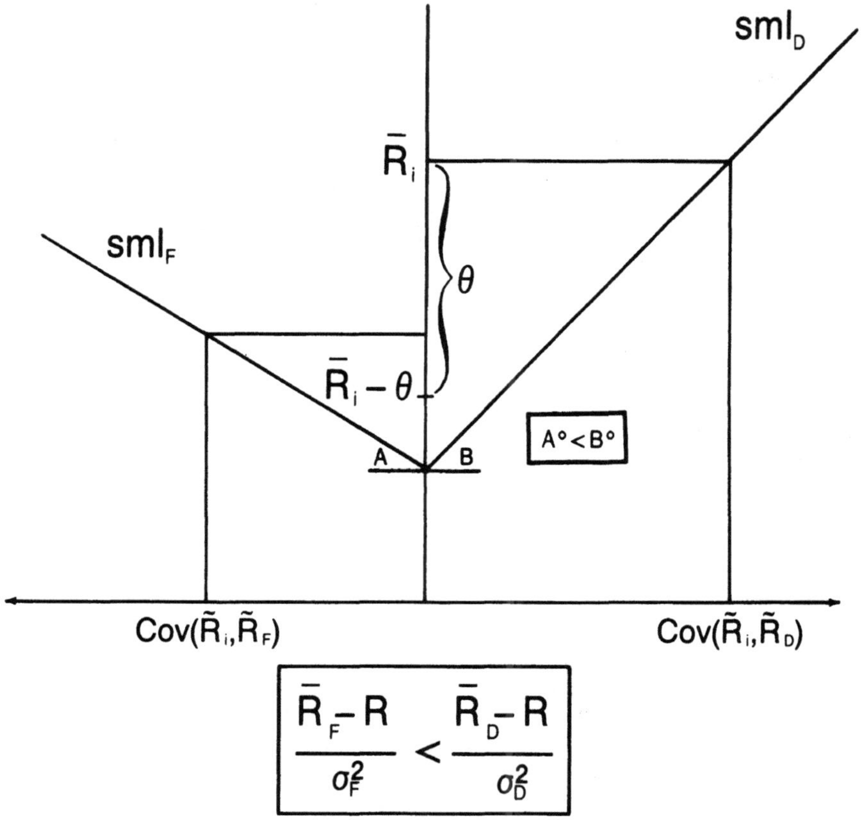

Figure 6–2. Impact of country risk on risk premium: Asset traded held exclusively by domestic investors.

the movement of the country along the curve. This result forms the basis for suggestions by Harberger, Aizenman, and others, that private foreign borrowing be limited or taxed. However, the same phenomenon also implies that private returns on activities that contribute to a country's ability to credibly commit to meet its obligations will be less than their social return and hence they should be subsidized! I return to this point in my concluding remarks.

Reduced Role of Market Incentives in Resource Allocation. A final efficiency cost of country risk is that in many cases it reduces or eliminates the role of market forces in the allocation of resources within the economy in question. The reason for this, as discussed above, is that when country risk is significant, sovereign finance, or, at a minimum, finance with an implicit sovereign guarantee, dominates unguaranteed lending, equity investment, and other forms of finance that link the lenders' fortunes to those of specific project or enterprise. As a result, lenders' will have a stake only in aggregate national outcomes and will have little or no incentive or ability to involve themselves in the selection or management of specific economic activities. While this may be attractive to the sovereign in that it minimizes foreign interference in the economy, it also eliminates the potential benefits of foreign expertise and places the full burden of micro-level allocation and management on the local bureaucracy. The minister of finance of Mexico or Brazil, for example, plays a much larger role in micro level allocation than the ministers of finance in the United States, the United Kingdom or even Japan.

6.4 Concluding Remarks

Country risk is a much broader and more complex phenomenon than the risk of default on external borrowings by sovereigns. It encompasses the full range of discretionary sovereign behavior in response to payments crises, which themselves are at least in part the result of previous policy choices. It affects domestic as well as foreign investors, curtailing out domestic private finance as well as foreign lending or investing. Given its differing incidence across assets and investors, and the resulting comparative advantage of different agents in bearing this risk, it appears to have contributed to a substantial skewing of patterns of international financial intermediation relative to those typical within countries. While we are far from a complete understanding of the mechanisms and effects of country risk, it is possible to identify certain steps that would reduce some of its apparently most costly effects.

Clearly, there remain many more questions than answers. It remains to be established that country risk is in fact a significant factor in limiting the diversification of risky assets across national boundaries. In contrast, there seems to be little question that in the case of LDCs, it has contributed to a crowding out in favor of sovereign financing of both domestic financing and penetrating foreign finance, but the precise mechanisms of this crowding out are not well understood.

Given this far from complete understanding of the mechanisms and effects of country risk, it might be argued that no policy conclusions should be drawn. However, the literature is replete with normative results derived from models that focus only on sovereign borrowing or, perhaps, sovereign borrowing and a single category of private foreign borrowing. Many recommendations for dealing with LDC debt crisis, for example, ignore possible implications of domestic financial intermediation and various types of penetrating cross-border claims.

Recommendations that private foreign borrowing be taxed or restricted because of its negative externalities, for example, should be accompanied by mechanisms for encouraging activities that through their net foreign exchange earnings generate positive externalities. Further, it should be recognized that such restrictions will create an advantage to domestic or foreign-based multinational firms relative to purely local firms since the former will be able to circumvent the restrictions via offshore borrowing accompanied by local investment.[20] The difficulty of implementing the resulting complex system of taxes and subsidies, though, suggests a greater reliance on market judgments, where firms are allowed to borrow abroad only to the extent that they can do so without explicit or implicit government guarantees. This would require credible mechanisms to protect sovereigns from being forced to assume the respective private obligations as happened in Chile and elsewhere. Ideally, the International Monetary Fund (IMF) would play this role, taking responsibility for the efficiency of international financial transactions rather than acting primarily as an enforcer of creditor claims.

What is needed is a much greater focus on institutional arrangements that would either reduce country risk or reduce its inhibiting effect on broad the functioning of financial markets. I suggest a few as points of departure for further analysis.

Among industrialized, capitalist countries, foreign claims are rendered enforceable largely by their free rider status vis-à-vis domestic claims coupled with the sanctions provided by the commercial and financial interpenetration of the various economies. Nevertheless, a movement toward greater global diversification by investors and/or an increase in net cross-border flows, especially those involving risky equity claims, would appear to threaten existing mechanisms that determine the distribution of rents among labor, capital, and government. Perhaps as a result, many governments limit foreign ownership of corporate equity. This, of course, results in a inefficiency in the bearing of macroeconomic and commercial risks. These limits on cross-border diversification can be relaxed to some extent by mechanisms that separate risk sharing from corporate governance, including institutional investment channels where governance is reserved for domestic players and futures and options markets that leave the underlying assets in the hands or domestic players while shifting the investment risks to others.

Sovereign risk as a barrier to cross-border investment will be eliminated only by limits on sovereign intervention, in return for regional or global rules regarding corporate governance. The snail's pace movement in this direction within the European Economic Community suggests that such a step will be a very long time coming across more diverse and less intertwined national economies, especially the United States and Japan.

The more pressing issues with regard to country risk, though, lie with the LDCs. Many current discussions of the LDC debt problem suggest that the major issue in international risk management is the mitigation and avoidance by lenders of risks of nonperformance by LDCs. However, another equally important dimension is the appropriate allocation among various lenders and investors of risks faced by LDCs. To solve only the first problem is analogous to addressing moral hazard by eliminating all fire and casualty insurance.

When viewed in terms of comparative advantage in risk bearing, the management of international risks inherent in the current structure of financing for LDCs is woefully inadequate and there is great room for improvement. While the existing structure is inefficient along many dimensions, there are a few key areas where a great deal of improvement is possible. These include a shift toward general obligation financing whose terms more closely match borrowers' ability to pay such as floating rate financing coupled with interest or currency swaps, price-level index or commodity price-linked bonds; increased stand alone finance where lenders/investors would be exposed to the commercial risks of projects or enterprises; and increased risk capital in the form of portfolio investment in equities and quasi-equities as well as direct foreign investment.

Many of these innovations involve the transfer of micro-level (commercial) risks to private, foreign, or domestic investors, lenders, or providers of services. Typically, this involvement will be by parties with a comparative advantage in managing such risks by virtue of their knowledge of specific industries, their ability to manage specific activities, and/or their relative ability to diversify away certain key risk elements.

However, these same parties—direct foreign investors, firms with alternative commercial linkages to specific projects such as licensing or other sales or service contracts involving contingent compensation, foreign institutional suppliers of risk capital, and local investor groups—typically are at a disadvantage in coping with macro-level noncommercial risks. Multilateral institutions, commercial banks, and national export credit agencies are natural parties to unbundle these two types of risks. They could, for example, simultaneously insure some of these macro risks and "take a place at the table" to exert leverage on behalf of these claims. They also could exert leverage within the international financial community, especially the World Bank (and the other MDBs) and the IMF, to accord at least equal treatment to project specific claims whether these were outright credits or contracts contingent on specific projects' success.[21] All of these steps would have the additional advantage of helping to create the conditions necessary for a viable private market in pure country risks.[22]

In addition to taking on more of the macro (noncommercial) risks faced by other parties, official financial agencies could also reduce their own exposures to adverse selection by exporters of capital goods or services by requiring (or encouraging through more favorable rates) that contracts be written in such a way as to transfer identifiable commercial risks to these firms. Such steps would go a long way to reintroducing appropriate micro-level risk management while maintaining or improving the management of macro-level risks.

Notes

1. See, for example, Eaton and Gersovitz (1981), Walter (1981) and Eaton, Gersovitz and Stiglitz (1986).
2. See, for example, Kobrin (1979).
3. See, for example, Lessard (1976), Agmon (1973), or Solnik (1973).
4. See, for example, Aliber (1973, 1978) and Dooley and Isard (1980).
5. This distinction between action and effect depending on the nature of the asset is introduced by Kobrin (1979).
6. See Gennotte et al. (1986) for further discussion of this point.
7. This point is developed by Eldor et al. (1986).
8. Even in this idealized setting, though, country risk would have the same effects as a tax, driving a wedge between private and social returns and hence distorting resource allocation.
9. Even with variations in real exchange rates and differing consumption preferences, all investors would continue to hold a common portfolio of risky assets, although each (national) consumption group would also hold a unique minimum variance portfolio as well as a portfolio hedging away the consumption risk specific to them in universal risky asset portfolio.
10. In the case of Mexico, for example, by 1985 external obligations were on the order of $100 billion, roughly double the value of domestic primary financial assets ($M1+M2$).
11. In the literature on international bank lending, the term "country risk premium" refers to the spread between the base rate (e.g., LIBOR or prime) and the lending rate for a particular country. It is an adjustment to the promised rate, but it does not necessarily imply a risk premium in terms of expected costs. In contrast, in the financial economics literature, a risk premium is defined as an adjustment to the expected rate of return to compensate for the costs of risk bearing.
12. The risk-adjusted promised rate, of course, may rise with the level of borrowing, since there will be an increased probability that the borrower will be unable to pay and the supply of credit (the present value of the expected payment) can decline quickly to zero as the promised payment is increased beyond a critical level.
13. With regard to the costs of default, two major strands are represented by Eaton and Gersovitz (1981), who stress the utility loss from not being able to employ external finance to smooth consumption, and Sachs (1984), who stresses the loss of productivity of assets through reduced trade. Bollier (1986) combines the two in a continuous-time utility-maximizing model. With regard to the credibility of penalties, most researchers simply assert them, though some are beginning to explore conditions under which a unitary lender would actually impose them after the fact and others, e.g., Sundaram (1986) examines the case where atomistic lenders would cooperate to impose them.

14. For an excellent discussion of the relative risk of a sovereign's explicit foreign obligations and its implicit domestic obligations, see Protopapadakis (1985).

15. For a rigorous development of this argument, see Ize and Ortiz (1983) and Eaton (1986).

16. This point is developed by Frieden (1981).

17. This also implies that the social cost of foreign borrowing may exceed the private cost, a point made by Harberger (1976) and further developed by Aizenman (1985).

18. A constraint on cross-border investments, imposed to mitigate particular policy risks that would increase with foreign ownership, can be modeled as a tax as well. In this case, the "tax" on cross-border investment would be shadow price of the constraint.

19. For numerical illustrations of the magnitude of cross-border taxes or barriers required to induce degrees of home biasedness in portfolio holdings, see Cooper and Kaplanis (1986b).

20. This point is developed in Agmon and Lessard (1976).

21. The proposed Multilateral Investment Guarantee Authority (MIGA) would play precisely this role.

22. By pure country risks, I refer to losses on scheduled general obligations. These would serve as a proxy for the transfer risk elements inherent in more penetrating contracts.

References

Agmon, T. (1973), "The Significance of the Country Risk Factor for Share Price Movements," *Journal of Business*, January.

——— (1985), *Political Economy and Risk in World Financial Markets*, Lexington Books, Lexington, MA.

——— and D. Lessard (1976), "The Multinational Firms as Vehicles for International Diversification: Implications for Capital Importing Countries," *Revista Brasileira de Mercados de Capitais*, December.

Aizenman, J. (1986), "Country Risk, Incomplete Information and Taxes on International Borrowing," Paper presented at Conference on Research in International Finance, June 19–20, Centre HEC-ISA, Jouy-en-Josas, France.

Aliber, R. Z. (1973), "The Interest Rate Parity Theorem: A Reinterpretation," *Journal of Political Economy*, **81** (6).

——— (1978). "The Integration of National Financial Markets," *Weltwirtschaftliches Archiv*.

Barnea, A., R. Haugen, and L. Senbet (1985), *Agency Problems and Financial Contracting*, Prentice-Hall, Englewood Cliffs, NJ.

Black, F. (1972), "Capital Market Equilibrium with Investment Barriers," *Journal of Business*, July.

Bollier, T. (1986), *International Debt, Repudiation and Opportunistic Behavior in an Uncertain Environment*, Ph. D. dissertation, Massachusetts Institute of Technology, Cambridge.

Buiter, W. (1983), "Implications for the Adjustment Process of International Asset Risks: Exchange Controls, Intervention, Policy, and Sovereign Risks," in R. Hawkins (Ed.), *The Internationalization of Financial Markets and National Economic Policy*, JAI Press.

Cooper, I. and E. Kaplanis (1986a), "Costs to Crossborder Investment and International Equity Market Equilibrium," in Edwards et al. (Eds.), *Recent Advances in Corporate Finance*, forthcoming.

——— (1986b), "Estimation of Barriers to International Investment," London Business School Working Paper IFA-91-86.

Dooley, M. and P. Isard (1980), "Capital Contols, Political Risk, and Deviations from Interest Rate Parity," *Journal of Political Economy*, **88** (2).

Dooley, M. (1986), "Capital Flight: A Response to Differences in Risks," *IMF Staff Papers.*

Eaton, J. (1983), "Country Risk: An Economic Perspective," in Herring *op. cit.*

——— (1986), "Public Debt Guarantees and Private Capital Flight," unpublished working paper, The World Bank, August.

Eaton, J. and M. Gersovitz (1981), "*Poor Country Borrowing in Private Financial Markets and the Repudiation Issue*," Princeton Studies in International Finance, No. 47.

Eaton, J., M. Gersovitz, and J. Stiglitz (1986), "The Pure Theory of Country Risk," *European Economic Review*, **30**.

Eldor, R., D. Pines, and A. Schwartz (1986), "Productivity Shocks and Home Asset Preference," mimeo. Boston University.

Errunza, V. and E. Losq (1985), "International Asset Pricing Under Mild Segmentation: Theory and Test," *Journal of Finance*, March.

Frieden, J. (1981), "Third World Indebted Industrialization: International Finance and State Capitalism in Mexico, Brazil, Algeria and South Korea," *International Organization*, **35** (2).

Gennotte, G., H. Kharas, and S. Sadeq (1986), "A Valuation Model for LDC Debt with Endogenous Reschedulings," *World Bank Economic Review*, forthcoming.

Harberger, A. (1976), "On Country Risk and the Social Cost of Foreign Borrowing by Developing Countries," mimeo.

——— (1980), "Vignettes on the World Capital Market," *American Economic Review*, May.

Herring, R. (Ed.) (1985), *Managing International Risk*, Cambridge Univ. Press, Cambridge.

Ize, A. and G. Ortiz (1983), "Fiscal Rigidities, Public Debt, and Capital Flight," unpublished working paper.

Kobrin, S. (1979), "Political Risk: A Review and Reconsideration,"*Journal of International Business Studies*, Spring/Summer.

Lessard, D. (1976), "World, Country and Industry Factors in Equity Returns," *Financial Analysts Journal*, July–August.

Lessard, D. and J. Williamson (1985), *Financial Intermediation Beyond the Debt Crisis*, Institute for International Economics, Washington, DC.

Lessard, D., R. Eckaus, T. Bollier, and R. Kahn (1983), "Country Risk, Capital Market Integration, and Project Evaluation: A Canadian Perspective," unpublished report prepared for the Corporate Finance Division, Canada Finance.

Protopadakis, A. (1985), "An Analysis of Government Credit 'Crises,'" Federal Reserve Bank of Philadelphia, Working Paper No. 85–14.

Sachs, J. (1984), "*Theoretical Issues in International Borrowing*," Princeton Studies in International Finance No. 54.

Solnik, B. (1973), *European Equity Markets*, Lexington Books, Lexington, MA.

Stulz, R. (1981), "On the Effects of Barriers to International Investment," *Journal of Finance*, September.

——— (1985), "Pricing Capital Assets in an International Setting: An Introduction," *Journal of International Business Studies*, Spring.

Sundaram, A. (1986), "Syndications, Debtors' Cartels and Equilibria in International Lending to LDCs," Paper presented at Conference on Research in International Finance, June 19–20, Centre HEC-ISA, Jouy-en-Josas, France.

Vernon, R. (1985), "Organizational and Institutional Response to Ineternational Risk," in Herring, *op. cit.*

Walter, I. (1981), "Country Risk, Portfolio Decisions, and Regulation in International Banking," *Journal of Banking and Finance*, March.

Commentary by Thomas D. Willett

Donald Lessard has given us a stimulating, insightful contribution. It not only presents a considerable amount of highly useful analysis, but also focuses attention on a major issue that has been relatively neglected in the recent discussions of the international debt crisis—the extent to which various developments associated with the debt crisis have acted to drastically reduce the influence of private sector decisionmaking in the microeconomic allocation of financial resources in the developing countries.

6C.1 The Decline of Private Micro-Level Lending in the Developing Countries

Capital flight from the developing countries has not only worsened these countries' international financial positions, it has also reduced the role of private sector participation in the allocation of funds within the economy. The increase in country risks combined with the increased priority given to repayment obligations of direct government borrowing from abroad, relative to private micro-level borrowing has led to a substantial reduction of private international lending for projects at the microeconomic level in the developing countries.

As Lessard points out, even among the industrialized countries, international lending is much lower than would be predicted by most of the currently used models in the finance literature. Furthermore, the cross-border investments that do take place are much more heavily concentrated on sovereign claims such as government bonds and Treasury bills relative to equity investments than efficient market models would predict. Thus, there is a general issue here to be explored. However, the most crucial policy issues in this area at the present time almost certainly have to do with the decline in the role of the private market in financial allocation in the developing countries. This has reached such a magnitude that even those economies that are quite skeptical of laissez-faire market ideology should be concerned by the degree of dominance in financial resource allocations played by governments in many developing countries.

Lessard's analysis convinces me that efforts to reverse this trend should be a major element in future discussions and negotiations related to the debt crisis. The primary responsibility for reversing this trend will have to lie with the developing countries themselves, just as their past policy decisions have been its major cause. The industrial countries have a responsibility to help in this process, but unfortunately so far this has not occurred to any significant extent. Indeed, by giving new loans exclusively to governments and insisting that they be placed high in the cue for repayment in the case of macro crisis, the industrial countries' governments and international institutions have actually helped to worsen this aspect of the problem by making microeconomic lending even more subject to overall country risk. We should understand by now that government credit guarantees are not costless. While they reduce risks to those making loans to the activities receiving the guarantees, this is at least partially offset by increasing the relative riskiness and cost of borrowing for those activities not receiving the guarantees. At low levels of government involvement these costs may be relatively minor, but in many of the developing countries government involvement has reached proportions where such effects can be of major significance.

The industrial countries have quite correctly focused attention on the need of the developing countries to adopt policies that reduce the incentives for capital flight. What may not have been fully appreciated, however, is the extent to which the lending policies of the industrial countries and international institutions may themselves have contributed to the incentives for such capital flight.

6C.2 Country Risk Management and the Scenario Analysis Approach

The majority of Lessard's chapter is devoted to discussing the various major types of country risks, their interrelationships, and ways of managing them. While lacking the drama of his concluding policy emphasis on the types of issues just highlighted, this analysis is quite useful. There is still a strong tendency in both the academic literature and managerial practice to treat various types of risk in isolation. Lessard has been in the forefront of the recent trend to stress the interrelationships of different types of risks. I would just add that in this process I believe that, as Arnold Zellner discussed earlier, scenario analysis techniques may prove to be very useful.[1] This approach helps to emphasize that the instability of many empirical relationships that have been used in risk management strategies has resulted because the variables involved, such as exchange rates and interest rates, are endogenous variables. Their statistical relationships will vary systematically depending on the patterns of underlying disturbances.

If domestic interest rates rise because of tight monetary policies we should expect currency appreciation, whereas if the increase in interest rates is due to an increase in inflationary expectations we should expect currency depreciation. To find more stable empirical relationships we need to probe deeper into the pattern of underlying developments, such as monetary and fiscal policies and oil shocks. As an example, consider the argument that borrowing by developing countries at variable short-term interest rates has been a poor risk hedge because such rates have been high in recent years while export earnings have slumped. While certainly a correct analysis of the recent period of disinflation, this may not be a good reason for developing countries to move substantially away from variable interest borrowing in the future. In a simple Keynesian IS–LM framework, real interest rates and economic activity will be positively correlated when IS curve shifts are dominant, and negatively correlated when monetary changes are dominant.

The recent period of disinflation was dominated by monetary tightness (with the interest rate effects increased by fiscal ease), giving the negative correlation mentioned above. This may well be reversed in future scenarios. Indeed, during both periods following the major oil price increases in the 1970s real interest rates fell, and indeed real short-term rates were negative ex post. This served as a partial hedge for developing countries during these episodes. My guess is that, on balance, developing countries would find considerably more scope for risk reduction through seeking greater diversification of the currencies of denomination of their debts away from the current very high proportion in dollars.

Some of the most valuable aspects of Lessard's risk analysis are his attention to the issues of policy choice versus chance in influencing risk and analysis of the comparative advantages of different types of private and official institutions in identifying and assessing, bearing, and mitigating risks. A major conclusion of this analysis is the need to seek ways to more effectively unbundle macro and micro risks so that various types of institutions may specialize more in those types of activities where they have comparative advantages. This failure has contributed substantially to the crowding out of micro lending by sovereign debt, which was discussed above.

6C.3 Analyzing Possible Financial Market Inefficiencies

Lessard follows this analysis of comparative advantage with a useful summary of a number types of possible influences in and barriers to international lending and a list of some of the possible types of policy and institutional innovations that might help to overcome them. Here the analysis can be sharpened a good deal. While often difficult to apply in practice, a conceptual distinction should be made between barriers that reflect genuine costs of transacting such as those of obtaining information and those that reflect artificial barriers whose removal would directly increase efficiency. Both types of situations will impose deadweight costs that will reduce international lending, but the former would not necessarily imply policy-relevant inefficiencies.

In dealing with such issues of possible market failure, good analysis is as much an art as a science. It is straightforward to show that many real world situations do not conform to the standards of efficiency derived from models with perfect information and zero transactions costs, but it is not always so easy to analyze whether actual institutional or policy innovations are likely to be able to improve outcomes by reducing information and transaction costs.[2] Before advocating policy proposals to correct perceived market failures, we need to attempt to develop an understanding of why the market has failed to develop the desired characteristics and analyze whether proposed innovations would in practice be likely to overcome these obstacles. Thus, for example, while the absence of widespread use of indexing contracts in the United States and international financial markets has often been treated either as prima facie evidence of the failure of private capital markets to operate with full efficiency or as the result of legal discouragements, recent literature has stressed the role of relative price variability in limiting the mutual advantages of indexing to both parties to the transaction.[3] While "optimal indexing" is far from a settled issue, this literature does give us insights into the ways in which we need to approach the broader issues of possible policy and institutional innovations to help improve international risk management and deal with the debt crisis more effectively.

Someone looking for an agenda of policy proposals that should immediately be adopted will not find satisfaction in this chapter. And that, I think, is very much to Lessard's credit. As was made particularly clear in his verbal remarks at the conference, his checklist of policy proposals should be read as part of an agenda of items for analysis, not immediate indiscriminate action. While the specifics of his discussions of issues contain many useful contributions, they are far from definitive, as I believe Lessard would be quick to admit. I would be inclined to put greater emphasis on the policy actions that can be taken by the developing countries themselves than does Lessard in his chapter. For example, with the blessing of current creditors, developing countries could be encouraged to give priority for repatriation to international lenders willing to take the microeconomic risks of lending directly for specific private sector activities.

In conclusion, while I have questions on some of the specifics of Lessard's analysis, I believe that it would be difficult to overestimate the value of posing the relatively neglected questions that he has emphasized. This and the illustrations offered of how one can usefully go about beginning to analyze the problems are what make this an unusually important chapter. It provides us with a fascinating and highly policy-relevant agenda for analysis. That's quite a contribution!

Notes

1. For further discussion of the interrelationship of types of risks and usefulness of scenario approaches, see Oxelheim and Wihlborg (1987) and Oxelheim et al. (1986).
2. This need to compare realistic alternatives when considering the possibility and alternative forms of government intervention has been emphasized by a number of economists writing from public choice and law and economic or property rights perspectives. See, for example, the contributions and references in Amacher et al. (1976).
3. For recent contributions and references to the literature on indexing of financial instruments and why it is not more widespread, see Dornbusch and Simonson (1983), Fischer (1986), and Weiner (1983).

References

Amacher, R., R. Tollison, and T. D. Willett (Eds.) (1976), *The Economic Approach to Public Policy*, Cornell Univ. Press, Ithaca, NY.

Dornbusch, R. and M. Simonsen (Eds.) (1983), *Inflation, Debt, and Indexation*, MIT Press, Cambridge, MA.

Fischer, S. (1986), *Indexing, Inflation and Economic Policy*, MIT Press, Cambridge, MA.

Oxelheim, L. and C. Wihlborg (1987) *International Macroeconomic Risk for the Corporation* Wiley, London.

Oxelheim, L. P. Sharp, C. Wihlborg, and T. D. Willett (1986), "Measuring and Managing Exchange Risk," presented at the International Futures and Commodities Institute Conference on *Monetary Uncertainty, Financial Futures and Economic Activity*, Geneva, Switzerland, November 1986, forthcoming in conference volume. Available as a *Claremont Working Paper*, 1986.

Weiner, S. (1983), "Why Are So Few Financial Assets Indexed to Inflation?" Federal Reserve Bank of Kansas City, *Economic Review*, May, pp. 3–18.

MIX
Papier aus verantwortungsvollen Quellen
Paper from responsible sources
FSC® C105338

FSC
www.fsc.org

If you have any concerns about our products,
you can contact us on
ProductSafety@springernature.com

In case Publisher is established outside the EU,
the EU authorized representative is:
Springer Nature Customer Service Center GmbH
Europaplatz 3, 69115 Heidelberg, Germany

Printed by Libri Plureos GmbH
in Hamburg, Germany